THE WINES OF GREAT BRITAIN

THE INFINITE IDEAS CLASSIC WINE LIBRARY

There is something uniquely satisfying about a good wine book, preferably read with a glass of the said wine in hand. The Infinite Ideas Classic Wine Library is a series of wine books written by authors who are both knowledgeable and passionate about their subject. Each title in The Infinite Ideas Classic Wine Library covers a wine region, country or type and together the books are designed to form a comprehensive guide to the world of wine as well as an enjoyable read, appealing to wine professionals, wine lovers, tourists, armchair travellers and wine trade students alike.

Port and the Douro, Richard Mayson
Cognac: The story of the world's greatest brandy, Nicholas Faith
Sherry, Julian Jeffs
Madeira: The islands and their wines, Richard Mayson
The wines of Austria, Stephen Brook
Biodynamic wine, Monty Waldin
The story of champagne, Nicholas Faith
The wines of Faugères, Rosemary George MW
Côte d'Or: The wines and winemakers of the heart of Burgundy, Raymond Blake
The wines of Canada, Rod Phillips
Rosé: Understanding the pink wine revolution, Elizabeth Gabay MW
Amarone and the fine wines of Verona, Michael Garner
The wines of Greece, Konstantinos Lazarakis MW
Wines of the Languedoc, Rosemary George MW
The wines of northern Spain, Sarah Jane Evans MW
The wines of New Zealand, Rebecca Gibb MW
The wines of Bulgaria, Romania and Moldova, Caroline Gilby MW
Sake and the wines of Japan, Anthony Rose
The wines of Great Britain, Stephen Skelton MW

THE WINES OF GREAT BRITAIN

STEPHEN SKELTON MW

infiniteideas

Stephen Skelton started his career in wine in 1975. After twelve months at Schloss Schönborn in Germany's Rheingau winegrowing region and two terms at Geisenheim Wine School, he returned to the UK in 1977 to establish Tenterden Vineyards in Kent (now the home of the UK's largest wine producer Chapel Down) where he made wine for 23 vintages. He was also winemaker at Lamberhurst Vineyards, then the UK's largest wine producer, between 1988 and 1991.

He became a Master of Wine in 2003 and won the prestigious Mondavi Prize for the highest marks in the written part of the examination. In 2005 he was awarded the AXA Millésimes award for his contribution to the work of the MW Education Committee. He was Deputy Vice Chairman of the Institute of Masters of Wine from 2014–16 and in 2014 was appointed to be in charge of the Research Paper, the final part of the MW examination. He also lectures on viticulture for the Wine and Spirit Education Trust's Diploma courses.

Stephen is a consultant to the English wine industry and is involved with planting vineyards for the production of both still and sparkling wines. Since 1986 he has written and lectured widely on English wine and has published four guides to UK vineyards, the 2001 edition of which, *The Wines of Britain and Ireland*, won the André Simon award for Wine Book of the Year. He has also written *Viticulture*, a primer on the subject for students, and *Wine Growing in Great Britain*, for growers.

First published in 2019 by
Infinite Ideas Limited
www.infideas.com

A CIP catalogue record for this book is available from the British Library
ISBN 978–1–905940–69–1

Front cover: Oast House Meadow vineyard of Hush Heath Estate with the oast house and manor house beyond. Staplehurst, Kent, England © Cephas/Mick Rock

Plate p. 1 (top), Breaky Bottom, courtesy of Axel Hesslenberg, thepebbles.com
Plate p. 2 (top), Flint Vineyard Winery, courtesy of Simon Buck Photography.
Plate p. 3 (bottom), Llanerch, courtesy of A.L.S. Photography, Vale of Glamorgan.

Printed in Great Britain

CONTENTS

INTRODUCTION

It has been over forty-five years since my interest in making wines in Britain was first aroused. A house-hunting expedition one Saturday morning included a property that had a small vineyard attached – it was Nettlestead Vineyards near Maidstone, now long-gone. We didn't buy the house, but when I got home, I was sufficiently intrigued about the idea to investigate and discover that there was an English Vineyards Association and, in due course, join it. In those days (1974) there were barely 200 hectares (500 acres) of vines and the quality of the (still) wines produced, based largely on two varieties, Müller-Thurgau and Seyval Blanc (with a smattering of lesser varieties, mostly German crosses and old hybrids), was patchy. Some producers did produce good wines, light, fruity with refreshing acidity, but hardly world-beating. The worst were dry, thin and often over-acidic. Some producers seemingly were wine-masochists and made wines that definitely tested even the most ardent Muscadet lover's palate. However, slowly but surely, as new vineyards were planted, sometimes by people who had done their research and had a modicum of training in both viticulture and winemaking, the proportion of good-to-acceptable wines rose and the proportion of poor-to-terrible declined. The arrival of Kenneth McAlpine's Lamberhurst Vineyards, with vines first planted in 1972, with its (for the time) space-age winery, professional winemaker and German-style *süssreserve* sweetened wines, changed the game. From the mid-1970s, as Lamberhurst and other vineyards started to produce much more consumer-friendly wines and the area under vine increased, wine writers, wine buyers and the public started to take notice. Over the next two decades the vineyard area rose until it reached a peak of 1,065 hectares

(2,632 acres) in 1993, after which it declined. However, a perfect storm whipped up by the arrival of New World wines to which the public took wholeheartedly, a lack of interest in German-style (and German-sounding) wines and too much English wine on the market led to growers grubbing their vineyards. Between 1994 and 2004 the area under vine in Britain fell by 304 hectares (751 acres), almost 29 per cent of the total planted. In addition, the retail prices of wines stagnated and, in many cases, fell: a case of over-supply meets under-demand with the inevitable consequences.

The story of the (second) revival of British viticulture, occasioned by climate change which allowed growers to successfully crop and ripen the classic Champagne varieties and make world-class and world-beating sparkling wines is told in much more detail in this book. The area under vine has risen dramatically from that 2004 low point of 761 hectares, to an estimated 2,750 hectares (6,795 acres) by 2018, with the prospect of another 10–15 per cent increase in plantings for 2019, 2020 and … who knows. By my estimate, 50–55 per cent of all producers whose vineyards are currently planted with Champagne varieties do not yet have sparkling wines on sale – either their vineyards are too young to crop or the wines so far produced are too immature to market. Where this wine will sell is the elephant in the room of English and Welsh wine. The exceptionally large 2018 harvest, estimated to be 15.6 million bottles, or three times the 2013–17 average of 5.2 million, will strain the marketing skills of still wine producers, whose wines need to be sold relatively quickly (compared to sparkling wines). The large harvest will also strain the bank balances of sparkling wine producers who must find around £45,000–50,000 per hectare for picking, winemaking, bottling and storage of their wines. The marketing challenge they will have to face is in the future.

The sparkling wine market in Britain, for so long dominated by Champagne, Cava, Asti and New World cheap sparklers, is in a state of transition. The arrival of Prosecco is one of the vinous phenomena of our era and sales in Britain of this fairly undistinguished sparkling wine have risen from an estimated 220,000 bottles in 2000 to over 120 million in 2017 to a point where the product is larger in value (and much larger in volume) than Champagne. The massive increase in Prosecco sales helped contribute to the rise in the sales in Britain of sparkling wines of all types between 2000 and 2018 from 71 million (75 cl) bottles to 215 million – just over three times as many. Although the Champenoise will not openly admit it, Champagne itself is undergoing something of a crisis. Sales in Britain, their biggest export market, stood at 36 million bottles a year in 2008 and 34.2 million in 2015, but had fallen to just under 27.8 million bottles by the end of 2017. One can cite the financial crisis, the Prosecco invasion and a number of other factors, but the fall in the sales of mid-to-upper range Champagnes (which are by far their most profitable products) has been partially matched by the rise in sales of English and Welsh sparkling wines. What message this sends to producers of English and Welsh sparkling wines is another matter. Can the wine market in Britain absorb a doubling, a trebling, a quadrupling of the amount of home-grown sparkling wine that will (not might, not could, but will) come onto the market? Exporting has been mentioned by many of the larger growers as a possible route to market, with some producers hoping to sell as much as 25 per cent of their production overseas. Whilst this is, in principle, a fine idea, in practice, as some producers who have tried it will admit, export markets need finding, nurturing and maintaining – all of which cost time and money. With the volumes of all but the very biggest producers being small in world terms, exporting might not prove to be the route to profits that some believe. For wine producers in Britain, still and sparkling, there are most definitely uncharted waters on the horizon.

However, what is not in doubt at all is the excellence of the products. Whilst still wines lag behind sparkling in terms of absolute quality and value for money, they have made great strides over the last two decades and the best are excellent and, what is more, sell at profitable prices. Sparkling wines continue to improve to a point where Britain now has a place in any line-up of the world's top sparkling wines. Take the very best from Champagne, California, New Zealand and Australia and pit them against wines from Britain and you can guarantee that those wines will be jostling for position in the top ten. Nyetimber's 2018 launch of its '1086' range of £125–150 per bottle wines to almost universal critical acclaim (on taste, on style and on presentation) is an affirmation that sparkling wines from British producers have really arrived on the world stage. However, in terms of production methods and techniques, sparkling wine producers are just beginning their journey. How old are most of the vineyards? Not very. Do we really know which sites and which soils will produce the best wines? Probably not. Have we discovered the best rootstocks and clones for our climate? Definitely not. How far are we along the tried and tested road of making true non-vintage wines? Not far. What's the position on the use of carefully selected reserve wines in both cuvées and dosage? Very limited. In short, whilst Britain's sparkling wines may be good now, there are many reasons to think they could get better in the future. In addition to the above, Britain now has well over 100 serious wine producers, both still and sparkling, and the critical mass will build. Although I have written several guides to the vineyards of England and Wales, this book differs from previous publications in that it contains twenty-one producer profiles, in-depth studies of these businesses intended to give readers an insight into how growing grapes and making wine in a challenging climate can be both a profitable and an enjoyable enterprise. The producers chosen, large and small, established and new, cover all the winegrowing regions. The arrival in Britain of two Champagne houses as vineyard owners (and the very real prospect of more to come), as well as vineyards owned by established and experienced wine producers from other countries, adds a whole new dimension to the business. Whilst Britain is still small in global terms – Champagne produces around 350 million bottles a year, 75 times the young pretender's current average yield – it could be big, very big, in high-end sparkling wine. The next few decades will be interesting ones to watch.

1

VITICULTURE IN THE BRITISH ISLES, PRE-ROMAN TO 1939

PRE-ROMAN BRITAIN

Whether or not vines were grown, grapes harvested and wine made in Britain before the arrival of the Romans is open to debate and as there are no reliable records pointing one way or the other, it is anyone's guess. The Belgae, who had established themselves in the east and south of Britain prior to the Roman invasion, did have a liking for wine, and amphorae[1] dating from before the Roman conquest have been discovered on sites in southern England.

ROMAN VITICULTURE – FACT OR FICTION?

Most books with anything to say about the origins of British viticulture state with absolute certainty that 'the Romans introduced the vine' to the island and then usually go on to give the impression that swathes of vines covered most of the slopes of southern England. Fields that look like they have been terraced by human hand – which in all probability

1 Amphorae were used for transporting all manner of liquids (wine, olive oil and fish sauce were the most usual) over long distances and their presence therefore does not necessarily confirm a connection with wine.

have naturally evolved or have been created by nothing more than hundreds of years of sheep tramping up and down on them – are especially prone to be said to have been 'a Roman vineyard' when absolutely no evidence for one exists.

Dr Tim Unwin, in his scholarly book *Wine and the Vine, An Historical Geography of Viticulture and the Wine Trade*, writes that: 'the northern limit of viticulture in the Roman era is widely considered to have been just north of Paris,' and that 'much of the evidence adduced in support of the cultivation of vines in Roman Britain has been shown … to be of dubious validity'. Hyams conjectures that: 'vines were introduced by the Romans more by way of an ornamental re-creation of the Mediterranean atmosphere, than for the grapes they yielded'. The Roman historian Tacitus, writing at the end of the first century AD in Vita Agricolae, declared that the British climate was 'objectionable and not at all suitable for growing vines or olives'. This could suggest that someone had at least tried to establish vines, even if they had been unsuccessful. Archaeological digs of Roman sites in Britain have also failed to uncover any implements specific to viticulture such as the double-sided vine billhook – the *falx vinitoria* – which are a feature of sites in continental Europe where the Romans grew vines. These are small, easily lost tools and one might have thought that at least a single example would have been found. (Plenty of the usual harvesting and cutting single-sided billhooks used in general agriculture have been found, however.) In addition, no winemaking equipment such as the bases of presses or treading troughs,[2] again a feature of sites where winemaking during the Roman era was carried out, has ever been uncovered. The absence of these is perhaps more understandable, as being floor-level constructions they would have normally been removed once they fell into disuse. Of course, the absence of these items neither proves nor disproves anything but it is generally recognized that there is considerable uncertainty about the scope and scale of Roman viticulture. There is plenty of evidence that wine was imported into Britain during the Roman era and it is said that there are streets in St Emilion paved with stones which came from Britain as ballast. The official Bordeaux wine museum, run by the CIVB (Conseil Interprofessional de Vins de Bordeaux), shows a picture

2 Although stone treading troughs and press bases have been found in continental Europe, there is plenty of evidence to show that the Romans preferred to press grapes in large, shallow wooden troughs, which would naturally not have survived for over 2,000 years.

of the Silchester wine barrel to illustrate their Roman wine industry! This barrel, made from a silver fir only found in the Alps, was discovered lining the walls of a Roman-era well in the town of Silchester, near Basingstoke.

What does not appear to be in doubt is the Romans' liking for wine, whether home-grown or imported. After Claudius' army invaded Britain in AD 43, wine drinking became more commonplace and when Roman villas, houses and garrisons have been excavated, archaeologists have nearly always found remains of wine amphorae and drinking cups. In addition, grape pips and stalks of bunches of grapes are occasionally found, although whether these are from imported or home-grown fruit it is not possible to say. What has never been found is remains of grapes – pips, skins and stems – in a considerable quantity in one place, which, had there been, might well have been evidence of grape pressing and therefore winemaking.

A Roman vineyard discovery?

The much-mentioned 'Roman vineyard' at North Thoresby, just south of Grimsby in Lincolnshire, is an interesting example of the wish for the existence of Roman viticultural activity taking second place to the evidence. In 1955 a landowner found a large quantity of pottery sherds (fragments of pots) on a 4.5-hectare field he owned and had ploughed. Upon investigation, these turned out to be of Romano-British origin dating from the third century with AD 277 being pinpointed as the nearest date for a substantial proportion of the sherds. It was also discovered, by aerial photography and by digging trenches across the site, that the land was covered with an irregular pattern of trenches (wide enough to perhaps be called ditches), about 1.52–1.83 metres wide, 0.91–1.48 metres deep and 7.62 metres apart (5 to 6 feet wide, 3 feet to 4 feet 6 inches deep and 25 feet apart). These trenches contained layers of old pottery and stones (many more than in the adjacent untrenched land) which would appear to indicate an attempt at draining what was (and of course still is) a fairly heavy clay soil. Phosphate levels in the lower levels of the trenches were also tested and found to be eight times higher than in the adjacent land. High phosphate levels are indicative of well-manured land, such as might be found on productive arable or horticultural land. In addition, the humus content of the trenched land was twice as high as untrenched land, again indicating both manuring and residues from plants that grew in the trenches. A report entitled: 'A possible Vineyard of the Romano-British period at North Thoresby, Lincolnshire' was written by the archaeologists who carried out the investigations, D. and H. Webster and D. F. Petch, and published in *Lincolnshire History and Archaeology* no. 2, in 1967. The evidence, the authors suggested, showed that because of the amount of work that went into digging the ditches and importing the stone and pottery to aid drainage, the crop would have had to have been a high-value one. Since olives can be discounted as a commercial crop at these latitudes and other fruits such as apples would not have been of high enough value, it was suggested that grapes were the most likely crop. This was despite the fact that the site was so far north, despite the heavy clay and despite the very wide rows – far wider than vineyards usually planted by Roman vinegrowers. Ray Brock (whose part in the revival of viticulture in Great Britain is fully detailed in Chapter 2) was consulted at the time and he too thought the evidence too flimsy to confirm that this site had been a vineyard. The authors of the report were also somewhat hesitant in declaring the site to have *definitely* been a Roman vineyard and concluded by saying: 'it is tentatively proposed, therefore, that the site at North Thoresby was an unsuccessful experimental vineyard' – hardly a ringing endorsement.

In AD 277 (some references say AD 280), the Emperor Probus repealed Domitian's earlier edict which prevented native inhabitants from planting vines in countries under the Roman yoke (specifically 'Gauls, Spaniards and Britons'). This may have provided the impetus needed for Britons to start growing vines and supplying both their rulers and perhaps some of the very early Christians with home-produced wines.

Salway, in *Roman Britain,* states at the end of his section on the Roman-era wine trade that: 'The evidence for British vine-growing is so far exceedingly thin, though there is some reason to think this may be partly due to inadequate recording in past excavations. Only at Gloucestershire [at Tolsey, Tewkesbury] is there anything remotely satisfactory, and that is from the report of a nineteenth-century find and has little detail. If there were British vineyards, we do not know if their production went beyond the small-scale operation that has revived in this country in recent years [this was written in 1991], nor whether it extended beyond domestic consumption to the commercial market.'

VINEYARDS AFTER THE ROMANS

When the Romans began to leave at the end of the fourth century, Christianity, which had been made the official religion in the empire by Constantine in AD 312, became more widespread and wine drinking, playing as it did an important part in Christian ceremonies, became more accepted. Whether this was of local or imported wine, it is hard to say. If there were vineyards, then they were undoubtedly attached to religious institutions such as abbeys and monasteries. As the Romans finally left Britain, the country was plunged into what we call the Middle Ages and invasions by the Jutes, the Angles and the Saxons destroyed much of the limited civilization that the Romans had established during their 300 years of occupation. These warring tribes had neither the time nor the inclination to settle down and become farmers and whatever vineyards there had been at this time undoubtedly became neglected. The early Christians, fleeing from these tribal disturbances, retreated to the corners of these islands – mainly to Wales and Cornwall – taking with them their skills as winegrowers. Whether they set up vineyards is not recorded, but many of these early Christian settlements (such as on the islands of Lindisfarne and Iona) were in areas not suitable, either then or now, for vines.

When Augustine (the first Archbishop of Canterbury) landed on the Kentish Isle of Thanet in AD 596, sent to Britain by Pope Gregory to convert the early Celtic Christians to a Roman way of Christian worship, he probably brought wine with him and would have obtained further supplies from continental traders. Whether he planted vineyards in England or not is unknown. It would be nice to think that he did and as Canterbury was (and still is) a favourable area for fruit growing, it is not an impossible thought. As Christianity spread into the climatically more favourable areas of Britain, old skills were revived and there is some evidence that vineyards were established. However, given that growing conditions on the continent were more suitable for commercial viticulture and that wine travelled, why would anyone want to establish a vineyard with all its attendant costs, unless they were perhaps members of an enclosed religious order? The fact is that trade with mainland Europe was increasing and it is well recorded that wine played an important part in that trade, thus lessening the need for home-grown product.

The Venerable Bede, writing in his *Ecclesiastical History of the English People*, completed in AD 731, stated that: 'vines are cultivated in various localities' (which Hyams renders as: 'it [Britain] also produces wines in some places', a slightly more positive statement than Bede's actual words). Regardless of the accuracy of the translation, Bede's words seem to have been taken by many as proof-positive that vineyards flourished all over the British isles. However, Dr Unwin notes that there is doubt about its accuracy and Bede's later assertion that: 'Ireland abounds in milk and honey, nor is there any want of vines' was challenged by a twelfth-century writer, Giraldus Cambrensis, who stated that Bede was wrong and that Ireland has no, and never had, vines. In any event, the Vikings, who raped and pillaged their way around much of the country during this period, destroyed many monasteries and once again skills such as vinegrowing and winemaking – had they existed – would have become lost.

King Alfred, the Anglo-Saxon ruler of Wessex from AD 871 to 899, who defeated the Danes at Edington in Wiltshire and saved the country from Scandinavian rule, helped re-establish the Christian religion, and in doing so, undoubtedly encouraged a revival of viticulture (although perhaps not of cake baking). It is often stated that he approved a law giving owners of vineyards compensation in the event of damage by trespassers and this is often taken – once again – as proof-positive that vineyards were definitely being cultivated. Dr Unwin questions this and states that in fact this reference to vineyards occurs in the preamble to Alfred's laws where he is quoting from the Bible (Exodus 20) and that there is *no* mention of vineyards in his own new laws. However, whether or not winegrowing was a feature of ninth-century Britain, there is far less doubt that by the tenth century, vineyards existed and wine was made.

In AD 956 King Eadwig (sometimes called Edwy), Alfred's great grandson, granted Dunstan, the Abbot of St Mary's Abbey, Glastonbury, a vineyard at Panborough in Somerset, and although the original document stating this is lost, it survives in a fourteenth-century copy in the Bodleian Library. Panborough, which has south-facing slopes, is only four miles from Glastonbury, where the Benedictine monastery was re-established in AD 940. Somerset appears to have been something of a centre of winegrowing and several vineyards were recorded there, including one at Watchet, overlooking the Bristol Channel, which King Edgar (the Peaceful) granted to Abingdon Abbey in AD 962 (Hooke 1990).

NORMAN CONQUEST TO THE BLACK DEATH (1066–1350)

By the time William the Conqueror set foot on British soil in 1066 and defeated King Harold at Hastings, monastic viticulture was at a fairly low ebb. Desmond Seward in his *Monks and Wine* says that there were probably no more than 850 monks in the whole of England at the time of the Norman invasion (although out of a population of just under 3 million this is quite a large number), so it is unlikely that monastic vineyards were widespread. However, not only did King William bring with him French soldiers and courtiers for whom wine was a daily requirement, he also brought French abbots and their monks who were experienced in vinegrowing. The year 1066 marked the start of an era of viticultural activity that would not be matched until the current revival, which began almost 900 years later.

King William's Domesday Surveys,[3] which started in 1086 (and were completed by his son William Rufus after William's death in 1087), covered much of the southern half of Britain and record vineyards in 42 definite locations, with references to vines and wines in another three. Ten of the vineyards had been recently planted, suggesting that the Normans were instrumental in supporting viticulture in their newly conquered country. Although in a few instances the sizes of vineyards are given in acres, they are mostly given in arpents (also spelt arpends) – a measure of area about whose exact size there is uncertainty but believed to be slightly less than an acre. Most of the vineyards recorded were in two main regions: around London and up into the eastern counties of Essex, Suffolk and Norfolk (the area covered by the more detailed Little Domesday survey); and in the western counties of Somerset and Dorset. Apart from three in Kent, at Leeds Castle ('two arpents of vineyard'), Chart Sutton, near Maidstone ('three arpents of vineyard, and a park of beasts of the forest') and at Chislet near Canterbury, and one in Surrey, at Staines, there were none recorded in the southern counties of Kent, Surrey, East and West Sussex or Hampshire, the home of a large number of today's vineyards. Was this to do with land ownership, with land

3 The two surveys, Little Domesday and Great Domesday, were by no means a complete survey of the whole of Britain and excluded Scotland, Wales and much of northern England, as well as the cities of London and Winchester. In some of these places there may well have been vineyards.

use or for some other reason? The probable reason is that these were very heavily wooded regions (timber and charcoal production were extremely important at this time) and the large-scale clearances of land for agriculture had not yet begun. The vineyard listed at Leeds Castle was on land that King William gave to his half-brother Bishop Odo of Bayeux and was given together with 8 acres of meadow.

It is also interesting to note that only 12 of the Domesday vineyards were attached to monasteries. The majority of vineyards belonged to nobles and they were undoubtedly cultivated to provide them with wine for their dining tables and altars, rather than for commercial sale. On almost all of the manors where Domesday vineyards were recorded, there were higher-than-average numbers of both slaves and plough teams, and Unwin suggests that these indicate that vineyards were situated on large and prosperous manors. Even King William himself was recorded as owning one at North Curry in Somerset (which had previously been owned by King Harold) which was, at 7 acres, the largest vineyard recorded in Great Domesday. In only one instance do the Domesday Surveys record a yield, that of a vineyard at Rayleigh in Essex. Here, six arpents (about 2 hectares) yielded 20 *modii*, each *modius* being a measure of liquid volume that Hugh Barty-King, author of *A Tradition of English Wine*, gives as equal to 36 gallons or 164 litres. This gives a yield of about 16 hectolitres per hectare which compares not unfavourably to yields in pre-phylloxera vineyards in France of the 1860s of 15–20 hectolitres per hectare.

The conquest of the country by the Normans led to a large influx of different religious orders. The pre-conquest Benedictine monks were soon joined by Cistercians, Carthusians and Augustinians, all of whom needed wine for their religious observances, and the number of vineyards known to be in existence expanded to new levels. There were two main areas of post-invasion monastic viticulture: the southern coastal areas of Kent, East and West Sussex and Hampshire, and Somerset, Gloucestershire, Herefordshire and Worcestershire. William of Malmesbury (a historian who, among other things, updated Bede's *Ecclesiastical History of the English People* and who died in 1143) claimed that Gloucestershire was 'more thickly planted with vineyards' than any other part of England. Henry II (1154–1189) had vineyards and the Pipe Rolls[4] of 1155 stated that: 'it moreover appearethe that tythe hathe

4 Pipe Rolls were the Exchequer's 'books', which recorded financial transactions and taxes.

bene payed of wyne pressed out of grapes that grewe in the Little Parke theare, to the Abbot of Waltham, which was parson bothe of the Old and New Wyndsore, and that accompts have bene made of the charges of planting the vines that grewe in the saide parke, as also of making the wynes, whearof somme partes weare spent in the householde, and somme solde for the kinges profit.'

The Diocese of Canterbury had vineyards at Teynham and Northfleet, both near the north Kent coast, on which the Archbishop spent considerable sums of money. His accounts of 1235 show that the expenses of the vineyard were somewhat greater than the income from it, another reminder that England was then (as today) on the margins for successful commercial viticulture. Kent seemed to be quite well endowed with vineyards. Apart from those already mentioned, vineyards were recorded at Great Chart, Chart Sutton, Halling, Snodland, Hythe, Folkestone, Barming, Tonbridge, Wingham and Sevenoaks. In Gloucestershire more than 20 vineyards are known to have been cultivated in the 1200s, all of them attached to monasteries. Many sources point out that the climate improved for a period of 300 years starting from about the time of the Norman invasion and citing this as the reason why so many vineyards were planted. However, not everyone found this to be the case.

In 1230 the Abbot of Glastonbury, Michael of Amesbury, who had a summer palace at Pilton, Somerset, had a vineyard planted on a sloping site there, appointing William the Goldsmith to manage it and make the wine in 1235. Although the Abbot liked Pilton – he had a new house built there in about 1240 – his vineyard was relatively short-lived and after 30 years the vines were taken out and the hillside converted into a park for game. It is recorded that the summers between 1220 and 1260 were particularly poor and several other vineyards in the country at that time were grubbed-up. By 1270, there were some 14,000 monks in the country (Seward 1979), still out of a total population of less than 3 million.

MIDDLE AGES TO THE END OF THE GREAT WAR (1350–1918)

The story of vinegrowing and winemaking during this long, almost 600-year period is one of change and gradual decline. Why viticulture did not really become a viable alternative for farmers and growers, as it did in other countries where monastic viticulture was common, is open to debate, but probable changes in the climate, together with commercial and practical considerations, have to have been important.

While vineyards were tended by monks and friars assisted by serfs and slaves who in truth had little option but to do what their masters required of them, the question of whether growing grapes and making wine was profitable was probably of little consequence. However, when workers required reward for their hire, the question of whether it was more economical to drink home-grown or imported wine became important. Before the Black Death arrived the religious orders had prospered, benefiting from a pliable and available workforce. However, finding their manpower depleted by the plague, they took to leasing their land rather than working it themselves, and their new tenants, dependent upon short-term cash-crops to pay the rent, did not want to grow vines, which then, as now, are expensive to establish and can really only be grown on a long-term basis. This was the time when rural populations declined, with sheep, and perhaps more importantly their wool, becoming the mainstay of British agriculture. The populations of towns and cities started to expand rapidly and the production of beer and ale became important.

The rise of beer

The rise of beer and ale as the drinks of the masses was probably another contributory factor in the decline of vineyards. Beer was flavoured with hops, whereas ale was 'unhopped', i.e. made without hops. (Today, ale is made with top-fermenting yeast and matures more quickly than beer, which is made with bottom-fermenting yeast and requires more ageing: both will usually be made using hops (or hop extract) to add flavour.) Barley, the main ingredient in both beer and ale, can be stored year-round, so brewing can take place week-in and week-out subject to demand. As the water for the brewing process has to be boiled, beer and ale were safer to drink than most of the water then available, as well as being both alcoholic and thirst quenching.

The last vineyard owned by the Archbishop of Canterbury was pulled up in 1350, the year the plague arrived in Kent. By 1370, the number of monks and friars had dropped to 8,000 compared to a high point of 14,000 one hundred years earlier. Although the Dissolution of the Monasteries, which occurred after the 1534 Act of Supremacy following the annulment of Henry VIII's marriage to Catherine of Aragon in 1533, is often cited as being the single event that destroyed medieval winegrowing and winemaking in England, it would appear that by this time many monasteries had already given up viticulture from either lack of manpower, indolence or a combination of both.

Climate change can also be introduced as a possible reason why the tending of vineyards started to decline. A wide number of sources state that northern Europe warmed up from about 550 BC until the end of the thirteenth century (known as the 'Medieval Warm Period'). This meant that in the period between 1100 and 1300, summers were warmer with average temperatures about 1–1.5°C higher than today's long-term average (although probably about the same as the average over the past ten years), but with colder winters. This equates to today's climate on the Mosel or in Champagne and Chablis. After the mid-1300s, it is said that the British climate generally became wetter, with cooler summers and milder winters, leading to less ripe grapes and more fungal diseases, both of which would have been disincentives to profitable grape growing and winemaking. Wine had been coming into the country from Bordeaux since Henry II (who had married Eleanor of Aquitaine in 1152) became king of England. As more and more wine (and other goods) came into the country from overseas, both transport conditions and speeds improved and the transport of wine became cheaper. Also, as techniques of preserving wine for long journeys improved, imported wines arrived in better condition. Thus poorer quality, lower alcohol (and mainly white) home-produced wine stood little chance against the competition. The love of the British for Bordeaux Clairete, the light red wines of Bordeaux, stems from this era. England signed trading treaties with Portugal from as early as 1353 and whenever the country was at war with France it was at peace with Portugal, which helped secure a supply of good wine (Fielden 1989). According to Seward, 3 million gallons (136,363 hectolitres) came into the country from Bordeaux in 1448–9, which on a per capita basis is higher than today's imports from the same region.

Other factors also played their part in viticulture's problems. The Black Death, which lasted from 1348 until the 1370s, not only cut the population dramatically, but also forced changes in agriculture which had far-reaching social and demographic effects. British fields, until then tended on the feudal strip system, were now divided up into larger fenced and hedged enclosures. Livestock – in particular sheep – required far less manpower than arable crops, and they became commonplace. The resultant drop in the production of grain was compensated for by a rise in imports from mainland Europe, where growing conditions were generally better and supplies could be obtained more easily. This led to an increase in trade of many other goods from overseas, including wine.

With these disadvantages, it is perhaps not surprising that commercial viticulture suffered and vineyard owners, unless they were prepared to support their efforts out of funds from other sources, found more profitable uses for their land. However, despite these problems, vineyards *were* planted and wines *were* made and there are many references to vineyards throughout the literature of the era. Barty-King's book *A Tradition of English Wine* is the most complete history of viticulture in the British Isles yet published and I therefore mention only a few that are of special interest.

James I, who ruled England from 1603 to 1625, had vineyards at Oatlands Park in Surrey, together with a 'vine garden' at St James's Palace, although it is not recorded whether they cropped well (or cropped at all) or whether the grapes were for the table or for winemaking. In 1610, Robert Cecil, the first Earl of Salisbury, asked the great botanist John Tradescant to go to Flanders to search for some suitable vines for his estate. The next year 20,000 vines (at '8 crowns the thousand') were sent from France, with more following in later years. Lord Salisbury's vineyard at Hatfield House, planted on the banks of the River Lea, was well known throughout the seventeenth century. The great diarist Samuel Pepys visited it on 22 July 1661 and commented that he 'walked all alone to the Vineyard which is now a very beautiful place again' (which seems to suggest that it had been neglected previously). He visited it again in 1667. In between these two dates he visited another vineyard owned by one Colonell [sic] Blunt near Blackheath. On 1 May 1665 Pepys writes that he went to Greenwich (by boat from Tower Wharf) and then 'to his house, a very stately sight for the situation and brave plantations; and among others, a vineyard, the first I ever did see!' Unless his previous diary entry was incorrect, it would appear that the Hatfield vineyard failed to make much of an impression on him. Blunt's vineyard was obviously famous (and perhaps a rarity), as several writers of the day visited and commented upon it. Pepys went again to Lord Salisbury's Hatfield vineyard and writes that on 11 August 1667: 'the church being done [it was a Sunday] we to our inn, and there dined very well, and mighty merry; and as soon as we had dined we walked out into the Park through the fine walk of trees, and to the Vineyard, and there shewed them that, which is good order, and indeed a place of great delight.'

John Evelyn, the writer and diarist, visited Blunt's house and gardens a few years before Pepys in 1655 and wrote that he 'had drunk of the wine of his [Blunt's] vineyard which was good for little!' Sir Thomas Hanmer (a well-connected Welsh Royalist and gardening authority) also visited it (in 1656). In 1659 Hanmer wrote in his *Garden Book* – one of the first and most important books on gardening in English – that: 'the vineyard was betwixt one and two acres and was on a hill which lyes full facing on the south'. Hanmer describes the system of growing in full and comments that: 'the Colonell sayth hee uses no dung or compost to this barren earth of his vineyard, which is very strange'. Evidently, 'the Colonell' had discovered what modern growers know only too well: vines in Britain's climate are often too vigorous and benefit from a lack of nitrogenous fertilizer. Hanmer makes no comments on the produce of the vineyard, so perhaps Blunt had stopped offering it to visitors, however grand. Samuel Hartlib, also writing in 1659, said: 'I dare say it's probable that vineyards have formerly flourished in England, and we are to blame that so little is attempted to revive them again' (Barty-King 1977).

In 1666 John Rose, 'Gard'ner to his Majesty [Charles II] at His Royal Garden in St James's', wrote a treatise (a bare 48 small pages long) on the cultivation of vines in England called *The English Vineyard Vindicated.* It was republished three times: in 1672, 1675 and 1691. It was also published, bound together with a translation by John Evelyn of *The French Gardiner* [sic] – an important work in its time – in 1669 and 1672. In his opening 'Epistle Dedicatory' Rose states: 'I know your Majesty can have no great opinion of our English Wines as hitherto they have been order'd'. He then goes on to say that he hopes 'that by his instructions and recommendations that precious Liquor may haply once again recover its just estimation'. In the preface, written by Philocepos (John Evelyn's pseudonym) it is stated that he (Evelyn): 'discussed with Mr Rose the Cause of the neglect of Vineyards of late in England and questioned why they had declined when one considered how frequently they were heretofore planted in this Country of ours.'

In his treatise, Rose discusses the question of site selection, vine varieties, pruning and training (with illustrations) and care of the vines up to the harvest. He was also a commercial nurseryman as on the front page of the treatise he states that it contains 'an Address where the best Plants are to be had at easie rates,' and ends it by advertising that he has 'a plentiful stock of sets and plants for sale and that readers may receive them of me at very reasonable Rates'. Rose, obviously a talented gardener, is generally regarded as the first person to grow an *Ananas* (pineapple) in England, which he presented to King Charles II in 1671.

In 1670, one Will Hughes, a servant to the Right Honourable Edward, Lord Viscount Conway and Kilulta, wrote a book entitled *The Compleat Vineyard: or An Excellent Way for the Planting of Vines According to the French and German Manner and Long Practised in England.* In the introduction he states: 'there have been plenty of vineyards in England heretofore; and it is very well known that there are now in Kent, and other places of this Nation, such Vineyards and Wall-vines as produce great store of excellent good wine'. In his book he gives explicit instructions on all aspects of growing vines: site selection and preparation, choice of varieties – 'the lesser and greater white Muscadine, the red Muscadine, the Frantinick, the Parsley-grape (more for show and rarity than profit) and the Rhenishwine vine' – how to stake and grow them, when to pick ('when they are ripe by their sweet and pleasant taste') and finally how to make the most of them in the winery.

Despite these exhortations from the good and the great of the time, vineyards do not appear to have been widely planted. However, a few were. Richard Selley in his book *The Winelands of Britain: Past, Present and Prospective* tells of a substantial vineyard at Deepdene, near Dorking. Here, Charles Howard, the fourth son of the Duke of Norfolk (whose descendant was to plant one a century later at the family seat, Arundel Castle), planted a vineyard which seems to have been popular with writers. John Evelyn made several visits to Deepdene between 1655 and 1670 but did not mention the vineyard, so perhaps it had not been planted by then. John Aubrey visited in 1673, by which time it had been planted as he produced a plan showing it to cover 7 acres, 1 rood and 1 pole[5] (2.94 hectares). In 1724 Daniel Defoe wrote in his book *A Tour thro' the Whole Island of Great Britain* that the vineyard had

5 A rood is an area of one furlong (just over 200 metres) long by one rod (just over five metres) wide. There are four roods to the acre. A pole is 1/160th of an acre.

produced: *most excellent good wines and a very great quantity of them.* By 1762, however, the vineyard appears to have been abandoned.

In 1690 or thereabouts, one 'D. S.' wrote a book called *Vinetum Angliae: or A new and easy way to make Wine of English Grapes, and other fruit, equal to that of France, Spain etc, with their Physical Virtues,* which was published by G. Conyers, at the Gold Ring in Little Britain (price 1 shilling). In chapter 1 of this little book, charmingly entitled *England's Happiness Improved: or, an Infallible Way to get Riches, Encrease* [sic] *Plenty, and promote Pleasure,* the author states: 'That Vineyards have been frequent in England is apparent, upon the account of the many places now bearing Corn and Pasture retaining that Name,' and continues by saying that 'it is the Opinion of the most experienced in this way, that the Southern parts of this Island, with the Industry of the Natives, might produce Vines [sic] equal to those of France, either Claret or White-Wines.' D. S. then sets out the precise way in which vines should be planted and manured (although surprisingly does not mention which varieties of grape would be best), continuing with a section entitled *To make Wine of the Grapes of the Growth of England* in which he details the complete winemaking process and finishing with the advice that 'the white grapes not too ripe give a good Rhenish-Tast [sic], and are wonderful cooling.'

In 1727, a 'Gentleman' known only by the initials S. J. published a relatively large handbook (192 pages) on growing vines (as well as a wide variety of other fruits).[6] It was called *The Vineyard* and in it S. J. writes: 'Tis not above a century or two of years since the planting of the Peach, the Nectrine, the Apricot, the Cherry and the Hop, were treated in as ridiculous a manner, as the Vine-yards at present are, in this Country,' and goes on to demonstrate in careful detail how vines would grow and fruit in the British climate. He continued by saying: 'the Want of Wine in England is not owing to the Unkindness of our Soil, or the Want of a benign Climate, but to the Inexperience of our Natives.'

6 Blanche Henrey in *British Botanical and Horticultural Literature before 1800* suggests that the author of this book was in fact Richard Bradley, Professor of Botany at Cambridge. Bradley's publisher, Mears (who also published *The Vineyard*) did publish a number of his works and included a similar title in a list of his publications. However, this is only an assumption based on circumstantial evidence as there is no obvious reason why Bradley would publish this anonymously as he was (apparently) a self-seeking, ambitious man, and there is no evidence of his travelling in France (the book makes frequent reference to French vineyards). Also, as Bradley was a well-known writer at the time, it is hard to believe that his publisher would fail to use his name in this work and lose potential sales. S. J. was most probably someone else entirely.

How experienced S. J. was is open to conjecture as he also advocated the growing of almonds and olives, fruits which even the most optimistic of growers would find difficult to grow today in the open air.

Painshill Place

One of the most famous vineyards of this era was that at Painshill Place, Cobham, Surrey (the Painshill junction on the A3 road is named after it) which was planted by the Honourable Charles Hamilton in 1740. Hamilton, the ninth and youngest son of the Earl of Abercorn, was an extraordinary character, as so many in this saga seem to be. In 1738, aged 34, he took a long lease on a 121-hectare (300-acre) property and started to construct one of the most fabulous gardens of its time. He landscaped it and filled it with follies including a ruined abbey, a Roman temple, a Turkish tent, a Temple of Bacchus, a fantastic shell-filled grotto, a hermitage complete with hermit,[7] and some Roman steps. The gardens also featured a vineyard.

Planted between 1741 and 1743 on a steep 45-degree slope, it overlooked a magnificent lake constructed so that it was 12 feet (3.66 metres) above the level of the nearby river Mole – to stop it becoming flooded – and kept at exactly the same level, summer and winter, by being constantly topped up by a 35-foot (10.67-metre) water wheel which brought water up from the adjacent river. Hamilton employed David Geneste, a Huguenot refugee from a winegrowing family from Clairac, a town near Agen in south-west France, to tend his vines and make his wine. Geneste appears to have started working for Hamilton by 1748 as according to letters he wrote to a friend in the October of that year, the vineyard then extended to fifteen *cartonnats* (about 2 hectares/5 acres) and Hamilton wanted to plant a further 4.05 hectares (10 acres) in the next year. Geneste commented that the vineyard was in a very poor state when he arrived but he soon set-to and by 1750 the vineyard contained several different varieties: Pied Rouge, Muscat Blanc, Muscat Rouge, Guillan Blanc, and Sauviot together with a few other *hatifs*

7 The hermit was to be paid 700 guineas (for a seven-year contract) and had to agree to the following conditions: He must remain for seven years with a Bible, optical glasses, a mat for his feet, a hassock for his pillow, an hourglass for his timepiece, water for his beverage, and food from the house. He must wear a camel robe, and never, under any circumstances, must he cut his hair, beard, or nails, stray beyond the limits of Mr Hamilton's grounds, or exchange one word with the servants. Perhaps not surprisingly, he found it difficult to adhere to these conditions and legend has it that after three weeks he was found in a drunken state in the local inn and was dismissed.

(early ripening varieties). Yields from the vineyard were very varied. The 1751 harvest was ruined by poor flowering and frost at harvest time, but in 1754 four barrels of wine were made, two of which were sold as 'vin de Champaign at 50 pièces' [7 guineas] a barrel.

In 1775, after Hamilton had given up the lease to the estate (see below), he wrote to a friend that the vineyard was:

> *... planted with two sorts of Burgundy grapes, the Auvernat, which is the most delicate, but the tenderest, and the Miller grape, commonly called the black cluster, which is more hardy. The vineyard at Painshill is situated on the south-side of a gentle hill, the soil gravelly sand. The first year, I attempted to make red Wine, in the usual way, by treading the grapes, then letting them ferment in a vat, till all the husks and impurities formed a thick crust at the top, the boiling ceased, and the clear Wine was drawn off from the bottom. It was so very harsh and austere, that I despaired of ever making red Wine fit to drink; but through that harshness I perceived a flavour something like that of some small French white Wines, which made me hope I should succeed better with white Wine. That experiment succeeded far beyond my most sanguine expectations; for the very first year I made white Wine, it nearly resembled the flavour of Champaign [sic]; and in two or three years more, as the Vines grew stronger, to my great amazement, my Wine had a finer flavour than the best Champaign I ever tasted; but such is the prejudice of most people against any thing of English growth, I generally found it most prudent not to declare where it grew, till after they had passed their verdict upon. [This advice, unfortunately, is probably just as true today as it was in 1775.] The surest proof I can give of its excellence is, that I have sold it to Wine-merchants for fifty guineas a hogshead; and one Wine-merchant, to whom I sold five hundred pounds worth at one time, assured me, he sold some of the best of it from 7s.6d to 10s.6d per bottle.*

In 1747, Philip Miller, writing in his *Gardener's Dictionary* (the first edition of which was published in 1731) said, 'that there have of late years been but very few vineyards in England though they were formerly very common and that at this day very few Persons will believe it [wine production] possible to be effected'. In the sixth edition, published in 1771, Miller recommends planting 'the Black Cluster or Munier [sic] Grape, as it is called by the French, from the hoary down of the leaves'.

(Barty-King surmises that the 'Dusty Miller', a synonym for Meunier, was named after Philip Miller himself. I find this less than probable and am sure that the name derives from the French word for 'miller' due to the floury look that the leaves of this vine have.) Miller's *Gardener's Dictionary* became a standard work on all things horticultural and went to nine editions, the last being published in 1835 with the inscription '*Ebenus Cretica*' – no more published (Gabler 1985). The sixth edition, although it has a large section on wine and winemaking (not only from grapes), has more on growing table grapes than on wine grapes under the entry for *Vitis*.

In 1786, Francis Xavier Vispré (quite a well-known painter at the time), who had owned a small vineyard in Wimbledon (and was later to have another one in Chelsea) and who had given a talk at the Society of Arts two years earlier called *A Plan for Cultivating Vineyards Adapted to this Climate*, wrote a small book on the subject – *A Dissertation on the Growth of Wine in England* – which gained some popularity, even notoriety. This was possibly because he challenged a Revd M. Le Brocq over a system of growing vines that he (Vispré) had been using for some years and which Le Brocq had patented. Vispré writes (with little modesty) that he was 'sufficiently satisfied with the prospect of being the restorer of Vineyards in this country,' and was obviously peeved that Le Brocq had stolen both his thunder and apparently his methods.

Despite all this writing and proselytizing about outdoor vineyards, they did not really become widespread or commercially successful. Painshill died out at the end of the 1800s and although there were others, the story was much the same. After the initial enthusiasm of the owners (mainly gentlemen of property and considerable income), the uncertainty of the climate and the variability of the crops in terms of both quality and quantity took their toll and the vineyards were abandoned. Tastes and fashions in wines also changed. Sweet, heavy, fortified wines from 'the colonies' (Australia and South Africa) were popular and home-grown wines could never match these. During the shortages of wine from mainland Europe in the latter part of the nineteenth century due to the damage done to vineyards by phylloxera, British companies, as did firms on the continent, started to make wines from both raisins and grape concentrate and the 'British Wine' industry was born.[8]

8 'British Wine' is wine made from imported grape juice, usually concentrated, and fermented and finished in Britain.

The Bute family and Castle Coch

The last great experiment into commercial viticulture – that is before the start of the modern revival – was that of Lord Bute at Castel Coch, to give it its Welsh name, although it is more usually called Castle Coch (or sometimes called in literature of the time Castle Cock). The third Marquess of Bute, John Patrick Crichton-Stuart, was a landowner and industrialist who had the wherewithal to indulge his visions and fantasies. His father, sometimes known as 'the creator of modern Cardiff', had died in 1848, leaving him not only vast properties all over the country, but also the ruins of Castle Coch, some 5 miles outside Cardiff.[9] In 1871, the 24-year-old Marquess, who was intrigued by the Middle Ages, commissioned the architect William Burges to restore the castle to its medieval glory. In 1873 he summoned Andrew Pettigrew, his head gardener at his main residence, Mount Stuart on the Isle of Bute in Scotland, and told him of his plan to complete his vision of the past at Castle Coch by surrounding it with a vineyard. He sent Pettigrew to Castle Coch to survey the site and report back.

Not one to do anything by half, the enthusiastic Marquess dispatched Pettigrew to France to see how vines should be grown. Pettigrew appears to have been well looked after, especially by a Champagne grower called Jacquesson who arranged for him to travel to Bordeaux in the company of one of his clerks, Scottish by birth but a fluent French speaker, who showed Pettigrew the 1873 *vendange* at Châteaux Latour, Lafite and Margaux. Following his visit, vines were ordered and in the spring of 1875, they were delivered, the varieties chosen being Gamay Noir and Millie Blanche (also sometimes called Miel Blanc). According to a report by Pettigrew in the Royal Horticultural Society's (RHS) *Journal* of 1895, only enough vines were procured to cover one eighth of the 3 acres selected to be planted, so Pettigrew took cuttings and had soon propagated enough to cover the full area. The land chosen was the southern slope below the castle, just 4 miles from the Bristol Channel. It had previously been cleared of weeds by taking a crop of potatoes and had then been trenched to help with the drainage. The vines were planted on a 3-foot (0.91-metre) square system, low trained to the ground on a 4-foot (1.22-metre) high trellis, in the manner suggested by Miller in

9 The Butes' fortunes were founded on their enterprise in building Cardiff Docks, together with the railways that brought coal and iron ore in from the mines. At one point Cardiff Docks handled a third of the world's exports (by weight) of all products.

his *Gardener's Dictionary*. (Millie Blanche did not prove to be a successful variety and it was eventually replaced with Gamay Noir.)

The years between 1875 and 1877 were good ones – warm and dry – and the vines were able to establish themselves well, while disease, especially *Oidium tuckeri*, was kept to a minimum. In 1877, the first small crop was harvested and made into wine at a winery established in Cardiff Castle (where the original press can still be seen). The grapes were crushed and a little water along with 3 pounds (1.36 kilos) of cane sugar to every gallon were added and the wine allowed to ferment for 20 days. In that first vintage only 240 bottles were made. Despite *Punch* magazine's assertion that if ever a bottle of wine was produced it would take four men to drink it – two to hold the victim and one to pour it down his throat – the wine was well received and likened to a still Champagne (as the wine from Painshill had been).

Lord Bute was pleased with the success of the original vineyard and asked Pettigrew to look for further sites on his estate. Over the next 35 years, the original site below Castle Coch was expanded and a further two sites were planted. One was at nearby Swanbridge, between Penarth and Barry, where, in 1886, 5 acres (just over 2 hectares) of vines were established. Another, a smaller one, was planted at St Quentins near Cowbridge, overlooking the Bristol Channel, but was abandoned owing to it being much too windswept. These two later sites were planted with Gamay Noir cuttings from the original Castle Coch vineyard.

Throughout the life of Bute's vineyards there were tremendous variations in cropping levels. In 1879 poor flowering weather caused all the flowers to drop off and no crop was taken at all, Pettigrew reporting that a total of 44.4 inches (1,128 mm) of rain fell on 196 days in the year. Likewise, cold weather caused total crop losses in 1880, 1882, 1883 and 1886. However, 1,500 bottles were made in both 1884 and 1885 and in 1887 3,600 bottles were made, the largest ever crop from the Castle site. Between 1878 and 1892 only white wines were made, but in 1893 the harvest was huge and a good red wine was made. In total, from all the vineyards,[10] 40 hogsheads were made (around 9,560 litres), yielding a total of 1,000 cases of a dozen bottles each (a yield of about 17 hectolitres per hectare/1 tonne per acre). It was calculated that at 60

10 The actual size of the Bute vineyards is open to question and various publications – contemporary and modern – give different acreages. My best guess is 5.26 hectares (13 acres) in total, not including the unsuccessful site at St Quentins.

shillings (£3) a dozen the potential income from the 1893 harvest alone was sufficient to repay all the expenses of the vineyards to date. However, as the usual practice was to leave the wine in barrel for three years and in bottle for four before it was sold, there was no prospect of instant income. The wine from the 1893 vintage, however, was not a great success. Pettigrew's son, also called Andrew, who succeeded him as Bute's gardener, said that although 'a deficiency of three degrees of saccharinity was recorded ... Lord Bute refused to allow the addition of sugar, with the result that only a vinegary liquor was produced.'

A mixture of incompatible sorts

Contemporary accounts vary as to the quality of the wine. At an RHS meeting in September 1894, at which Pettigrew (a Fellow of the RHS) gave a talk, samples of the wines were available. Mr Lance, another Fellow and a chemist to boot, said: 'the samples of wine on the table were most excellent as a British production; not only full of alcoholic strength, but containing an agreeable amount of natural acid tartrate, as well as aroma, being far in advance of Grape wines generally manufactured in this country.' However, a Mr W. Roupell, present at the talk, said that 'experiments should be conducted with a view to producing a wine with a character of hock not sherry,' indicating that some of the wines tasted were both high in alcohol and quite sweet (dry sherry being a relatively modern invention). Pettigrew said that the standard winemaking practice was: 'to bring the must up to 30° proof [approximately 15 per cent alcohol] before putting it in the barrel'. However, Tod, writing in 1911, says that he was a regular visitor to the vineyards and had drunk several vintages. He drank the 1881, listed as a 'still Champagne', in the Angel Hotel, Cardiff (a Bute-owned establishment), so it would appear that there were at least two different styles produced. Tod was not really impressed with the Bute wines and later wrote that there 'was a want of definiteness of style and character in the wines and that they remind one of a mixture of incompatible sorts.' Hardly a seal of approval.

Pettigrew continued to look after the vines for Lord Bute and despite a run of dreadful years, continued to be optimistic. The wines were sold locally and the 1881 was sold at the usual price of 60 shillings per dozen – some even higher. A price of 115 shillings (£5.75) a dozen was achieved at auction when the contents of a local doctor's cellar were sold.

The wines were also stocked by the London firm of Hatch, Mansfield & Co. and listed as 'Canary Brand, Welsh Wines' with the 1887 vintage available in four different styles all priced 'at 44/- [£2.20] the dozen ... payment of carriage to any railway station in Great Britain or Port in Ireland' included. Interestingly, the styles of wine described mainly appear to be sweet; the four 1887 wines are described as: 'Full Golden Rather Sweet, Dark Golden Medium Sweet, A Luscious Golden Wine and Light Golden Mellow.' Considering that Gamay would be considered a difficult variety to ripen today and knowing the usual natural sugar levels of suitable varieties of grapes grown in South Wales today, it is not surprising that considerable amounts of sugar had to be added to the juice before fermentation. Whatever these tasted like, it is fairly certain that they can have borne little relation to the light fruity wines that are produced in South Wales now.

The third Marquess of Bute died in 1900 and was succeeded by his 19-year-old son, who was equally enthusiastic about the vineyards. Poor vintages, however, coupled with bad attacks of oidium, put the whole venture at risk. Even so, Tod visited the vineyard in 1905 and noted that he found 63,000 vines in fruit which at 9 square foot per vine meant there were some 13 acres (5.25 hectares) cropping. The summer of 1911 was apparently good and wines were made, but even so (according to Barty-King), 3.5 pounds (1.59 kilos) of sugar to every gallon was required, which by my calculations would have raised the potential alcohol by 20 per cent over its natural level. This would indeed have given a very sweet, high-alcohol wine.

The 1911 appears to have been the last successful vintage at Castle Coch. The Great War brought many shortages, and sugar, which then as now, was required to bring the alcohol up to acceptable levels, could not be spared. No wine was made during the war and in 1920 the vines were grubbed-up. Pettigrew junior, speaking to the Cardiff Naturalists' Society in 1926, was fairly clear as to why the vineyards previously under his and his father's care had not survived, saying: 'here [in Glamorgan] viticulture holds out no promise of success. There is obviously something wrong with the climate when even in the most favourable of seasons it has been found necessary to resort to the artificial addition of sugar or (as in some cases) of alcohol.' He also added that in only seven out of the 45 years had the grapes fully ripened.

The Bute vineyards at Castle Coch and Swanbridge were the last vineyards of anything approaching a commercial size to be planted in Great Britain expressly for the production of wine before the modern revival began in the 1950s. In between 1911 and 1952 (when the first 'revival' vineyard was planted at Hambledon) there were two world wars and the economic upheaval of the Depression of the 1930s. It is perhaps not surprising that planting vineyards and making wine did not occur on a commercial scale during this 40-year period.

TWO THOUSAND YEARS OF GRAPE GROWING

Anyone looking back over the almost two thousand years from the Roman occupation to the end of the Bute vineyards, would have to admit that outdoor viticulture for the production of wine grapes had been tried and had not proved itself commercially viable in the British Isles. The historical evidence is of brave attempts – some might even say foolishly brave attempts – at establishing vineyards, only to have them, ultimately, fail. Whatever successes growers did have in growing and ripening grapes, the quality of the wine was never good enough to sustain the vineyard longer than the enthusiasm of the man (and in all this history I can find no record of a female *vigneron*) who initially planted and supported it.

The revival,[11] if that is what it is, had to wait for the arrival of some brave – again, some would call them foolhardy – pioneers who wanted to disprove the theory then abroad that wine could not be made from grapes grown outside in the British climate. A combination of new varieties, more suitable growing techniques, better disease control and an acceptance by the public of the style of wines that those varieties produced, were the key elements in that revival.

11 I have never been totally comfortable with referring to the twentieth-century recurrence of grape growing as a 'revival', as the wine produced in earlier times was usually not intended for sale and the vineyards were very non-commercial. However, everyone likes to hark back to golden eras (often in reality not especially golden), so I will go with the flow on this one and keep referring to it as a 'revival'.

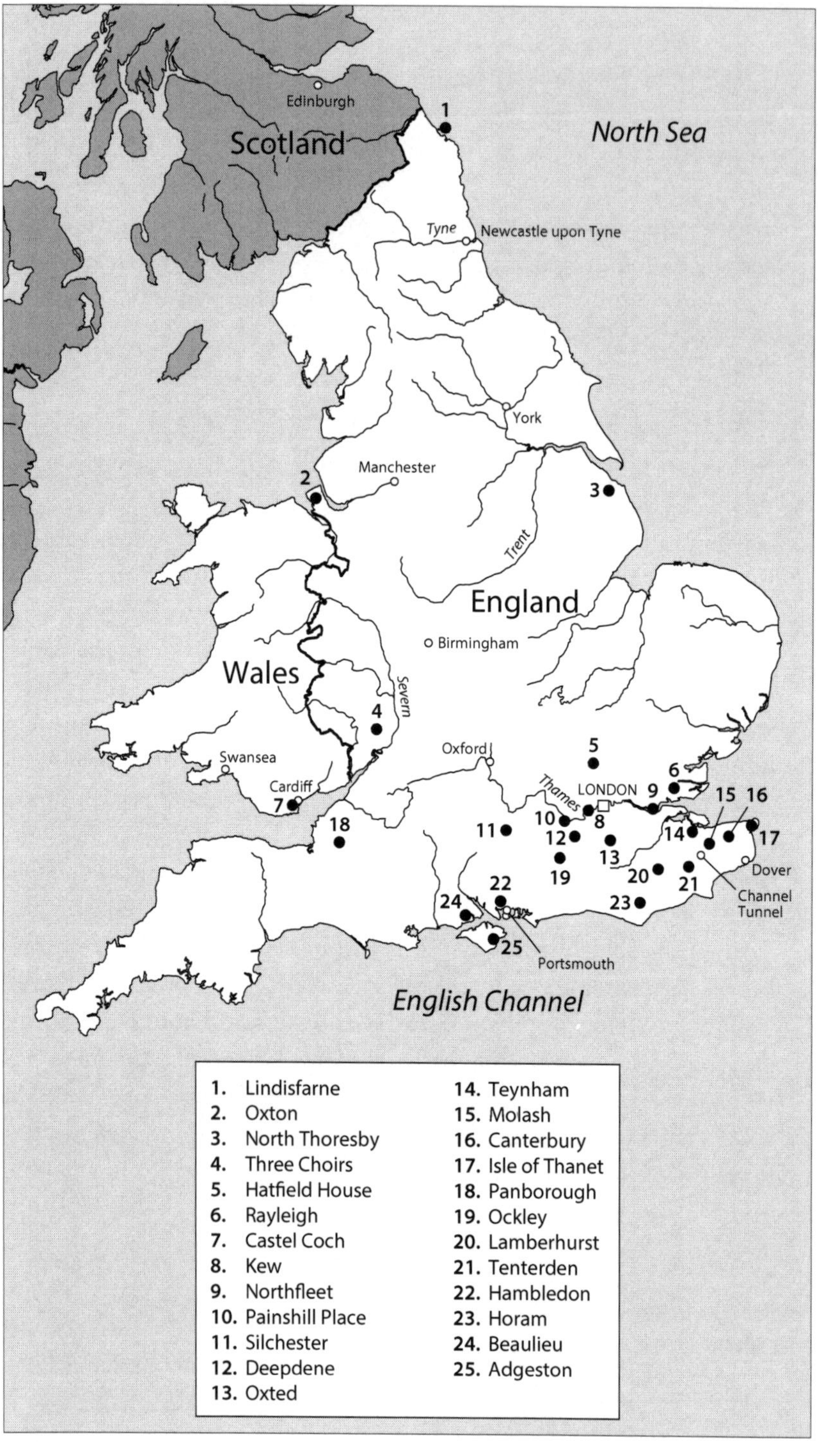

English and Welsh wine: sites of historical interest

2

THE REVIVAL, 1939–1951

To say that vinegrowing in the British Isles totally disappeared after the end of the Marquess of Bute's efforts in South Wales would be incorrect. Yes, it would appear that the growing of vines for commercial wine production ceased, but this did not stop there being a lively interest in the growing of grapes for both home-made wines and for the table. No doubt because of the state of the economy after the First World War and during the recession of the late 1920s and 1930s, many more people had vegetable gardens, allotments and smallholdings in which they raised a wide variety of fruits, vines included. In addition, there was a very wide use of glass cloches to protect tender plants, and two manufacturers, Horticultural Utilities Ltd of Liverpool and Chase Protected Cultivation Ltd of Shepperton, did much to promote the cultivation of vines under glass, both before and after the Second World War. There were also commercial growers in several places, Worthing in West Sussex and in the Channel Islands to name but two, who still grew grapes for the table under glass (Black Hamburg, Muscat of Alexandria and Gros Colmar were the standard dessert varieties) and who sent the fruit, carefully packed in baskets, up to Covent Garden for sale.

ROLAND LEE AND THE CHESHIRE VINEYARDS

A small booklet called *Growing Grapes in the Open* by Roland Lee, published in 1939, throws some interesting light on the situation before the experimental vineyards at Oxted were planted by Ray Brock (of whom more later). In this booklet (which Brock gave me when I visited him shortly before he died), Lee states that 'the urge to cultivate the grapevine was handed down by my forebears,' and says that he came from a long line of vinegrowers, claiming that as long ago as 1249 an ancestor, one Robert Dacre, was 'Keeper of Vineyards by Letters Patent'. He also stated that the first vineyard owned by the Lee family was 'established by James Lee in about 1720 ... at Hammersmith,' although his business logo clearly states 'First Established in 1770'. Barty-King (1977) throws some light on the Lee family and says that they co-owned London's famous 'Vineyard Nursery'. This was started in about 1745 on the site of what had been a vineyard, where today the Olympia exhibition centre stands. This continued to be owned and operated by the Lees and their descendants until the 1890s. J. C. Loudon's *Encyclopaedia of Gardening* of 1834 says that there had been a vineyard on the site, owned by Lee and Kennedy, and that 'a considerable quantity of burgundy wine was made year by year'.

It is obvious from both the text and the photographs in Lee's booklet that he was serious when it came to growing vines out of doors. At Oxton (near Birkenhead) in Cheshire, he had a 1-hectare (2.5-acre) vineyard (said on the back of the booklet to be the 'only Outdoor Vineyard Nursery in Great Britain') of 12,500 grafted vines aged three to four years of the varieties Alicante and Black Campanella (the latter being a black variety which he claimed as his own crossing), together with a vine nursery containing over 90,000 young grafted vines 'ready for lifting and sale'. Apart from Alicante and Black Campanella, Lee recommended two other black varieties, Black Hamburg and Reine Olga; and three whites, Roland's Muscatel (another exclusive variety), Royal Muscadine (also known as Chasselas Doré) and Queen of Vineyards. On the inside of the back of the booklet Lee quotes many newspaper and magazine articles (*Daily Mail, The Times, Daily Herald, Ideal Home, Popular Gardening* and several more) all of which take the same line: that they were surprised, but pleased, that someone was showing that table grapes (and nowhere in the booklet are wine varieties mentioned) could be successfully grown outside and ripened without glass. The booklet also contains a report of a radio broadcast (BBC National Service, at 2 p.m. on Sunday 23 October 1938) in which Mr Middleton (C. H. Middleton, a popular radio broadcaster of the time) and a Mr F. Jordan gave a talk on 'Outdoor Vines, Peaches and suitable Fruits for Walls' which 'has done much to popularise outdoor Vines'. This twenty-minute talk, sandwiched between 'Troise and his Banjoliers' and 'Charles Ernesco and his Quintet' (how times have changed), was reported in *The Listener* (a weekly magazine published by the BBC). It made no mention, however, of vines for winemaking.

What happened to Roland Lee and his vineyards remains something of a mystery. In 1939 his company appears to have been taken over by Cheshire Vineyards Ltd, who also claimed the only 'Outdoor Vineyard Nursery in Great Britain' (presumably the same one). It is known from a letter dated 1949, sent to Ray Brock by the well-known vine nursery owned by the Teleki family in Austria, that they sent 'important quantities of grafted vines' to Liverpool in 1939 and Cheshire Vineyards may well have been the destination. (Unfortunately, all Teleki's records were destroyed through Second World War bombing so they could not be certain where the vines had actually been sent.)

After 1939 the trail more or less goes cold. Hyams, in a note after the preface to his book *The Grape Vine in England*, published in 1949, apologizes for 'having failed to mention, among recent British vineyards, the Cheshire vineyard of hardy hybrids which was established successfully before the late war,' but gives no further details. Brock mentions neither Lee nor his proprietary varieties in any of his (Brock's) publications even though Lee's booklet was in his possession. Both Hyams and Brock mention Horticultural Utilities Ltd of Rigby Street, Liverpool who, in catalogues from 1951, claimed that in Formby they had 'The Principal Vine Nursery of England' (which might imply that there was at least one other). Since Birkenhead and Formby are but 12 miles away (as the crow flies) one has to assume that by then Lee's vineyard had, if not totally disappeared, significantly diminished. Horticultural Utilities published two small pamphlets *Vines Under Glass and in the Open* (c. 1951) and *Successful Growing of Grape Vines* (c. 1954) both written by S. E. Lytle. In the 1951 booklet virtually all of the varieties offered for sale were for table grape production, whereas by 1954, both *viniferas* and hybrids (including Seyve Villard 5276) are offered, reflecting the early trials being carried out by Brock at Oxted.

By the mid-1940s, with the country at war, growing grapes commercially to make wine must have seemed a fairly remote prospect. If English and Welsh viticulturalists were ever to succeed, they were certainly by now in need of a Moses to lead them to the promised vineyard. In fact, two people appeared who, in their own ways, brought about the start of the revival which resulted in the planting, in 1952, of the first commercial vineyard of modern times at Hambledon in Hampshire. These men were Ray Brock and Edward Hyams.

RAYMOND BARRINGTON BROCK 1908–99

Ray Brock must be considered as one of the founding fathers – if not *the* founding father – of the revival in wine production in the British Isles. At the start of the war he was in a reserved occupation – he was managing director of Townson and Mercer Ltd, a well-known firm of scientific instrument makers – and wished to move away from Croydon where he and his wife lived and which at the time was being heavily bombed.[12] In 1941, they moved to a house called Summerfield which had been built in 1938 by a lady called Doris Foster who, on account of the bombing, wanted to move to Cornwall. Summerfield, at Rockfield Road, Oxted, Surrey, is situated at an altitude of 122–137 metres (400–450 feet) on the South Downs, overlooking the Weald. With considerable enthusiasm and dedication – and aged only 33 – he took to gardening and, as recorded in his meticulously kept garden notebooks, planned and set out a substantial garden, including a large area devoted to fruit trees of all types. In March 1943, on one wall of the house, he planted the first of what was to be many vines – a Brandt which came from Hilliers of Winchester. He noted when it arrived that it was 'very badly pruned'.

Among his fruit collection were several peach trees which, he recorded, even at that altitude, ripened their fruit well. As the received horticultural wisdom of the time was that peaches needed at least a south-facing wall, if not a proper peach house, to ripen them, Brock started to consider what other 'exotic' fruits he might grow. His thoughts turned to grapes. In the preface to his book *Outdoor Grapes in Cold Climates* (1949) he writes: 'it is now difficult to remember just why we originally decided to start a Vineyard, although we are now very frequently asked this question. We think that primarily we were so interested to discover the ease with which Peaches could be ripened on bush trees out-of-doors, despite all the old gardening literature on the

12 In fact, their house in Croydon never suffered damage while the Brocks lived there, but soon after moving to Oxted, a Heinkel dropped a stick of bombs in the garden and blew quite a few tiles off their roof. Always one to see an advantage where others might see a misfortune, Brock excavated the hole and built himself a swimming pool.

subject [which said it was impossible to ripen them] that we felt equally sceptical about the comments on Grapes.'

The Oxted Viticultural Research Station

Brock's vineyard, initially called the Beebrock Vineyard, but later renamed (with typical Brock confidence) the Oxted Viticultural Research Station, was conceived with great care and a 'grand plan' was drawn up. The vineyard was located on two separate plots. A small part was in his existing garden and this he prepared in July 1945. The larger part was established on an additional 0.4 hectares (1 acre) of land that adjoined his garden and which his accounts for 1944/5 show he purchased for £980.[13] Brock noted in his garden diary that he: 'Spent two whole days (four in all) clearing Vineyard site. Managed to burn everything and got up a lot of Brambles.' On 28 November 1945, Ernie Walker, a man he had taken on to help with the work (and who had been offered the job while still a serving soldier building Bailey bridges in Germany), ploughed the land.[14]

The major task facing Brock in 1945 was that of locating and obtaining different vine varieties to plant. The effort and diligence – as well as time and money – which he put into this task was formidable and with the benefit of hindsight one can safely say that the real achievement of Brock's vine growing was the assembling and trialling of some 600 different vine varieties over the 25 years of the research station's life. Brock mounted what can only be described as a one-man crusade to collect as many different vine varieties as he could. He was a member of the RHS – he was invited to serve on their Fruit Group Committee in 1946 – and through their magazine, *The Garden*, he asked members to send hardwood cuttings of vines in their gardens and greenhouses to Wisley (RHS headquarters), which, when they had been rooted, were sent on to Oxted. Hundreds of cuttings arrived, many of them misnamed, many of them duplicates. By 1947, Brock had 1,400 vines of 29 varieties and by 1950 this had expanded to over 7,000 vines of 60 different varieties. He visited Switzerland in 1946 (and again in 1947) and made good contact with Mr Leyvraz at the Swiss Federal Vine Testing Station at Caudoz-sur-Pully. For several years they sent him (free of charge)

13 At a later stage, Brock decided that he needed more land for the vineyard and was able to buy an additional 2 hectares (5 acres) of land adjacent to the house.

14 Brock always referred to Walker as his 'vinearoon'. See p. 41 for the origin of this term.

cuttings of a large number of varieties from their collection including the two which would, in future years, become the backbone of the early English and Welsh wine industry: Müller-Thurgau (then called Riesling Sylvaner) and Seyve Villard 5276 (Seyval Blanc).

Import licences were obtained from the Ministry of Agriculture, Fisheries and Food (MAFF) and in the spring of 1947, the first vines arrived and were inspected by a Mr Rhodes, the local MAFF plant health inspector, and pronounced 'healthy'. Some of the most interesting and fruitful contacts Brock made were with the German vine breeding stations at Geilweilerhof and Alzey. In 1957, Brock was sent hardwood cuttings from Alzey of three named varieties, Müller-Thurgau, Siegerrebe and Scheurebe, and two unnamed varieties known only by their breeding titles *Sämling* [seedling] 7672 and *Sämling* 23469. These five varieties were rooted and set out in the vineyard.

Brock's 1960 report on the varieties

Müller-Thurgau: 'Appears to be identical to Riesling Sylvaner received from the Swiss [it was] and giving excellent flavour and bouquet.'

Siegerrebe: 'Exceptionally early and the grapes have a strong bouquet.'

Scheurebe: 'Giving big crops, but appears to be very late ripening. Even in 1959 [which was a very hot year] it only ripened after the late varieties.'

Sämling 7672: 'Giving large crops which ripen with Riesling Sylvaner. Considered to be a promising variety.'

Sämling 23469: 'Has not produced any flowers and cannot be recommended at all.'

To start with, the parentage of the two unnamed seedling varieties was unknown, but a letter to Dr Zimmerman (who later became Director of the Alzey station) produced the information that *Sämling* 7672 was a freely pollinated seedling of Madeleine Angevine and *Sämling* 23469 was Lubeck x Triomphe. (Interestingly Siegerrebe, which at one time was credited with being a Madeleine Angevine x Gewürztraminer crossing, was unmasked by Heinz Scheu, Georg's son, as also being a freely pollinated Madeleine Angevine seedling.) The naming of *Sämling* 23469 never became an issue as it performed badly and Brock soon abandoned it. However, as *Sämling* 7672 was showing promise,

Brock started calling it Madeleine x Angevine 7672 for the sake of convenience. Unfortunately, as vineyards started to be planted with this variety and wine was made, the 7672 was left off labels and it soon became referred to simply as 'Madeleine Angevine'.

As information about the work Brock was doing at Oxted spread, so did his circle of contacts. In June 1961, he heard from Nelson Shaulis, Professor of Pomology (inventor of the Geneva Double Curtain (GDC) training system and Dr Richard Smart's mentor) at Cornell University, Geneva, New York, who said that he would be coming to Britain in September and wished to visit Oxted. Shaulis paid a visit, and in a letter sent in November that year thanked Brock for his hospitality, saying that the noon meal 'was very delightful, especially the ginger beer shandy' (home-made no doubt). Shaulis also said that he was just concluding the harvest at Geneva and yields had been between 3 and 9 tons per acre. What Brock must have made of Shaulis' views on trellising is not recorded, but it would be interesting to know. Brock's standard planting distances for wine grapes were by that time 0.91 metres (3 feet) between the rows and 1.22 metres (4 feet) between the vines – 8,941 per hectare (3,620 per acre) – with vines Guyot trained low to the ground. The standard GDC is based on 3.66 metres by 2.44 metres (12 feet by 8 feet) spacings – 1,121 per hectare (454 vines per acre) – and is a high-wire cordon system. Brock remained convinced throughout the life of the Oxted Station that close planting encouraged root competition and that vines close to the ground ripened their fruit better as they absorbed heat from the soil. He was certainly not a GDC man.

Brock also had correspondence with Pierre Galet, long-term Director of the Montpellier School of Viticulture and author of several massive works on vine varieties and the science of ampelography (vine identification). In a letter dated May 1961, Galet thanked him for his *Report No. 3* and hoped that Brock would get in touch if he needed help, partly because he was always interested in other people's researches into vines, but also because, 'je suis Anglais par la famille de ma Mère' (I am English from my mother's family) – what better reason? When one looks back at the remarkable amount of effort and energy that Brock put into his search for vine varieties, all undertaken in the days before the internet and email, even before many people had access to a telephone, and when communication was mostly conducted by letter, it seems an almost impossible task. Yet, one can see the results and one has to be in awe of his achievements.

First harvest at Oxted

The first harvest from the 1946 planted vines in the trial plots did not come until 1948 and owing to tremendous problems with diseases – powdery and downy mildew and botrytis – as well as birds and rabbits, yields were small and the grapes were either eaten, sold or given away. The situation in 1949 was different. More timely use of Bordeaux Mixture to control downy mildew and sulphur dusting against powdery mildew, together with better bird control (using both netting and a new shotgun – a Webley and Scott .410 – bought from the Army and Navy Stores in December 1948 for £14.10.0) meant that on 9 October 1949 Brock picked about 45 kilos (100 pounds) of grapes. These were taken over to Edward Hyams' cottage at Molash in East Kent and, together with others from Hyams' own vineyard, were crushed, pressed and eventually fermented, using a yeast culture – Johannisberg 43 – sent to Hyams by the Wädenswil Research Station in Switzerland. (Hyams had offered his winemaking skills as he had been making home-made wines for some years.) However, when Brock arrived with his grapes, the press was not ready and much of the juice was lost. When Brock tasted the Shottenden Rosé (as they called the wine, Hyams' cottage being on the Shottenden Road) shortly after it had finished fermenting, he commented: 'flavour very poor and yeasty'. After some of it had been bottled and kept for almost a year, it was tasted again and the comments were no more favourable: 'distinctly sedimented, yeasty and decidedly off-flavour. Rejected as of no promise. Used both bottles for Fire Water' (which meant it was distilled). Hyams' prowess as a winemaker did not impress Brock!

Brock harvested the remainder of his 1949 grapes a week later and had a go at turning them into wine himself at Oxted. He seems to have had all kinds of problems with the wine, which was fermented on the skins as many of the grapes were red. He also used the same Johannisberg 43 yeast which was so active that the fermentation was finished before Brock thought it had even started. He tried heating it twice to get it to start, but merely destroyed what character it originally had. He wrote that he 'left the skins in contact with the wine for far too long'. The wine was over-acidic and some calcium carbonate was added to reduce the acidity. This helped soften the wine, but it still tasted harsh and tannic (due Brock thought to the heating he had given it) and the end results were not spectacular. Some was bottled, but the remainder used for a trial into vinegar production (which appears to have been as unsuccessful as the winemaking) or for distillation.

In 1950, Brock seems to have got himself better organized for winemaking and the results were more promising. He also sent grapes over to Hyams and this year the wine was described as 'definitely a good normal light wine. One of the best with real character.' Brock's remarks, made in his fermentations book, are heavily underlined and one can almost sense the relief that something drinkable had at last come from his years of hard work, to say nothing of the expense. Brock seems to have had the services of a Mr Rivollier who acted as his winetaster and came by from time to time to pass judgement on various wines. Perhaps he had good reason, but some of his comments seem very harsh. Over the next three years, Brock seems to have had his fair share of problems in the winery. Much wine seems to have been destroyed because of oxidation or films of mould and fungus forming on top of the wines, or just because they tasted terrible, usually far too acidic. For many, distillation was the only course. In 1954 the new winery was under construction and no wine was made at all. By the 1955 harvest, the new winery was complete and Brock at last started to make some batches of trial wines that could be bottled and put away to see how they matured.

Brock's winemaking

With a total lack of winemaking experience, it is perhaps not surprising that Brock's early efforts were less than perfect. Whether he was helped or hindered by Hyams' involvement – who can say – the wines produced by Hyams seem to have been no better than those Brock initially made himself. Hyams' section on winemaking in his 1949 book *The Grape Vine in England* is fairly rudimentary and it is obvious from his instructions that winemaking was not his first discipline. In the 1953 book *Vineyards in England*, which Hyams edited, the winemaking chapter was written by Dr Alfred Pollard of the Cider Department at Long Ashton Research Station, then part of Bristol University where in 1965 a half acre of vines was established. This chapter gives far more technical (and accurate) information than Hyams' own 1949 book and while today some of the instructions look very old-fashioned, no doubt at the time they were current industry practice. Bottling wines with residual sugar was obviously something that winemakers of the day had not cracked and the art of sterile bottling using very fine filters (developed in about 1947 by the Seitz Filter Company in Germany) had clearly not been heard of in Britain. This meant that wines that were bottled with residual sugar either had to be so heavily dosed with free sulphur as to render them objectionable or were subject to chance refermentation which inevitably led to spoilage or explosion (or both). One of the most useful tools in the English or Welsh winemaker's locker today is the ability to soften fresh, fruity wines which have what one might call a 'crisp' (i.e. high) acidity with a few grams per litre of residual sugar. This can only really be achieved through sterile bottling. Brock also made bottle-fermented sparkling wines, a few bottles of which survived until the 1980s.

Brock's work on vines must be seen as really quite remarkable. That he should decide to establish a private research station to study a crop that did not have a natural home in the British climate is quite a feat in itself; that he should do so with such effort, energy and diligence for little or no personal gain, apart from the satisfaction of seeing it done properly, is another matter. In retrospect, the site he chose could have been better – closer to sea level and less exposed – and undoubtedly this would have resulted in riper grapes and better wine. He knew his site had limitations, but always countered this by saying that he felt comfortable in recommending a variety that had performed well at Oxted, knowing that it would therefore ripen on almost any site in the south of the country. The legacy of the Oxted Viticultural Research Station is to be seen in today's English and Welsh wine industry. While minute by the standards of other (more climatologically blessed) countries, it owes its existence in great part to his work. He lived to see an industry that was producing an average of two and a half million bottles of wine a year and slowly gaining recognition. He died on 14 February 1999, aged 91. Ray Brock was a truly remarkable human being.

EDWARD SOLOMON HYAMS 1910–1975

Edward Hyams, who first appears in the Oxted story at the harvest in 1949, shares with Brock the honour of being one of the fathers of the viticultural revival. Although his winegrowing and winemaking activities were never on the same scale as Brock's, through his writing and speaking he did much to publicize the subject and make the public aware that the revival was under way. In 1938 Hyams and his wife had bought a small house – called Nut Tree Cottages – and 1.21 hectares (3 acres) of rough garden in Molash, a village between Faversham and Ashford in the eastern part of Kent. At the beginning of the war, as Hyams was away serving in the forces and his wife was in the Land Army and living on a farm elsewhere, the house lay empty. At first, it was commandeered for evacuees, but later let to a local farmer who was a less-than-perfect tenant. By the end of the war, the cottage lay empty and almost derelict. It had been broken into and the contents stolen or vandalized.

In March 1946, Hyams was demobbed from the Royal Navy and he and his wife returned to Kent. Hyams, then 36, and his wife decided that: 'the values by which we had lived before the war were morally, intellectually and spiritually unprofitable,' and they therefore, 'decided to dispense with any more income than could be earned by work that was congenial, therefore liberating.' In this spirit of self-sufficiency, they started to clear the land and establish a vegetable and fruit garden which contained, among other things, their own small tobacco plantation. Before the war, Hyams and his wife had talked about planting some vines and as soon as this became a practical possibility, he set about contacting likely sources for suitable varieties.

From the outset, the intention was to plant both table grapes and varieties to turn into wine, with Hyams estimating that he needed a litre per head per day to keep him and his wife happy. He made contact with some of the same institutions and nurseries with whom Brock was in touch and ended up with some of the same varieties. Hyams made contact with Brock in 1948 and visited Oxted on 5 September of that year. After his visit he wrote to Brock asking for various varieties, including Riesling Sylvaner (Müller-Thurgau) which had been sent to Oxted in 1947 from Switzerland. Brock replied saying, 'there is not likely to be any big demand for this variety yet,' and offered him plenty of cuttings as a present. These were sent the next year. In 1950, Hyams received cuttings of three new varieties from Professor Dr B. Husfeld who ran the Geilweilerhof research institute at Siebeldingen bei Landau-Pfalz in Germany. These were Madeleine Angevine x Gutedal No. 3 28/28, Madeleine Angevine x Sylvaner F2 31/16/52 and Madeleine Angevine x Sylvaner III 28/51. Two cuttings of each of these were passed on to Brock who put them into his collection. Although the first two of these proved less than satisfactory and were abandoned in 1958/9, the Madeleine Angevine x Sylvaner III 28/51 proved to be very effective and at one stage Brock rated it as one of his best. Brock shortened the name to Madeleine Sylvaner and it can still be found, albeit rarely, in a few British vineyards.

Hyams also went searching for old varieties already growing in Britain and through an appeal in one of his many articles, was told about a vine growing on a cottage wall at Wrotham in Kent. The cottage was located and cuttings taken to Brock at Oxted and propagated. As its leaves resembled those of Meunier, Hyams named it Wrotham Pinot, a name that survived Britain's entry into the Common Market in 1973, when it became one of the country's 'Approved' varieties. Brock trialled it at Oxted and reported that it had 'a higher natural sugar content and ripened two weeks earlier' than supplies of Meunier obtained from overseas. Brock sold cuttings and it became quite popular in the early days of the revival.

Hyams and his wife left Kent in 1960 and moved to a new home, Hill House, near Ashburton in Devon, taking with them 1,500 unrooted cuttings which Hyams proceeded to root in their kitchen garden. The next year he proceeded to plant another small vineyard, the history of which is recorded in *An Englishman's Garden* published in 1967. Despite Hyams' experience with vines, the Devon vineyard was not a success, and after only a few years he reduced it in size and really only kept a few hardy hybrids for old time's sake and for decoration. He blamed the much wetter growing conditions of Devon (compared to east Kent) which led to too much lush growth, too much disease and poor fruit set.

Promotion of British winemaking

Hyams' greatest contribution to the advancement of viticulture in Great Britain was undoubtedly the massive amount of publicity he created through his writing and broadcasting. C. J. Greenwood of his publishers, The Bodley Head, suggested quite early on that he write a book on vineyards and in 1949 *The Grape Vine in England*, with a foreword by the well-known gardener and author Vita Sackville-West (of Sissinghurst Castle fame), was published. This book marked a milestone in the early years of the revival. It was, and remains to this day, a scholarly work on the subject and contains chapters on the history of the grapevine in England, the work of Brock at Oxted and the cultivation of the vine and winemaking. Given that viticulture was at a very undeveloped stage at the time, it shows that Hyams had a genuine interest in and regard for the subject.

In 1948 Hyams had read Richard Church's book 'Kent' and noted what he (Church) had written about the possibility of a revival of viticulture in the county. In August 1949, Hyams wrote to Church to let him know what he was up to at Molash and informed him that a book on the subject was about to be published. Church then mentioned both Hyams' vineyard and his forthcoming book in his weekly article for the *Spectator* magazine on 2 September 1949. This alerted first the local and then the national press to Hyams' experiments. Church then suggested to *Country Life* that they commission Hyams to write an article, which he did, further fanning the flames of interest.

On 3 August 1950, Hyams gave a talk on the BBC's *Third Programme* called *Vineyards in England* which engendered yet another round of publicity. Hyams was very generous in recognizing the part played by Brock in the whole story and ended his radio talk with a dedication, saying: 'If it were the practice to dedicate radio talks, I should have dedicated this one to Brock, because any man who spends so much of his leisure time, his energy and money, not to speak of intelligence, on reintroducing a fruit plant, and that plant the source of wine, deserves all the honour one can give him.'

Hyams' interest in vines and wine stayed with him throughout his life. In 1952 he wrote *Grapes Under Cloches* which drew heavily ('rather too heavily' Brock told me) on Brock's two published works: *Outdoor Grapes in Cold Climates* (1949) and *More Outdoor Grapes* (1950). Hyams dedicated this book to Brock, thanking him for his extraordinary generosity in making his research available and calling him 'a notable vinearoon' – a term Hyams liked to use to mean *viticulteur* or *vigneron.* (Hyams had discovered this hitherto unknown word in a letter written by Lord Delaware in 1616 from New York to his Company in London when discussing the possibility of planting vines in Virginia.) In 1953 Hyams edited *Vineyards in England*, a masterly work which consisted of 20 chapters, many written by different specialists (although Hyams himself wrote six of them and Brock two) covering every conceivable aspect of grape production in the British Isles. It included chapters on the history of viticulture, several on varieties including one on new French hybrids, soils and manures, climates, cloche and greenhouse cultivation, pests and diseases and winemaking. The book stands today as one of the most important for anyone contemplating growing vines in England or Wales and despite being published over half a century ago, much of it, apart from the choice of varieties, remains relevant.

Hyams was an extremely prolific writer and kept up a tremendous output of both fiction and non-fiction: books, articles in journals, magazines and newspapers all flowed from his pen. He wrote a weekly column in *The Illustrated London News*, in its day one of the most widely read magazines, especially among those interested in gardening and the countryside. In 1975, two months before he died, he wrote a well-researched article in it about vineyards in Great Britain (which my father cut out and posted to me when I was training in Germany), in which he appears to have changed his mind somewhat about the financial viability of viticulture. At the end of this long article he wrote: 'the undertaking should be profitable if you can produce 2,000 bottles of wine per acre and very profitable at 3,000 bottles. There is no doubt that English vineyards in the right places can produce fine white wines, and that such wine should be the object of English viticulture.' By then of course the revival – of which he was in no small part responsible for instigating – was well under way.

Between them, Brock and Hyams had questioned why it was that outdoor viticulture in the British Isles had all but died out and had shown how it might be revived. Although they had not discovered all the answers, they had, through a combination of practical demonstration, scientific research and publicity, generated sufficient enthusiasm for those with the inclination to start planting vineyards again. The first modern vineyard, Hambledon in Hampshire, planted in March 1952, was the tangible evidence that a revival was under way. Mention should also be made of George Ordish, a Kentish entomologist and economist who took a private interest in viticulture and planted a small vineyard at his home in Yalding, Kent in 1939. He wrote *Wine Growing in England* in 1953 which helped spread the word about the revival. He also wrote *The Great Wine Blight*, a book about phylloxera, in 1972, and *Vineyards in England and Wales,* a well-researched and informative book, in 1977.

3

COMMERCIAL VITICULTURE, 1952 ONWARDS

THE EARLY VINEYARDS 1952–1965

The planting of the Hambledon vineyard in March of 1952 by Major-General Sir Arthur Guy Salisbury-Jones GCVO, CMG, CBE, MC DL (to give him his full name, title and decorations for the first and last time) marked a turning point in the history of winegrowing in Great Britain. This was the first vineyard to be planted specifically to produce wine for sale since Andrew Pettigrew planted the Marquess of Bute's at Castle Coch in 1875. Furthermore, the main varieties planted, Seyve Villard 5276 (Seyval Blanc), Seibel 5279 (Aurore) and Seibel 10.868, all French–American hybrids, stood a good chance of resisting mildew and botrytis and of ripening their fruit, problems which up until then had so troubled previous vineyard owners that all had, eventually, given up the battle. Why Salisbury-Jones chose these three varieties one can only speculate. He had visited Oxted and in Brock's first two *Reports*, Seyval Blanc, which Brock and Hyams had been growing (albeit only since 1947/8), had been recommended as 'promising'. Perhaps one of his contacts in Burgundy was a member of FENAVINO or subscribed to *La Viticulture Nouvelle*? Who knows? Whatever it was, Seyval Blanc (if not perhaps the other two varieties) was an inspired choice and in retrospect, while it could possibly be seen as unadventurous, it did enable Salisbury-Jones to harvest crops of clean fruit with sufficient regularity to make wine every year.

Salisbury-Jones had ordered 3,620 vines, grafted onto 41B, 5BB and 161-49 rootstocks that he said 'were required because the chalky soil at

Hambledon resembled that of Champagne' and those were the rootstocks used there. The vines were trained in a very Burgundian way, with narrow 1.22-metre (4-foot) rows with the vines planted approximately 0.91 metres (3 feet) apart and trelliswork of around 1.22 metres high. The area planted was almost exactly 0.4 hectares (1 acre). The vines grew well and produced their first crop in 1955. The wine – history does not record what it tasted like – was the first commercial vintage to be made in Great Britain since the 1911 Castle Coch. The fact that wine *was* now being produced created much interest and Salisbury-Jones was besieged by the press and media, anxious for a story. He was an imposing figure, with a colourful and honourable past, a name to conjure with and the ability to hold an audience. This made him much in demand as a guest speaker. The name Hambledon soon became synonymous with English Wine and Brock's dream of re-establishing commercial wine production in Great Britain, some ten years after he started his trials at Oxted, became a reality.

The expansion of vineyards after the planting of Hambledon was painfully slow. Jack Ward, who had co-founded the Merrydown Wine Company at Horam in East Sussex, became interested in the subject. Being a cider and country winemaker, he looked at wine made from home-grown grapes as something which his company might get involved in. Ward made contact with Brock at Oxted and went to see what he was doing. In 1954 Ward planted six vines – really just to see how they would do at Horam – in the grounds of the Merrydown winery, known as Horam Manor, although the manor house had long before burnt down. The varieties chosen were Müller-Thurgau, Madeleine Royale and Gamay Hâtif des Vosges. No sooner had he done this than a property known as The Grange, a house across the road from the winery with several acres of garden, came up for sale and was bought by the company to provide accommodation for some of its employees. Ward's plans for establishing a vineyard were promptly brought forward and in 1955, taking charge of the gardens, he planted a 0.8-hectare vineyard – the second commercial vineyard of the revival. Apart from Müller-Thurgau, it is not known what other varieties were planted, although it would be surprising if Seyval Blanc was not also included. In later years, Ward, who had studied music at the Frankfurt Conservatorium before the war and spoke fluent German, visited Geisenheim and was instrumental in introducing varieties such as Reichensteiner, Huxelrebe and

Schönburger to Britain. He was very much a driving force in the industry and was elected to be the first Chairman of the English Vineyards Association (EVA) when it was formed in 1967.

The third vineyard to be planted in modern times was that of the Gore-Brownes at Beaulieu. In 1956 Lieutenant-Colonel Robert and Mrs Margaret Gore-Browne, who had recently returned to Great Britain from Africa, rented a house called The Vineyards on the Beaulieu Estate (the owners of which, the Montagus, were old family friends). On asking Lord Montagu why the house was so-called, they were told that the land behind the house had been the site of a vineyard planted by the Cistercian monks who had established Beaulieu Abbey in 1204.[15] Despite initial reluctance from the Colonel, but no doubt encouraged by the success of the nearby vineyard at Hambledon (planted by a fellow soldier) the Gore-Brownes decided to re-establish the vineyard. In the spring of 1958 they planted four rows of Müller-Thurgau and Seyval Blanc as well as a few Gamay Noir Hâtif des Vosges, Précoce de Malingre and Madeleine Sylvaner III 28/51, all of which they bought from Brock at Oxted. Brock's account books show a sale to the Gore-Brownes on 24 December 1957 (perhaps a Christmas present?) of £112 worth of vines. The vineyard was gradually expanded with more of the same, plus some Wrotham Pinot. By 1960/61 they had planted almost 2.23 hectares (5.5 acres). Their first vintage, in 1961, was a rosé and was apparently well received. They also experimented with Baco No. 1, Brandt, Pirovano 14 and Cascade – this last variety despite the fact that Mrs Gore-Browne had heard that it was prohibited by the Common Market 'as it is said to have an injurious effect upon the liver', a common scare story put out by the anti-hybrid growers in France. By 1967 however, they had decided to eliminate the experimental varieties – no doubt due to poor performance. Margaret Gore-Browne is now best remembered for the very stylish silver rose bowl she gave to the English Vineyards Association in 1974, and which is awarded annually to the top wine in the industry's Wine of the Year Competition.

Winemaking in those early days was, from all accounts, a fairly hit and miss affair. Both Salisbury-Jones and Gore-Browne, as well as

15 In the 1960s, Lord Montagu received a 'cease and desist' letter from the Californian company Beaulieu Vineyard, founded in 1900, demanding that he stop using the word Beaulieu. He replied pointing out that wine was first produced on his estate over six hundred years ago and heard no more.

others in years to come, were helped by Anton Massel, a young German who had come across to work for the Seitz Filter company in Britain in 1956. In 1961 Massel opened his own laboratory at Water Lane in London which he moved to Ockley, a village to the south of Dorking in Surrey, in 1969. Before the first vintage at Hambledon (the 1955) Salisbury-Jones had built a small winery and equipped it cheaply with simple equipment and the first two vintages were made in what one might certainly call 'primitive conditions'. This showed in the results. When Massel appeared on the scene and offered his services, the first thing he did was persuade Salisbury-Jones to invest £6,000 in better equipment, including a small Willmes air-bladder press – the first of many to enter the country. This press is believed to be still in use. It was first sold to Sir Reresby Sitwell, Bt at Renishaw Hall near Sheffield and subsequently to a grower in the south of the country. Massel also persuaded Salisbury-Jones that the vineyard needed to be at least three acres in size to be viable and to make use of the equipment that now sat in the winery. In fact Salisbury-Jones enlarged the vineyard to 1.82 hectares (4.5 acres). The Gore-Brownes likewise built themselves a winery and used Massel as their consultant. Being already involved with fermentation of cider and fruit wines Merrydown had their own winemaking equipment – albeit on a rather larger scale than they needed for their small vineyard – and did not need the services of a consultant.

Tasting notes

What these very early wines were like is open to question – very few tasting notes survive and people's memories tend to be selective. Those who do remember them recall wines of high acidity, lean in structure and lacking fruit. The early growers battled to control disease, powdery mildew and botrytis being the worst, and undoubtedly picked too early in order to get to the grapes before the birds or the rot. The wines were usually made in a fairly natural, dry style, with little or no residual sugar, and left to soften with age. Hambledon thought nothing of offering wines of five or more years old and almost prided itself on the wines' long cellaring potential. The idea of bottling wines with a little residual sweetness to temper the acidity was something of an anathema to the early pioneers and this practice, now widespread, had to wait a few years.

The establishment of these three vineyards between 1952 and 1958, and the appearance of English wine on sale, was proof-positive that viticulture in the British Isles had been revived. While it would be an exaggeration to say that the industry then 'took off' there is no doubt that the number of both actual and potential vineyard owners suddenly expanded and small trial plots of vines appeared in all kinds of unlikely places. The real expansion of vineyards from which commercial quantities of wine for sale could be made started in the early to mid-1960s. People such as Trevor and Joy Bates at Nettlestead outside Maidstone, Norman Cowderoy at Rock Lodge, near Uckfield in West Sussex, Robin Don at Elmham Park in Norfolk, Nigel Godden at Pilton Manor in Somerset, Messrs Gibbons and Poulter at Cranmore on the Isle of Wight, the Montagus at Beaulieu, Gillian Pearkes in Devon, Major Rook at Stragglethorpe Hall near Lincoln, Pam Smith at Flexerne, East Sussex and Philip Tyson-Woodcock at Brede, near Rye in East Sussex, all planted vineyards. Wales too became the home of several vineyards: Lewis Mathias at Lamphey Court, George Jones at Pembrey, plus several others belonging to or with advice from Margaret Gore-Browne (who was Welsh by birth).

This spread of vineyards geographically, coupled with a diversity of owners, sites, training and pruning systems and, above all, of vine varieties, meant that at last valuable experience was being gained across the whole country. Thus, potential winegrowers were better able to judge what varieties and what training systems were actually working, how vines should be managed and – last but by no means least – how grapes could be turned into palatable wine.

VINEYARDS BECOME MORE COMMERCIAL 1966–1975

Once wines from the early vineyards started to be produced in saleable quantities and could be bought, tasted and assessed by the wine trade and consumers alike, the publicity surrounding English and Welsh wine really started to gather momentum. It soon became clear that making wine in Britain, even with its marginal climate, was no longer entirely the joke it had long been considered and that grapes could perhaps be viewed as a commercial crop.

The real expansion of the vineyard area and the establishment of both sizeable vineyards and wineries started in earnest in the late 1960s and it was an era of rapid growth. One of the features of English and Welsh viticulture is the diversity of backgrounds of those who plant vineyards. In other countries where new vineyards are being planted, one would expect to see existing landowners – most usually those with land in the vicinity of established vineyards – planting up, together with a smaller number of entrants with no experience of growing at all, but with serious funds, usually made in a completely unrelated industry. In Britain, those planting vineyards came from a much wider cross-section of the community: a sprinkling of retired service people, a few farmers and landowners looking for alternative – hopefully more profitable – crops, some 'lifestyle' smallholders (generally under-funded) keen to be part of the 'Good Life' brigade, as well as those with a few acres attached to their houses in the country who liked the idea of having their names on a wine label. Only one thing really seems to have united them: an almost complete lack of experience in growing vines (and in many cases of growing anything) or of making wine. Sadly this lack of experience often (although not always) showed in the quality of both the vineyards they planted and managed and of the wines they produced.

In the late 1960s a new crop of vineyards appeared: Ken Barlow at Adgestone, Isle of Wight, Richard and Joyce Barnes at Biddenden, Kent, Graham and Irene Barrett at Felsted in Essex, Walter Cardy at Pangbourne in Berkshire, the Crossland-Hinchcliffes at Castlehouse in East Sussex, Jack Edgerly at Kelsale in Suffolk, Ian Grant at Knowle Hill in Kent, Bill Greenwood at New Hall, Purleigh in Essex, Anton Massel at Ockley in Surrey, Gruff Reece at Gamlingay, Bedfordshire, Bernard Theobald at Westbury, Berkshire and T. P. Baillie-Grohman at Hascombe, Surrey (whom some of us dubbed 'T. P. Barely-Growing', such was the state of his vineyard). These new ventures were in many cases quite substantial and their owners, several of whom were mildly (and in some cases quite wildly) eccentric, helped do two things: spread the word that establishing commercial vineyards was possible in the British Isles and reinforce the idea that to do so, in Britain's climate, was something rather unusual and novel.

The next five years (the first half of the 1970s) saw yet another frenzy of planting: Sam Alper at Chilford Hall in Cambridgeshire, Bob Blayney at La Mare on Jersey, R. M. O. Capper at Stocks in Worcester, David Carr Taylor at Westfield near Hastings and William Ross at Barnsgate Manor, Crowborough, both in East Sussex, Peter Cook at Pulham St

Mary in Norfolk, J. R. M. Donald at Tytherley in Wiltshire, Colin and Sue Gillespie at Wootton in Somerset, Peter Hall at Breaky Bottom, Lewes, East Sussex, Kenneth McAlpine at Lamberhurst in Kent, Mary Macrae at Highwayman's near Bury St Edmunds, Basil Ambrose at Cavendish Manor and Ian and Eleanor Berwick at Bruisyard, all in Suffolk, Alan McKechnie at Three Choirs at Newent in Gloucestershire, Andrew and Ian Paget at Chilsdown in West Sussex, Chris Stuart at Aeshton Manor in Wiltshire and Bob Westphal at Penshurst in Kent. The above is by no means a comprehensive list of all those who planted vineyards – just the more substantial plantings – and scores of other growers were experimenting with smaller vineyards across the whole of the south of Britain. By the end of 1975, the total British vine area was recorded by MAFF as being 196 hectares.[16]

Help from a heatwave

The fabled summer of 1976 which, according to legend, was the hottest and driest on record (there were nine days over 30°C, which was a record at the time), gave further impetus to vinegrowing. In fact, although some vineyards did pick large crops in 1976 others were badly damaged by mid-April frosts and most vineyards suffered greatly from botrytis as it started raining at the end of August, and September and October, the main ripening and harvesting months, were very wet. This, however, did not stop the general public believing that at last the Almighty had smiled on the country's winegrowers, further fuelling the interest in English and Welsh wines and with it the planting of more and more vineyards.

16 Until 1989, requests for information about the planted area of vines were only sent out to farmers and growers having a MAFF 'Holding Number' and who had recorded vines as part of their 'other crops' on their December returns (which each farmer is legally required to make). As these vine returns were voluntary, not all vineyard owners completed them. In addition, many vineyard owners, especially those with vines in back gardens, allotments and small paddocks, were not registered with MAFF and thus escaped scrutiny altogether. This means that the pre-1989 figures must be treated with suspicion. Post-1988, the data on vineyards and wine production has been collected by the Wine Standards Board (WSB), since 2006 the Wine Standards (WS) team at the Food Standards Agency (FSA), and because it covers all registered vineyards is much more reliable, although as vineyard owners do not have to register until they start producing a 'wine sector product' i.e. grapes, juice or wine, there is often quite a delay in registering and then collecting the data. A vineyard must be registered when it is 10 ares (1,000 square metres or 0.1 hectares) or more in size. Vineyards under this size are not registered or recorded, although plenty exist in Britain.

VINEYARDS ESTABLISHED 1976–1993

The years between 1976 and 1993 saw a large number of vineyards planted, including some very sizeable ones. Growers such as Mark Lambert at Barkham Manor, Piltdown, East Sussex, Jon Leighton at Valley Vineyards (now Stanlake Park), Reading, Berkshire, Stuart and Sandy Moss at Nyetimber, Pulborough, West Sussex, the Quirk family at Chiddingstone, Edenbridge, Kent, the Sax family at Battle, East Sussex, Andrew Vining at Wellow, Romsey, Hampshire and Adrian White at Denbies, Dorking, Surrey all planted vineyards in excess of 8 hectares (20 acres) in size, the largest (Denbies) growing to 107 hectares (265 acres). In addition, existing vineyards such as those at Adgestone, Carr Taylor, Chilford, Highwayman's, Lamberhurst, New Hall and Three Choirs all increased in size as the market for their wines expanded. It was also in 1976 that I returned from Germany and in the spring of 1977 started planting vines at what was then called Spots Farm, which turned into Tenterden Vineyards and is now home to English Wines Group plc and more generally referred to as Chapel Down Wines.

The reasons for this spurt in planting were several-fold. A rumoured vine planting ban in 1990/91 persuaded many growers that if they were going to plant it had better be soon, and between 1992 and 1993 an abnormally large number of vines were planted. Other reasons were the general buoyancy in the economy, coupled with a growth in wine-drinking in Britain, which seemed to make people with a spare bit of land think that owning a vineyard would be fun. English and Welsh wine continued to get plenty of publicity and this further fuelled the fires of vineyard planting. The official Wine Standards Board[17] (WSB) figures for 1993 showed that the national vineyard area had reached 1,065 hectares (2,632 acres), of which almost 28 per cent was not yet in production, and that there were 479 separate vineyards. This area total remained the highest until eclipsed by the 2008 figure of 1,106 hectares.

To say that vineyard planting since the mid-1970s had followed a pattern of any recognizable sort would be brave, mainly because up

17 Set up when the British joined the European Union in 1973 to look after the legislation covering wine, this was partially funded by the Vintner's Company. The Vintners felt that this was a good chance to put something back into the wine trade, from which they had become somewhat separated, and offered the WSB both office space and funding. The Vintners contributed 40 per cent of the funding, which in 2005/6 amounted to £450,000 a year.

until 1989 accurate data did not exist. A voluntary survey of 1975 by MAFF revealed a total of 196 hectares (484 acres) of vines, but this was undoubtedly on the low side. By the time MAFF undertook its second survey in 1984, the figure had risen to 430 hectares (1,062 acres), but again, this was artificially low. The third survey in 1985/6 came up with 488 hectares (1,205 acres) and finally the fourth survey, in 1987/8, revealed a total of 546 hectares (1,349 acres), triggering the need for a statutory (compulsory) survey so that a 'Vineyard Register' could be compiled.[18] In 1989 the first statutory vineyard census was undertaken and a much truer figure of 876 hectares (2,164 acres) was recorded. This showed that previous surveys had greatly underestimated the extent of vineyard plantings in Britain.

DECLINE IN VINEYARD PLANTING 1994–2004

The period between 1994 and 2004 saw a gradual decline in overall plantings, with the total area falling from the 1993 high of 1,065 hectares to a low of 761 hectares in 2004, a drop of almost 29 per cent. What is perhaps more telling is that the percentage of vineyards 'not in production' fell from 34.5 per cent of the total in 1991, to 18 per cent of the total in 2003. The area of vines 'in production' did not vary quite so spectacularly and reached its zenith in 1998 with 842 hectares and its nadir in 2004 with 747 hectares – a drop of a mere 11 per cent. Likewise, the number of vineyards fell by a massive 30 per cent from 479 in 1993 to 333 in 2003. What this shows is that the smaller vineyards disappeared more rapidly than the larger, and the larger ones that remained tended to get bigger.

The factors behind this large fall in the planted area and the number of vineyards are not hard to find and can be summed up thus: wrong varieties, wrong sites, poor winemaking, poor quality and lastly, and most importantly, marketing difficulties.

Most of the vineyards up to this period had been planted with German

18 A 'Vineyard Register' is required in all EU member states that have 500 hectares or more of vines. This records the location of every 'parcel' of vines together with the variety, clone and rootstock, plus other information about the altitude, aspect, soil type etc. The WS attempts to keep this up-to-date and relevant, but the information they make available is often some years out of date.

crosses plus Seyval Blanc, varieties which (with one or two honourable exceptions) were getting beyond their sell-by date. The 1990 WS vine varieties survey showed that Müller-Thurgau, Seyval Blanc, Reichensteiner, Bacchus, Schönburger, Madeleine x Angevine 7672, Huxelrebe, Ortega, Kerner and Würzer together accounted for 729 hectares (78.5 per cent) out of a total planted area of 929 hectares. At this time, Pinot Noir and Chardonnay were fairly minor varieties and together only accounted for 51.9 hectares or 5.6 per cent of the total, most of which was planted on about three sites.

English and Welsh vineyards were finding it increasingly difficult to sell the wines they produced based upon these Germanic varieties, mainly because the public had been introduced to new styles of wines from places such as Australia, New Zealand, South Africa, Chile and the USA (principally California) and English and Welsh wines, with their Hock and Mosel bottle shapes and colours and their Teutonic varietal names required too much effort to get them to move off the shelves. Pricing too was always an issue and as costs rose, English and Welsh wines found themselves at even more of a disadvantage. Excise duties and VAT (value-added tax) doubled between the late 1970s and 1991, while retail prices seemed (almost) to stand still. Taken together, these factors pushed many of the small vineyards, as well as quite a few of the larger ones, into oblivion.

It is a sobering thought that of the 352 vineyards in my 1989 book *The Vineyards of England*, fewer than half – 150 to be precise – were still around to be included in my 2001 book *The Wines of Britain and Ireland* and of those 150 only 57 are still in existence today. That's almost 300 dreams, to say nothing of the cost and the hard work, destroyed. Among those that have disappeared are some 21 vineyards of 4 hectares (10 acres) or more – Barkham Manor, Bruisyard, Chiddingstone, Highwayman's, Pilton Manor, Pulham, Wellow and Westbury to name the biggest and best known. They went mainly because they were just unable to cope with the problem of selling their wines at anything approaching the right price – a price that gave both profit and return on capital. The wine trade in Britain was fairly averse to English and Welsh wine and considered it, one has to say with some justification, as being mainly produced by amateurs who made indifferent wines and expected the wine trade to sell them at unrealistic prices. Even those vineyards which did produce reliable, good-quality (for the price) wines and had a realistic price structure that gave both wholesalers and retailers a proper margin, struggled.[19]

So if size wasn't a guarantee of success – was quality? When one looks at the roll-call of Gore-Browne Trophy winners – presumably some guide to excellence – between the Wine of the Year Competition's inception in 1974 and 1999 (the last year before the Champagne-variety based sparkling wines started winning it) it would seem apparently not. Of the 15 vineyards that won it in these 26 years, only five – Biddenden, Carr-Taylor, Wyken, Stanlake Park and Tenterden – remain in anything like rude health; another three linger on in a much changed format – Adgestone, Chiltern Valley and Lamberhurst – and seven have disappeared altogether – Barton Manor, Brede, Felsted, Kelsale, Pilton Manor, Pulham St Mary and Wootton. It is a very sad fact that very few vineyards survive from the early 1970s and even fewer survive under their original owners: Beaulieu, Biddenden, Bolney, Breaky Bottom, Carr Taylor, Chilford, and New Hall come to mind – there may be a few others, but not many.

The surge of planting during the 1980s and early 1990s resulted in larger national yields and the average annual level of wine production for the eight years between 1989 and 1996 was 18,959 hectolitres, a shade over 2.5 million bottles (of still wine) a year. The 1992 national average yield of 37.7 hectolitres per hectare remained the largest ever achieved until the stellar vintage of 2018 when yields are estimated to be around 60 hectolitres per hectare. This increase in the supply of home-grown wine came at a time when demand appeared to be lessening and competition from overseas wines growing. Britain has one of the most sophisticated wine markets in the world and wines have to represent very good value for money if they are to succeed. The retail market is dominated by a small number of large chains of wine merchants and supermarket groups whose massive purchasing power allows them to squeeze keener and keener prices out of producers. Growers in marginal areas and whose production costs are relatively high and yields relatively low (such as Britain), are therefore at a very definite disadvantage. High levels of excise duty, levelled at a flat rate rather than on the value of the wine, also create further pressure in the market as certain

19 For three years, 1988–91, I was winemaker and general manager at Lamberhurst Vineyards, then the largest and most professional English wine producer. Under winemaker Karl-Heinz Johner their wines had won countless awards and medals and Lamberhurst was certainly the best-known vineyard name. Even with all this behind it, the only way that their wines made it onto supermarket and wine shop shelves was by attractive pricing.

'price points' have to be met and wines have to be correctly priced in order for them to move off the shelf. In addition, the creation of the European Union Single Market meant that British consumers could travel to the continent and import more or less unlimited quantities of wines at rates of excise duty of virtually nil, which also put pressure on English vineyards and wineries, especially those situated in the counties bordering the Channel where access to the ferries to the contintent is easiest. At one time there were several vineyards in East Kent, near the Channel ports, but they were all grubbed and until quite recently, this region was devoid of them. Taken together, these factors go some way towards explaining the miserable success rate of many vineyards planted in the late twentieth century.

Some vineyards were planted with the wrong varieties and on the wrong sites, and the problems of getting grapes to ripen under these circumstances were just too great. Others had fallen by the wayside through natural causes such as retirement, divorce and death. Quite a few vineyards, started by entrepreneurs in the boom years of the mid-1980s, were subsequently grubbed-up when their other interests came under pressure or failed. While many would like to believe it, not all vineyards that fail do so because the vineyard itself is in trouble. Other quite normal factors are often to blame. However, the desire to sink substantial sums of money into vineyards and wineries in Britain, where wine production has climatic and marketing problems that other countries do not share, has been quite remarkable. The profitability of growing grapes and making wine in Britain has always been open to debate and very many vineyards (mainly the smaller ones) have only survived because of a very high proportion of farm-gate sales at full retail prices, coupled with the ability of the owner to support the enterprise out of his or her own pocket in lean times. However, once a vineyard's production becomes too large to sell most of it over the farm gate and the wine has to be sold through the normal wholesale and retail distribution channels that exist in Britain, the problems of marketing begin.

Before the first Hambledon vintage of 1955, no market for English and Welsh wines existed. To start with – probably up until the early 1970s – overall volumes were extremely small, English and Welsh wines were still a novelty and most growers could sell all they produced with little problem. However, as the number of vineyards expanded, so the amount of wine available for sale increased. A combination of relatively high prices, reflecting the difficulty of growing grapes in Britain and the scarcity of the product, and some wines of dubious quality, reflecting the inexperience of some growers and winemakers, made the wine trade, i.e. wholesalers and retailers, somewhat wary of the product and they found it difficult to market. This led to some vineyards experiencing real problems with selling their wines at anything approaching a price that was required to fund their enterprises and they subsequently gave up the struggle. Many of these, it has to be said with the benefit of hindsight, completely misread their ability to market the volumes of wines they were able to produce. The wine market in Britain is a harsh place and English and Welsh wines have had to battle hard (and continue to battle hard) to maintain their place on the shelves against the endless stream of competing products.

One way out of the problem of selling wine has been for vineyards to take the decision to sell some or all of their grapes to other, mainly larger concerns, whose marketing skills and abilities left them short of wines made from their own, home-grown grapes. Chapel Down was the original exponent of this method of securing grapes although now is far from the only winery to do so and several others, large and small (including some very well-known ones), buy grapes to supplement their own supplies. Come harvest time, there is a fair trade in grapes and lorry loads travel (mainly) from east to west seeking a home.

VINEYARD PLANTINGS INCREASE FROM 2004

The upturn in planting started in 2004, spurred on by two factors: the weather in 2003 and what I have called 'the Nyetimber effect'. If anyone thought that climate change was not really affecting Britain, then the summer of 2003 was a wake-up call. With ten days in the year when the temperature rose over 29°C, nine days over 30°C, five days over 33°C and two days over 35°C – the first year in the more than 360 years of record keeping when this last temperature had been reached – it was evident that growers were entering into uncharted territory. In Champagne, the situation was even worse. Apart from the most damaging frost for 80 years – the temperature fell to –11°C on 11 April – August saw the temperatures rise to 43°C, again a record, and grapes ripened far too quickly, losing the valuable acidity which is the hallmark of great sparkling wines.

The general opinion was that little wine of note would be made in Champagne that year and if this was the shape of things to come, *vignerons* and the *Grande Marque* Champagne houses better find somewhere a bit cooler to plant their vines. Where? Well, to go cooler, you need to go further north and where better than the home of their largest export market – England. The general feeling was that climate change had definitely arrived and the southern half of Britain was no bad place to establish a vineyard. Thus started the Champenoise's interest in viticulture in Britain.

The other factor in the planting upturn was 'the Nyetimber effect'. Planted between 1988 and 1991 by two reclusive Americans, Nyetimber kept itself to itself for several years and just picked grapes and made wine, stacking up the vintages waiting for it to mature. The first release was the *1992 Blanc de Blancs Première Cuvée* (a 100 per cent Chardonnay wine) which hit the ground running and won a gold medal and the English Wine Trophy in the 1997 International Wine and Spirits Competition (IWSC). Not content with this initial success, their next release, the *1993 Classic Cuvée* (a Chardonnay, Pinot Noir and Meunier blend) went one better and won a gold medal, the English Wine Trophy *and* the Bottle Fermented Sparkling Wine Trophy in the 1998 IWSC. Suddenly, everyone woke up to the fact that good wine, even stunningly good wine, could be made from hitherto seemingly unworkable varieties – Chardonnay, Pinot Noir and Meunier – and what was more, the wine could be sold at a premium price. Nyetimber went from strength to strength, winning the Gore-Browne Trophy in 2001, 2003, 2004, 2005 and 2006 and the IWSC International Sparkling Wine Trophy in 2006, 2008 and 2009.[20]

Ridgeview

The second major producer making sparkling wines from the classic Champagne varieties was Sussex-based Ridgeview, which started planting in 1995. Their first release, the 1996 Cuveé Merret Bloomsbury, was in fact a wine made from grapes sourced from other growers, Surrenden Vineyard near Ashford, Kent (who had been growing Champagne varieties since 1984) being the main one. This wine, released in 2000, won the Gore-Browne Trophy in that year, and added further impetus to the realization that this was the way forward. Ridgeview also won the Gore-Browne in 2002, 2009, 2010 and 2011.

20 Since then, they have declined to enter most wine competitions.

From 2005, the national area under vine, after eleven consecutive years of decline, showed a modest net increase for the first year of 32 hectares, thus starting a trend which continues today. Official WS figures show the planted area rising between 2004 and 2018 inclusive by over 300 per cent, from 761 hectares to a total of 2,329 hectares. My guess is that total plantings are larger than that and I estimate that the figure for the total planted area today (including 2018 plantings) is nearer 2,750-hectares. The majority of new plantings since 2004 have been with Champagne varieties, mainly Chardonnay and Pinot Noir, with a lesser amount of Meunier, to a point in 2018 where these three varieties represent 63 per cent of plantings (and probably nearer 70 per cent of production).

Over the past fifteen years what has been notable is not only the growth of plantings but also the increase in the average size of vineyards, up from 2.24 hectares in 2004, to an estimated 3.8 hectares in 2018. This has largely been due to producers such as Nyetimber, Chapel Down, Gusbourne, Hambledon and Rathfinny planting and/or expanding their vineyard holdings. If you add onto this list Denbies – still the same size as it was when first planted in 1986 – the average size (in 2018) of these six growers is over 126 hectares (311 acres) each, with Nyetimber the largest at 258 hectares (638 acres). In what might be termed a 'second tier' of producers, there are twenty-four growers totalling 584 hectares (1,443 acres) with an average size of 24.35 hectares. Together these thirty producers own around 50 per cent of all the vineyards in Britain. Both Chapel Down and Nyetimber have stated that their aim is to plant another 200 hectares (500 acres) each, and with the arrival of the two Champagne houses, both of which are set to grow to 50 hectares (124 acres) or more, average vineyard sizes are not going to fall anytime soon. Plus there are others starting to take an interest in British viticulture and winemaking. Mark Dixon of Château de Berne – a 121-hectare (299-acre) square-bottle Provençal rosé estate – who made his fortune from Regus serviced offices, has already bought two established vineyards, Kingscote and Sedlescombe Organic, and taken a lease on a third, Bodiam Vineyards (where he will plant 30 hectares in 2019) and is said to be looking to expand his vineyard holdings to 400 hectares (1,000 acres). He was the underbidder on the 157-hectare (388-acre) parcel of land at Boxley, Maidstone, which Chapel Down leased in September 2018 and will plant between 2019 and 2021.

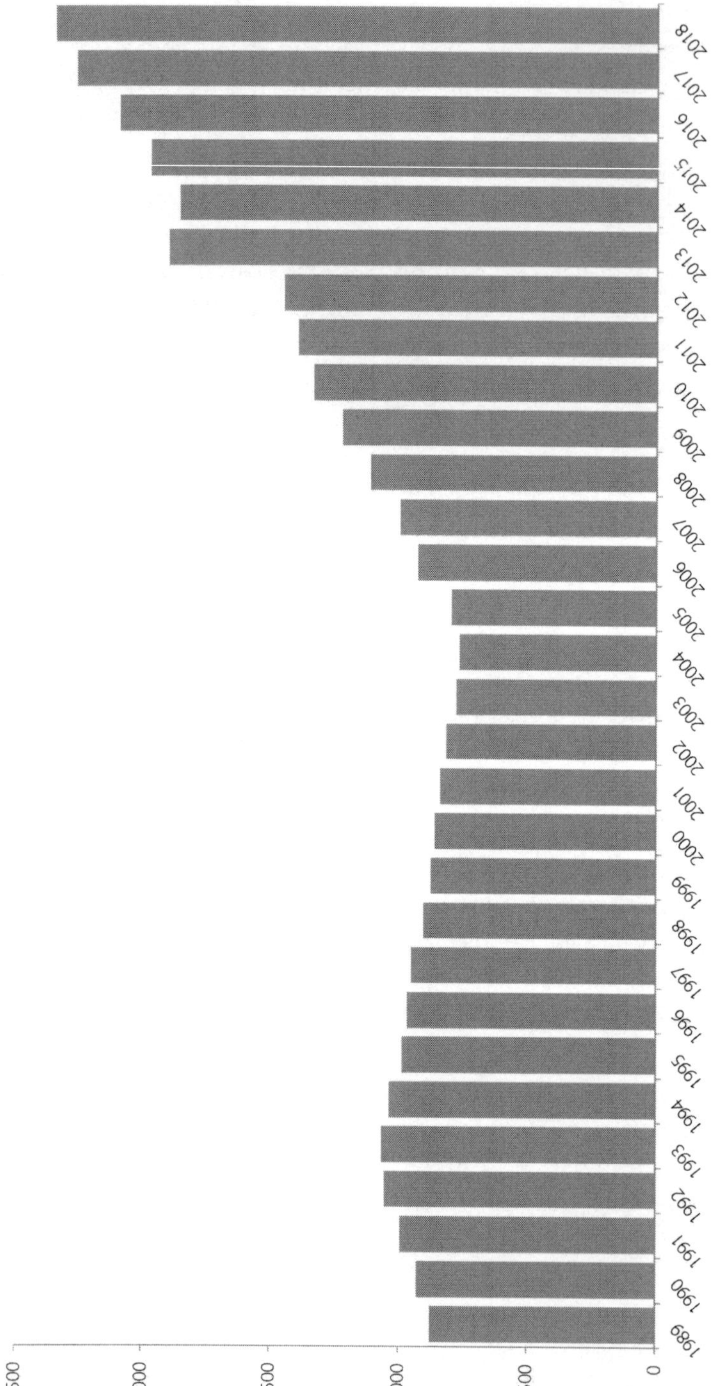

Planted hectares of vineyards 1989–2018

Britain certainly saw a massive increase in vineyard plantings in the three years between 2016 and 2018 when almost 750 hectares (1,853 acres) was planted. This is as much as was planted in the previous six years and shows little sign of slowing down. Plantings of course mean grapes, and grapes of course mean (eventually) wine – where it will sell is the conundrum everyone in the industry will have to get to grips with eventually.

THE EFFECT OF CLIMATE CHANGE ON BRITISH VITICULTURE

The factor that has most influenced viticulture in Britain in the last three decades is that of climate change. In 1989, when I wrote *The Vineyards of England*, it didn't merit a mention. Why? Because it hadn't happened then. Sure, there had been warm years. The year I returned from Germany, 1976, was certainly, at the time, the driest and hottest it had ever been since accurate records had been kept but that was a highly abnormal year and would not be repeated until 2003, almost 30 years later. Between 1959 and 1988, there were a total of forty-four days when the temperature rose to 29°C or higher, an average of just under 1.5 days per year. This period includes 1975 and 1976, both warm years, which together account for twenty of the forty-four days in the total – take these out and the average falls to exactly one per year. Between 1977 and 1982 – the first six years of my winegrowing career in Britain – I didn't see a single day when the temperature climbed above 29°C. Then things started to warm up and in 1989 and 1990 we had a total of thirteen days of 29°C or higher. These two years were probably the first time that British winegrowers realized that perhaps, just perhaps, the climate was looking up. The vintage in 1989 was very early. I started picking Schönburger on 19 September and pressed the last picking of Seyval Blanc on 12 October. In 1990 it was a similar story, but a much heavier harvest: started on 4 October and finished on 23 October. (In contrast, in 1988, a much cooler year, I only started picking Müller-Thurgau on 18 October and finished the Seyval Blanc on 4 November.)

The next three years, 1991–1993, were cool and British winegrowers saw only one day of 29°C or higher: 'back to normal,' we thought, but then something very strange happened. In 1994, the weather improved and apart from 1998 and 1999, the temperature rose to 29°C or above in every year up to and including 2006 (which had the highest average annual temperature ever). In 2007 things reverted back to normal, with no days of 29°C or higher and one of the wettest, coolest and most dismal summers ever, even though the average temperature for the year as a whole was, after 2006, the second highest since records began. Much the same pattern was seen in 2008, with no days of 29°C or over and a very low degree-day total (around 750), although sugar levels were exceptionally high, as were acid levels – an unusual combination. With the highest sugar levels ever then recorded in the history of modern British winegrowing (that is, until 2018), 2009 was a remarkable year. Chardonnay and Pinot Noir achieved 11–12% potential alcohol with near-perfect acid levels and some excellent yields. Even though the summer temperatures were not that high (only two days at 29°C or over), there was a very good spring and early summer with high temperatures in June and a flowering period to die for (which coincided with one of the driest Wimbledon tennis tournaments on record – no need of that new roof). July was wet and warm, August much the same, but September and October were largely dry and warm. But why – you may ask – is 29°C of such significance?

I have been convinced for many years that what made Britain such an unusual place (and sometimes a very unsatisfactory place) for growing grapes was the absence of really hot days in midsummer. The country's growers had quite a long, mild season with good light levels, long summer evenings, and summer temperatures and degree days that didn't differ too much from some other winegrowing regions, yet several things were obvious: natural sugar levels were lower, acids were higher (and more malic), dry extracts were lower and, very importantly for the economics of the business, yields were lower and more variable than in any other winegrowing region. In addition, the British spectrum of varieties was based around the ultra-cool-climate varieties: German crosses with the odd hybrid thrown in for good measure. None of the classic cool climate varieties – Chardonnay, Chenin Blanc, Pinot Noir, Riesling and Sauvignon Blanc – really got a look-in, since none of them would ripen for still wine. Champagne, Britain's nearest foreign winegrowing region, used to have very similar degree days to Kew in London, around 925 and 885 respectively, and the average temperature of the warmest month (July) was 17.8°C in Reims against that of 17.6°C in Kew. Yet it is plain to see that growers in Champagne could ripen 12–15 tonnes per hectare of Chardonnay and Pinot Noir and make sublime sparkling wines, whereas British growers struggled to ripen half to a third of that weight of varieties that often produced second-rate wines. What then was the difference?

The idea that high summer temperatures are needed to grow a good crop of grapes which will ripen fully is not mine. In *Viticulture Volume 1 – Resources* (2nd edition 2005) edited by Peter Dry and Bryan Coombe, reference is made to work done by J. A. Prescott in 1969 and Smart and Dry in 1980, both of which take the mean temperature of the warmest month (MTWM) – January in Australia, July in Europe – as the single factor that governs the suitability of a site to grow certain varieties. And what governs the level of the temperature of the MTWM? – the number of days when the temperature rises into the high 20s or low 30s. You can take anywhere between 28°C and 31°C, the theory holds good at any of these temperatures.

The past three decades have seen a gradual rise in the number of days when the temperatures rose above 29°C and 30°C, with a consequent rise in the average July temperatures which, for England as a whole, have risen from around 13.5–14.5°C in the 1970s and 1980s to 15–16.5°C – a rise of around 1.5–2°C in the past ten years. What this has meant to viticulturalists is that once marginal varieties – Pinot Noir and Chardonnay being the most widely planted – have suddenly started to move into the mainstream. Natural sugars have increased, acids are still high, but nowhere near as high as they were (for these varieties), the malic–tartaric balance is better. The other change in the climate – apart from the higher temperature midsummer days – is the rise in night-time temperatures (just ask the salespeople in any British bedding shop how many 13.5 tog duvets they sell these days). This means that vines warm up sooner, reaching the temperature where leaves can start photosynthesizing earlier, meaning that they can spend more time producing sugar. That is my theory anyway. However, the one element that hasn't changed much, in fact there is evidence that it has got worse, is yields, in both absolute and variability terms.

Since 2009, the British weather has been quite mixed, with vintages likewise. As in other parts of the world, what are known as 'extreme weather events' have occurred more often, with both cold and hot weather, floods and droughts, gales and high winds, all of an out-of-the-ordinary type. The winters of 2009–10 and 2010–11 were some of the hardest ever seen in Britain, but with relatively good summers, above-average yields and high sugars. At 5.98 hectolitres per hectare average yield and a total harvest of just over 1 million bottles, the lowest figures ever recorded, 2012 was the worst year on record for British vineyards. Nyetimber, Britain's largest producer, announced that it was not picking that year as the grapes were not of good enough quality. Flowering, véraison and harvesting were all late in 2013, with Chardonnay still being picked in a few vineyards in late November. In general sugars were low and acids high. An exceptionally good year, 2014 was frost-free, with early and good flowering and a perfect harvest, much like 2009. Average yields at 31.5 hectolitres per hectare were the highest of the modern era (since 1996 and up to 2017) with 6.32 million bottles being produced. Sugars were high, acids balanced and the wines exceptionally good. In 2015, which was again frost free, a cool spring and early summer made flowering two weeks later than usual and only an exceptionally good late September and October saved the day. In 2016 the story depended on which half of Britain you were in. The eastern and south-eastern half of the country had good growing conditions (Gravesend in Kent recorded one of its highest temperatures ever at 33.9°C) and managed to harvest good crops, even above-average ones, but the wetter, windier western half suffered badly from – well – wetness and windiness, and many Cornish and Devonian vineyards picked very little. Very high late-March and April temperatures got 2017 off to a memorable start but these were followed by some of the deepest spring frosts ever recorded in fruit growing regions – down to -7°C in some parts of East Anglia and the South East on 19 and 20 April and again on 26 and 27 April. Many vineyards with early budding varieties (including Chardonnay) got hit hard and yields in these vineyards were often (though by no means universally) low. Some vineyards, despite apparent frost damage which looked total, managed to catch up and produce good, even very good yields. June saw temperatures rise to 30°C and above for three or four days in a row – something not seen in Britain since 1976 – and flowering went through very early (16–21 June) and very quickly in amazing weather. The summer was indifferent, but September and October much better, leading to an early harvest. In the end, despite some vineyards losing 50 per cent of their primary buds, average yields were 23.8 hectolitres per hectare, slightly higher than the average of the previous ten years, and a total of 5.32 million bottles were produced.

For several reasons, 2018 was a remarkable year. A late start with no frost was a blessing, but at the beginning of May, as the season got under way, growth was generally two to three weeks behind. Then everything changed and in four weeks, went from late to early (by two to three weeks) with flowering starting on 9 June for early varieties and some growers even reporting flowering starting in Chardonnay on June 12, an unprecedentedly early date for the variety. By the beginning of Wimbledon fortnight (2 July 2018), a date when flowering typically *starts*, it was all over and most growers reported a 100 per cent set of flowers. With June and July temperatures being 2–2.5°C over the long-term average, the vines were able to grow their flower clusters, both pre- and post-flowering, leading to extra-large bunches at harvest. Instead of a typical 100–120 grams per bunch, some growers reported bunches of over 200 grams with some monsters at over 500 grams. The result was a massive (and early) harvest with yields of 10–15 tonnes per hectare (4–6 tonnes per acre) common, and some varieties – Reichensteiner, Rondo and Seyval Blanc – even surpassing 20 tonnes per hectare (8 tonnes per acre). Sugar levels were also at all-time highs with some wineries demanding that growers pick Pinot Noir early as the sugars were too high for sparkling wine, and some Pinot Noirs and Chardonnay for still wine coming in at over 13 per cent. With many vineyards reporting double (in one case quadruple) their best results ever, and with 1,924 hectares (4,794 acres) cropping, the largest ever cropping area, the final total is estimated to be 15.6 million bottles, three times the previous five-year average.

YIELD VARIABILITY IN BRITISH VINEYARDS

One might have thought that with rising temperatures, both average and maximum, yields in British vineyards, never very good at the best of times, might show a rise over the years. In fact, taking such reliable evidence as we have, the opposite is true. However, first a word of warning: British yield data is less than reliable and does not always give a true picture of the situation in well-sited, well-established and well-managed vineyards.

The only really consistent and reliable data source is the WS's annual production figures, produced as a requirement of Britain's membership of the EU and collected on a statutory basis. This means that if a grower or wine producer declines to give their production figures they can, in theory, be prosecuted and fined (possibly even imprisoned). Of course, this has never happened – neither fining nor imprisonment – and undoubtedly a few minor miscreants (who probably produce little wine anyway) escape the net. The figures are expressed in terms of hectolitres per hectare, not kilos per hectare, which would be better as volumes of liquid per hectare can be misleading due to different pressing practices in different wineries. Some sparkling producers, possibly wishing to claim superior practices by doing so, say that they only extract the first 500 litres per tonne from their carefully pressed whole bunches, junking the other 200–225 litres per tonne available. Others, usually ones producing a range of both sparkling and still, may well follow the same 500 litres per tonne 'only cuvée' practices, but squeeze the grapes dry and add the rest to lower-level wines both still and sparkling. Chapel Down, for instance, follow this latter practice, and their entry level still wine, *Flint Dry*, made using a combination of different (perhaps unfashionable) German-cross varieties, plus *taille* juice from sparkling wine varieties, is one of their real success stories.

One other factor that needs to be taken into account when looking at the WS figures is that returns are required from growers whatever quantity of grapes is harvested from their vineyards. This means that young vineyards where yields are necessarily lower in the first one or two cropping years and vineyards where management isn't to the highest standard, and disease, rot and bird damage (to say nothing of badgers or foxes) have lowered yields, still have to provide a return. In other words, pick a few buckets of grapes from your lovingly planted and tended vineyards in year two and send them to the winery of your choice to be pressed and in theory, their winery's production has to record this as a horrendously low yield. In a vineyard region like Britain's, which has been expanding by very significant percentages in recent years, the proportion of first-time cropping vineyards can be very high. Between

2007 and 2010, the percentage of first-crop vineyards was as high as 25 per cent (owing to new vineyard planting taking off in 2004) and this will have depressed the yield averages. However, taking all of the above into account, the figures are still worth looking at. I have always taken the view that good growers with well-established and well-managed sites ought to be able to crop at two and a half to three times the official yield figure. Thus when the average yield is 21 hectolitres per hectare (around 3 tonnes per hectare or 1.25 tonnes per acre), which it was for the ten years between 2008 and 2017, good growers ought to be cropping at 7.5 to 9 tonnes per hectare (3 to 3.6 tonnes per acre) at which level their vineyards are economic. Anything much less than this and one should question their long-term existence. Of course, many overseas growers marvel at the fact that British vineyards crop at all, let alone produce wine worth drinking.

So, now for some yield figures. In the five years between 1989 and 1993, i.e. between the years when the first (relatively accurate) statutory harvest returns were collected and the year before the vineyard area started to decline, the average yield was 28.02 hectolitres per hectare. This was the era when Britain was growing almost entirely German crosses and Seyval Blanc, and Chardonnay and Pinot Noir accounted for around 6–7 per cent of the total planted area. As has been said above, in the ten years between 2008 and 2017 – when Champagne varieties accounted for between 40 and 58 per cent of the planted area and all those big, well-managed, well-funded, sparkling-wine-only vineyards planted between 2004 and 2014 could be expected to be fully cropping – the average yield was 21.23 hectolitres per hectare, a drop of almost 24 per cent. This is the difference between having a viable, sustainable vineyard producing a return on investment and one that is probably not. Of course, the massive 2018 harvest has significantly changed the average data and taking the ten years between 2009 and 2018 and a national yield figure of 50 hectolitres per hectare for 2018, the average yield has jumped to 24.95 hectolitres per hectare with the five-year average (2014–18) standing at 29.51 hectolitres per hectare, the highest five-year average since accurate records began to be collected in 1989. Whether 2018 will turn out to be a flash in the pan or a portent of things to come, only time will tell.

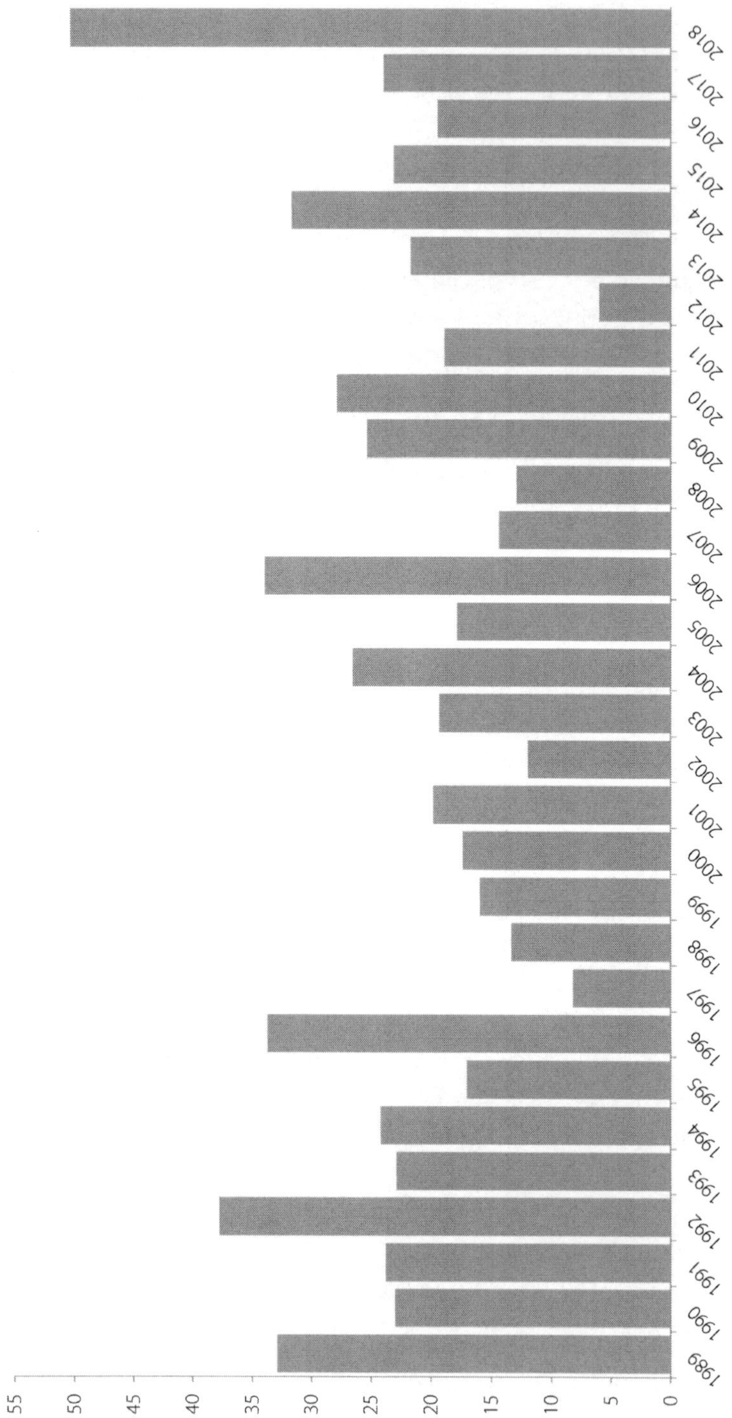

Yields in UK vineyards in hl/ha 1989–2018

CHANGES IN WINE STYLES

The past 30 years have seen a marked change in wine styles and types sold in Britain. In the late 1960s and 1970s, when English wines started making an impact on consumers, the biggest selling wines in Britain were Liebfraumilch and other German or Germanic styles. While there is no doubt that price played a great part in their popularity, these wines did find favour with a large sector of the wine-buying public who liked this easy, unpretentious style. In many respects the better English wines were similar – light and fruity, with a little residual sugar and not too heavy in alcohol – and they met with the approval of many consumers. In the 1980s, the tastes of wine drinkers in Britain started to change. Consumers seemed to want drier wines, perhaps because wine was appearing more and more at meal times, perhaps because palates were becoming more sophisticated. Wines from Australia, New Zealand and California started making a big impact on consumers and gradually the liking for German style wines reduced so that today's largest selling brands in Britain are the Australian Hardy's range and the Echo Falls and Blossom Hill ranges from California.

English and Welsh wines have reflected these changes in the market, and today no producer would risk bottling their still wines in tall German-style Hock or Mosel bottles. The preference today is to use the non-country-specific Burgundy (in brown or green) and Bordeaux (in green or clear) bottles. The few growers still using Germanic varieties such as Müller-Thurgau, Reichensteiner, Schönburger, etc. now tend to give their wines non-varietal names believing (correctly in my view) that Germanic varietal names are both confusing and off-putting to the consumer. Those making wines from varieties such as Bacchus, Ortega and Pinot Noir, which appear to be more acceptable names to consumers, continue to do so. Bacchus, which occupies 8.45 per cent of the area under vine, is definitely the best white still wine variety grown and as growers and winemakers gain experience with it, the wines get better and better. Its Sauvignon Blanc-like taste profile and its un-German name (no umlaut) make it attractive to regular wine buyers.

As the climate has warmed, the spectrum of still-wine varieties has also widened and now Pinot Blanc and Pinot Gris wines can be found with regularity. Sauvignon Blanc is starting to be used, although results to date show that in most years it's a hard variety to ripen and most growers blend it with Bacchus or Reichensteiner. A very few growers are trying Albariño, with mixed results – again, ripening problems tend to see it blended with other varieties; Riesling, that other cool-climate favourite, resists all attempts to be grown successfully in Britain. Rathfinny bravely planted 1.5 hectares (3.71 acres) of Riesling vines in 2012 and another 0.73 hectares (1.8 acres) in 2013 and the owners, Mark and Sarah Driver, trumpeted that they were 'looking forward to pouring the first glass of Cradle Valley Riesling in 2014,' and hoped 'to release a limited quantity of this richly complex, aromatic still white wine next year.' They said, 'the climate and soil in East Sussex are perfect for growing Riesling grapes,' but admitted defeat in 2016 and grubbed-up all the vines. This experience is not dissimilar to that of Denbies, which also planted Riesling in the late 1980s, but their only viable crop with the variety in twenty years was in the very warm year of 2003 and they too eventually grubbed it up.

SPARKLING WINE

The production of sparkling wine in Britain – although not from home-grown grapes – is verifiably over 350 years old, and we know from the two papers read at the newly founded Royal Society in December 1662 that sugar added to a fermented product and sealed in a bottle with a tightly bound stopper produced a 'brisk and sparkling' product. The Reverend John Beale's 'Aphorisms on Cider', read to the Royal Society on 10 December 1662, says that 'bottling is the next best improver' for cider and that 'two to three raisins into every bottle' plus 'a walnut of sugar' – a recipe guaranteed to produce a secondary fermentation – works wonders on the cider. A week later, on 17 December, it was the turn of the now famous Dr Christopher Merrett to read his paper, 'Some Observations Concerning the Ordering of Wines', and describe how Britain's seventeenth-century 'wine coopers' were making their wines 'brisk and sparkling' by the addition of sugar. This practice was certainly happening before 1662 and followed the development of the strong *verre Anglais* bottles which Sir Kenelm Digby had been perfecting since the 1630s.

Exactly when the first sparkling wine made from English grapes was produced is open to debate. Certainly wines being made in England in the 1750s were considered comparable to Champagne and as has been mentioned earlier, the wines produced at Painshill Place between 1741 and 1779 were often described as such. Of course, Champagne in those days was not always the sparkling wine that we know today. I have a wine list from the *Magasin de Vins Fins Chez Terral* from Pontac, a village just outside Bordeaux, dated 1760, which lists *Champagne mousseux* and *Champagne non-mousseux* both at the same price.

The first recorded production of bottle-fermented sparkling wines – made from British-grown grapes – is probably that carried out by Raymond Barrington Brock at his Oxted Viticultural Research Station in the 1950s. The *Daily Mirror* of 17 August 1950 carried an article entitled 'A bottle of Maidstone '49' which praised the work of Brock and that other viticultural pioneer, Edward Hyams and ended by saying: 'perhaps ten years hence you'll be raising a glass of sparkling Canterbury in honour of the men who made an English wine industry possible'. In September 1959 Brock welcomed members of the wine trade to a tasting and offered a number of different wines, including sparkling wines, to them. I have a letter dated 11 September 1959 sent to Brock by John Clevely, then a young Master of Wine, in which he thanks Brock for the visit and tasting and ends with a postscript saying: 'Moët must look to their laurels if you really start going "commercial" with that sparkling wine. I thought it was wonderful.' Praise indeed. Some of these sparkling wines survived undisturbed in the Station's cellars until the 1980s.

Sir Guy Salisbury-Jones at Hambledon, whose initial (1953) plantings included 20 Chardonnay vines, experimented with the production of a bottle-fermented sparkling wine, and in 1969 Bill Carcary, his vineyard manager, produced a batch of 60 bottles. Salisbury-Jones expanded the plantings of Chardonnay in 1970 with a further 1,000 vines but whether to make still or sparkling wine is not known. In 1979 his winemaking consultant Anton Massel helped produce a batch with apparently favourable results and as Salisbury-Jones also grew Auxerrois and Meunier, which ripened more easily, these became the basis of their sparkling wine cuvée. However, Sir Guy considered that the production costs were too high and the length of time the wine needed to mature was too long to make the product commercially viable and production ceased.

The first producers to make commercial quantities of bottle-fermented sparkling wines were Nigel (de Marsac) Godden at Pilton Manor in Somerset – first planted in 1966 – and Graham Barrett at Felsted Vineyards in Essex – first planted in 1967. As was quite usual at that time, the main varieties grown were Müller-Thurgau and Seyval Blanc and it is probable that it was these that were used. Their wines – never produced in large volumes – were certainly interesting, maybe even worth drinking and in the 1979 English Wine of the Year Competition (EWOTYC) the 1976 Felstar Méthode Champenoise won a silver medal and the NV Pilton Manor De Marsac Brut Méthode Champenoise won a bronze. These early successes, however, didn't seem to help sales much and their production faded out.

The next appearance of a bottle-fermented sparkling wine in the EWOTYC (ignoring the carbonated 1983 Barton Manor Sparkling Rosé that won a gold medal in the 1984 competition – delicious though it was) was in 1987, when the first Carr Taylor sparkling wine won a medal. David and Linda Carr Taylor first planted vines at their vineyard in Westfield, near Hastings, East Sussex, in 1973 and until 1983 their grapes were sent to Lamberhurst Vineyards for winemaking. From their huge 1983 vintage, however, when Reichensteiner cropped at 15 tonnes per acre and their total output came to 186,000 bottles, they decided to start making bottle-fermented sparkling wines. They engaged Clement Nowak, a Champagne-based Polish-French consultant winemaker, whose name at one stage actually appeared on the neck-label. For a few years Carr Taylor became the major producer – in fact almost the only producer – of bottle-fermented sparkling wines in Britain and achieved considerable success. Their Vintage Sparkling won a gold medal in the 1988 EWOTYC and their Non-Vintage Sparkling won the Jack Ward Trophy (best large volume wine) in the 1989 EWOTYC. In 1993 they won the IWSC English Wine Trophy with their 1987 Vintage Sparkling. They also entered their wines into overseas competitions – a rarity in those days – and did surprisingly well. Their 1988 Vintage Sparkling Wine was awarded a gold medal at the prestigious Concours European des Grands Vins beating 1,800 Champagnes and other bottle-fermented sparkling wines from around the world, and in 1999, in the same competition, their 1996 vintage was awarded a gold medal, this time out of 4,300 entrants. A fact that tends to get forgotten in these days of Britain's mega-vineyards planted with Champagne varieties is that the Carr Taylors were certainly the first to make serious commercial quantities of bottle-fermented sparkling wines. They did, however, only ever use what might be termed 'native' varieties for Britain: Reichensteiner, Schönburger, Kerner and Huxelrebe being the most important ones. This reliance on non-classic varieties, whilst it gave their wines a point of difference from other Chardonnay- and Pinot-based wines, also gave the wines a character more akin to Sekt or Asti than Champagne, something not all critics and commentators liked.

Britain's first Champagne-variety sparkler?

In 1985, Karl-Heinz Johner, then winemaker at Kenneth McAlpine's Lamberhurst Vineyards, started making sparkling wine for Piers Greenwood at New Hall Vineyards in Essex, a major grape supplier to Lamberhurst. He used mainly Pinot Noir (98 per cent) plus 2 per cent of what the Greenwoods 'thought was Chardonnay' for this wine, which Greenwood says, 'was released in December 1986 after ten months on the yeast'. This wine was therefore probably the first 'Champagne variety', bottle-fermented sparkling wine to be produced in Britain. It might also be the same wine as the 'Vineyard Choice' wine I listed in my 1989 book *The Vineyards of England*, which said '1984/5 New Hall Sparkling Wine Medium Dry £9.95'. When I took over as winemaker at Lamberhurst in May 1988 there was a stock of bottle-fermented sparkling wine in the cellars and I was told that this was made from Pinot Noir, Pinot Blanc and Chardonnay grown at New Hall. After getting Tom Stevenson to taste the wine and give it his seal of approval, it was released as 'Lamberhurst Brut' in 1988 or 1989. Whether this was from the same 1984/1985 grapes as New Hall's or from a subsequent vintage, I am unsure.

The next on Britain's sparkling wine scene was David Cowderoy who, working at his father's winery at Rock Lodge, produced the 1989 Rock Lodge Impresario[21] which won the IWSC English Wine Trophy in 1991. When David joined forces with others to create Chapel Down Wines (in 1992) one of their first wines, the non-vintage Epoch Brut, made from a blend of Müller-Thurgau, Reichensteiner and Seyval Blanc, was in fact a re-badged Rock Lodge wine. The fact that Chapel Down was not using the classic Champagne varieties (which, with the exception of New Hall Vineyards, were not being grown in enough quantity for them to buy) gave them something of a marketing advantage and

21 It had originally been called 'Rock Lodge Imperial' until Moët & Chandon complained as Impérial is one of its brands.

enabled their prices to remain reasonable – under £10 – although at the time this was at least twice that of still wines. In the end though, once Chardonnay- and Pinot-based wines started to appear in 1997–98, this marketing edge disappeared and their Müller-Thurgau, Reichensteiner and Seyval Blanc based wines, although very good and well-priced, were always playing second fiddle to the Champagne lookalikes in quality (and quality perception) terms. At much the same time, John Worontschak, winemaker at Thames Valley Vineyard (today's Stanlake Park) made a sparkling wine using Pinot Noir from Ascot Vineyard, a 1-hectare (2.47-acre) vineyard planted in 1979 on Crown land near Sunninghill Park and owned by Colonel Robby Robertson. Called Ascot Brut NV, it was released in 1992 and won a silver medal in the 1994 EWOTYC. Worontschak produced a number of Ascot sparkling wines from both Pinot Noir and (unusually) Gamay Noir, winning several silvers and bronzes between 1994 and 2004.

The production of sparkling wines using the three classic varieties – Chardonnay, Pinot Noir and Meunier – started in the mid-1980s when growers like Piers Greenwood (see above), Martin Oldaker at Surrenden Vineyard, near Ashford (planted between 1984 and 1986) and Karen Ostborn and Alan Smalley at Throwley, near Faversham (planted in 1986),[22] both in Kent, all started growing Chardonnay and Pinot Noir with the encouragement of Christopher (Kit) Lindlar. After leaving the Merrydown Wine Company,[23] based in Horam, East Sussex, where he had been one of the winemakers since 1976, Lindlar set up as a contract winemaker, firstly at Biddenden Vineyards, and then, in 1986, at his own High Weald Winery at Grafty Green, near Ashford, Kent. Lindlar, who also supplied vines, persuaded the two Kent vineyards above to experiment with these varieties, which had until then been very unsuccessful in Britain. Brock had grown Chardonnay in his collection at Oxted but could never get it to ripen properly. Ian and Andrew Paget at Chilsdown Vineyard planted Chardonnay and also had no luck getting it to ripen. In 1981, a very dismal year for British vinegrowers,

22 The 1989 Throwley Chardonnay Sparkling won the IWSC English Wine Trophy in 1992.

23 Merrydown was partially owned by Jack Ward, who was its MD, as well as being Chairman of the English Vineyards Association. Merrydown owned a small vineyard, Horam Manor, but more importantly operated a cooperative winemaking scheme for British vineyards, where in exchange for a percentage of the grapes, they made your wine.

the acidity (in grams per litre) in their Chardonnay was higher than the degrees Oechsle. Ouch. Extreme unripeness was a common finding among those early growers who persevered with it, although most decided to give up and removed the offending variety. Only in really hot years would Chardonnay produce anything like ripe grapes and tolerable wine. Pinot Noir, like many of the black varieties then being grown, suffered from terrible botrytis and was very difficult to ripen without huge losses. It is only since the arrival of better anti-botrytis sprays – initially Rovral and Ronilan, but more recently Scala, Switch and Teldor – that growing fungus-sensitive varieties like Pinot Noir has been possible. Meunier, in the guise of Wrotham Pinot, had always been grown in small amounts, but never used for anything other than blending with other, riper, reds. Lindlar's biggest, and subsequently best-known clients, were Stuart and Sandy Moss who decided, in 1988, to plant a vineyard at Nyetimber near Pulborough in West Sussex.

The Mosses had, by all accounts, been looking at various locations to plant a vineyard – California was at one time the front runner – but it was Sandy's love of (and business in) early English oak furniture that persuaded them that England was the place. In 1985 Hambledon Vineyards was up for sale and the Mosses viewed it and made a bid for it, but lost out to another bidder, John Patterson, who owned it until 1994. Bill Carcary, who had been at Hambledon since 1966, got to know the Mosses quite well at the time and when they then bought the 49-hectare Nyetimber estate in 1986, they asked Carcary to come and work for them as estate manager and eventually as winemaker and got so far with this idea as to refurbish a cottage for him and offer him a contract of employment. In his discussions with them about planting a vineyard on the land at Nyetimber, Carcary remembers it being his idea that they should plant the Champagne varieties for sparkling wine production, something he had long wanted to do at Hambledon, but which, as has been stated above, Salisbury-Jones had ruled out on cost grounds. In the end, Carcary decided for family reasons not to leave Hambledon and stayed, working for the new owner. Whoever actually came up with the idea to produce bottle-fermented sparkling wines on this (for the time) very large scale is uncertain, but the Mosses went ahead and planted the classic Champagne varieties, something which at the time was revolutionary – some said bonkers.

Hectares of Chardonnay, Pinot Noir, Meunier and Pinot Noir Précoce in UK vineyards 1990–2018

Variety	1990	1999	2004	2005	2006	2007	2008	2009
Chardonnay	20	34	36	49	91	120	180	202
Pinot Noir	32	44	49	62	85	121	185	218
Meunier	6	8	10	14	23	27	32	49
Pinot Noir Précoce	0	0	0	0	0	8	15	17
Total of above	58	86	95	125	199	276	412	486
UK planted area ha	929	872	761	793	923	992	1,106	1,215
% of total area	6	10	12	16	22	28	37	40

*Estimated figures. Source: Wine Standards Branch of the FSA 2015, UK Vineyards Guide 2017

The vines for the Nyetimber plantings between 1988 and 1991 were sourced from France and it was to Lindlar's High Weald Winery that the first commercial vintage, the 1992, was taken for processing under the watchful eye of consultant Jean-Manuel Jacquinot. As Lindlar modestly says, 'while they did hire Jacquinot, the winemaking buck stopped with me; that is to say, had those early vintages flopped it would definitely have been down to me.' Given the importance of the Mosses' enterprise, which when all was said and done was still something of an experiment, one has to give praise to Lindlar where it is due. After Nyetimber's first release, the 1992 Blanc de Blancs Première Cuvée, won the English Wine Trophy in 1997, and subsequent releases went on to garner further awards (see. p. 56), the English wine world started to take notice.

A few years after the Mosses planted, another Lindlar client, Mike Roberts, also decided to establish a dedicated classic-variety, bottle-fermented sparkling wine business at Ditchling in East Sussex. Ridgeview Winery was established in 1995 with thirteen clones of Chardonnay, Pinot Noir and Meunier and today it covers 6.48 hectares (16 acres), although it has access to grapes from a much larger area. A modern winery, with underground storage cellar, was built and equipped with the contents of the High Weald Winery, which was acquired when Lindlar closed the winery. In order to kick-start Ridgeview's production line, Chardonnay

2010	2011	2012	2013	2014	2015	2016	2017	2018	2019*
249	285	304	327	375	425	475	584	638	800
248	258	278	305	360	425	475	558	618	775
53	56	58	69	76	100	120	145	183	225
18	20	20	20	22	28	30	34	39	45
568	619	660	721	833	978	1100	1321	1478	1,845
1,324	1,384	1,437	1,503	1,565	1,813	1,956	2,267	2,328	2,750
43	45	46	48	53	54	56	58	63	67

and Pinot Noir grapes were bought from other growers, including Surrenden, and the 1996 Cuveé Merret Bloomsbury was produced. This wine won the 2000 EWOTYC Gore-Browne Trophy, awarded for wine of the year. Since that first release, Ridgeview has produced a range of wines, all named after London squares or areas – Belgravia, Bloomsbury, Cavendish, Fitzrovia, Grosvenor, Knightsbridge and Pimlico – and the tally of awards has been impressive. They won the Gore-Browne Trophy in 2000, 2002, 2009, 2010 and 2011 and regularly win gold and silver medals in the major wine competitions. Their most notable success was probably winning the Decanter World Wine Awards International Sparkling Wine Trophy (beating four very prestigious Champagnes in the process) with their 2006 Grosvenor Blanc de Blancs.

When first Nyetimber and later Ridgeview started selling wines and achieving the sort of prices that many in the wine business in Britain had thought impossible, the way forward for home-grown sparkling wines started to look a lot different. Following their significant commercial and competition success, plantings of the three classic Champagne varieties in Britain increased year on year and since the very warm year of 2003, several significant vineyards have been planted. Nyetimber changed hands twice and under its current ownership has expanded on various sites from its original 15.8 hectares to a whopping 258 hectares (638 acres) and growing. Owner Eric Heerema told me he was looking

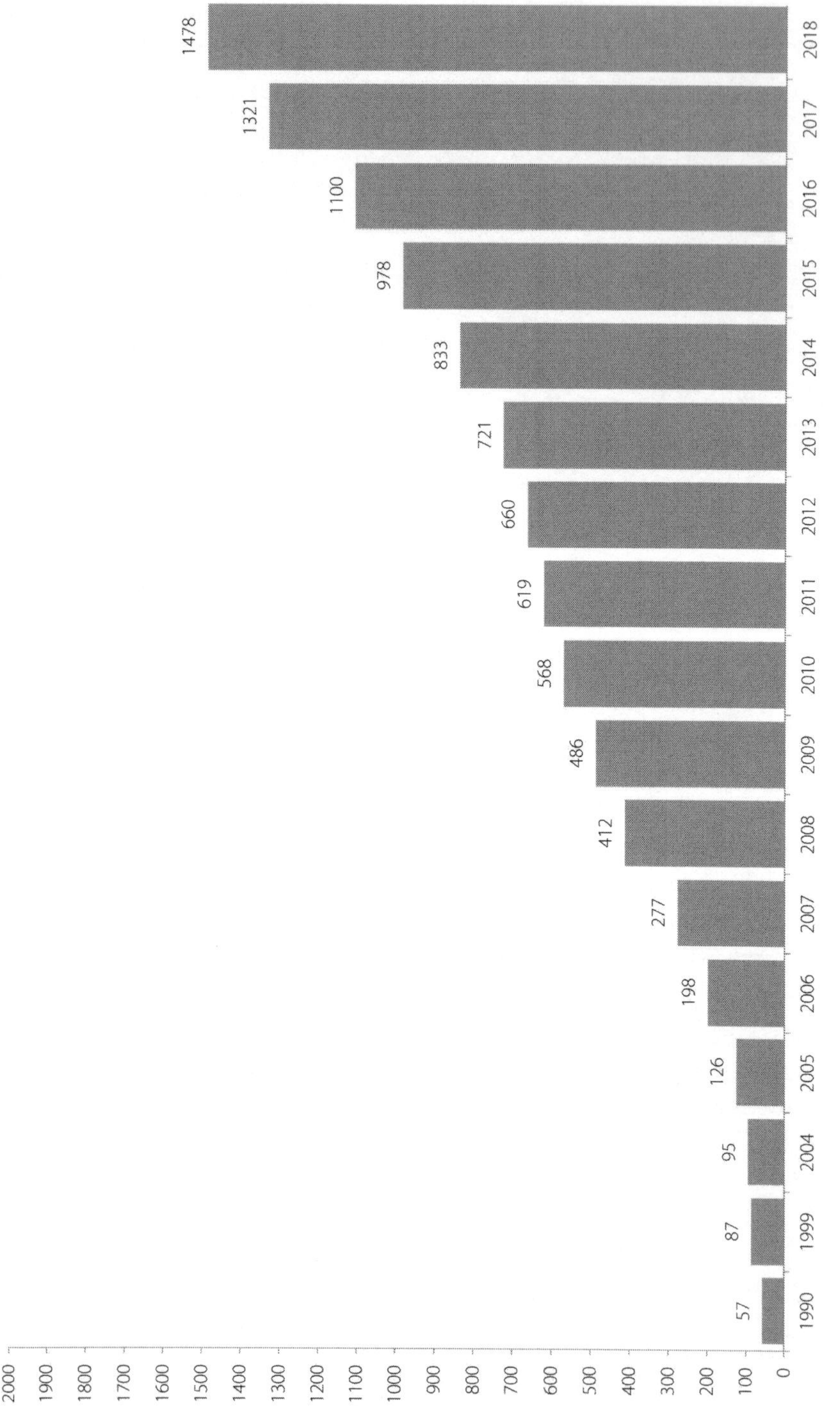

Hectares of Chardonnay, Pinot Noir, Meunier and Pinot Noir Précoce in UK vineyards 1990–2018

for another 200 hectares (500 acres). Other large sparkling wine producers include the largest, Chapel Down, with access to 300 hectares of Champagne variety vineyards; Gusbourne with 93 hectares; Ridgeview with 90 hectares; and Hambledon with 90 hectares. Other major sparkling players include Bluebell Estates, Bolney, Camel Valley, Coates and Seely, Laithwaite's, Langham Estate, Exton Park, Furleigh, Greyfriars, Hambledon, Hundred Hills, Hush Heath, Rathfinny, Simpsons, Southern Wines, Squerryes and Tinwood. Together, there are around 30 British producers who control 50 per cent of Britain's vineyard area and probably nearer 65 per cent of its sparkling wine production. The two French-controlled producers, Domaine Evremond (Taittinger) and what is currently called Pinglestone Estate (Vranken-Pommery) will be added to this list in time.

THE FRENCH CONNECTION

French producers, both from Champagne and elsewhere in France, have been interested in wine production in Britain for around 15 years. In 2003, following the hottest and earliest ever harvest in Champagne, a grower and winemaker from Avize, Didier Pierson, and his then wife, British-born Imogen Whitaker, entered into a joint venture with a Hampshire farmer, and in 2004 and 2005 planted 4 hectares of the three classic Champagne varieties on a somewhat isolated, exposed and high (up to 203 metres above sea level) site. The vines were planted very much *à la méthode Champenoise* with narrow rows and low trellising (ideal height for pheasants), and farmed using the only *enjambeur* tractor in Britain. The vineyard, known as Meonhill, was subsequently bought by nearby Hambledon Vineyard following the break-up and divorce of the Pierson-Whitakers.

In around 2004–5, Champagne producer Duval-Leroy instructed the Canterbury office of Strutt & Parker (well-known land agents with strong farming links) to seek out suitable land for planting. Their brief was short, if slightly eccentric: the land must be within one hour of the Channel Tunnel, the soil must be chalky and there must have been no livestock on the land in recent years. This last request baffled most of those involved, who were told that there might be residues in the soil which would interfere with the fermentation process. (I suspect there was something lost in translation.) Although several sites were found and one selected (Squerryes Estate) and lengthy negotiations entered into, nothing came of Duval-Leroy's quest and they retreated back to Épernay.[24] In 2006 (on an exceptionally wet and windy June day) I took Louis Roederer boss Frédéric Rouzaud, his winemaker Jean-Baptiste Lecaillon and Mark Bingley MW, their British agent, on a tour of English vineyards simply to show them what we were up to. Whilst this visit fuelled a lot of speculation about their intentions, it had only ever been a fact-finding trip and I never expected it to be anything else.

In 2007 Champagne producer Billecart-Salmon, in a joint venture with London wine merchants Berry Brothers & Rudd, found land in Dorset for the creation of an English sparkling wine brand. They were all set to go, but the financial crisis of 2008, when Champagne sales took a sudden dive, put them off the whole idea and it was shelved. When well-known wine writer and taster Steven Spurrier wanted to plant a vineyard on his wife's farm in Dorset, he first approached Duval-Leroy, who (again) proved difficult to negotiate with; then he tried teaming up with the Burgundy producer Boisset (whose sparkling wine house Louis Bouillot produce around 10 million bottles of Crémant de Bourgogne a year). However, Boisset were convinced that home-grown English sparkling wine couldn't sell for more than £12.99 a bottle (this was in around 2006/7) and wouldn't take things any further. Spurrier subsequently went ahead on his own, planting 10 hectares under the Bride Valley label.

The first Champagne house to actually take the plunge was Taittinger who, after over two years of discussions and negotiations, put their mouth and their money behind Domaine Evremond. This decision was put in motion following a visit to me by Patrick McGrath, a fellow Master of Wine who is MD and part-owner of Hatch Mansfield Agencies Ltd (Taittinger's British agents amongst other things). As a successful wine wholesaler they had decided that they should have an English Sparkling Wine on their books. How should they go about this? Should they look at buying an existing producer? Should they go the Champagne route – buy grapes and create a blend which they would market exclusively? What were the options? Buying an existing producer I said was out. The best were not for sale and you wouldn't want the rest. Buy grapes? Forget it – too many of the large wineries were already chasing them and supplies were too erratic and – more importantly – too

24 Squerryes Estate subsequently planted up and today have around 21 hectares of vineyards.

expensive. Why not go the whole hog, I inquired? Buy land, plant vines, harvest grapes, make wine, bottle wine, wait three years and – hey presto – wine for sale? Is that a practical option, asked McGrath? That's what I help people do, I said. When do we start looking for land?

The next two years were spent finding a suitable site. The South East was chosen as our target area and Kent the favourite county as I knew it well, it was near the Channel Tunnel and I considered it to have the best sites and best growing conditions for vines in Britain. As Hatch Mansfield were agents for Taittinger, they had to be consulted and Pierre-Emmanuel Taittinger, grandson of the founder and most definitely an Anglophile, agreed that Taittinger would become an investor. Eventually the Taittinger board decided that if they were to be involved, they needed to be majority shareholders and agreed to take around 55 per cent of the equity with the other 45 per cent owned by some significant minor shareholders, plus around thirty very small shareholders, mostly Hatch Mansfield employees, plus myself.

Sites were looked at and rejected, but eventually what I consider to be a perfect site, south-facing, less than 100 metres above sea level, well sheltered and with mainly chalk soil, was found between the villages of Selling and Chilham, eight miles south-west of Canterbury. After lengthy negotiations with the landowners, buying land they didn't want to sell and not buying blocks they wanted to sell, a deal was done and on 16 November 2015 the purchase was completed (it should have been the previous Friday but that, being the thirteenth, was rejected by the French as being inauspicious). The press launch was held on 9 December 2015 in the magnificent surroundings of Westminster Abbey, final resting place (in Poet's Corner) of Charles de Saint-Evremond. He was another Anglophile and Champagne lover who did much to introduce late-seventeenth-century Londoners to sparkling Champagne, which was becoming more popular than the predominantly still wine that was the norm at that time. The next 15 months were spent getting the site prepared, removing the apple, pear and plum trees that covered most of the site. The first 20 hectares (50 acres) of vines were planted in May 2017, another 8.08 hectares (19.97 acres) in 2019 and more will be planted as land becomes available, some of the land they bought being under a short farming lease to the original owners. Architects are working on plans for a winery and visitor centre and the first (small) harvest was taken in October 2018.

Following Taittinger, the floodgates hardly opened, but certainly tongues were set wagging in Reims and Épernay and it wasn't too long before French feet were heard in England again, this time in Hampshire. Champagne Vranken-Pommery bought (from Malcolm Isaacs, owner of nearby Exton Park Estate, for, it is said, £20,000 an acre) a 40-hectare site near Old Arlesford and planted 19 hectares in 2018, with 25 hectares to be planted in 2019. In the meantime, they have collaborated with near neighbours Hattingley Valley to produce some English sparkling wines under the *Louis Pommery* brand name, the same name as they use for their Californian '*méthode Champenoise*' wine (no doubt they wish they could call it that in Britain).

It will be interesting to see how many more Champagne and other foreign-based producers decide to invest in British vineyards. As has already been mentioned, Mark Dixon of Château de Berne has recently been increasing his land holdings in Britain (see p. 57). Boutinot, a major British-based wine wholesaler, bought Henners Vineyard in 2015 and the South African Benguela Cove Winery established vineyards in West Sussex in 2016 and 2017. Other southern French, Italian and even Californian producers have also been on reconnaissance missions and although they are all surprised how cheap vineyard land is compared to where they come from, their main discovery is how low yields are. With still wines selling in the £10–15 range and sparkling wines retailing between £16 and £35, can you really make money when you only harvest 5 tonnes per hectare (2 tonnes per acre)? Those yields might be OK if you are selling high-priced Champagne, Bordeaux or Burgundy, or New World wines with more than 95 Parker points, but they don't work for these relatively modestly priced wines. Still, this yield–price imbalance hasn't deterred home-grown producers expanding with the area of Chardonnay, Pinot Noir and Meunier rising year on year. By late May (after the planting season) in 2019, the total area under vine is expected to be near 3,000 hectares (7,413 acres) of which the Champagne varieties will account for around 65–70 per cent.

The future for production in Britain of sparkling wine – which in truth is the only category that really matters now – is an interesting one and I really wish my crystal ball was more reliable. I have got a bit wary of making predictions about the English wine scene, so rapidly have things changed in fifteen years. Until the bulk of the wines produced from vineyards planted in the past ten years come on the market and test the theory that they can be sold at sensible prices (£20–£30), then I cannot see the planting boom stopping. Years when very poor flowering weather (2012) and severe frosts (2017) cut yields dramatically in many vineyards will have tested people's resolve, but with deep pockets and good farm-gate sales, many producers believe they can get by on such yields as they can achieve. If the demand for grapes is anything to go by, then some producers certainly believe that high prices are here to stay. In 2017 such was the demand for almost all varieties, but especially Champagne varieties, that prices rose to nearly £3,000 a tonne with some paying a rumoured £3,800 a tonne for top-quality Chardonnay. At these prices and if you follow the rules laid down by the Comité Interprofessionnel du vin de Champagne[25] (CIVC) and only press 512.5 litres per tonne, then your cost per bottle for grapes alone is more than £5.50, around the same as in Champagne. Add on your production costs, bottling costs, storage costs and finance costs for ageing and you are probably getting to over £10 a bottle. If you sell direct to consumer from the gate at £25–£35 a bottle (£18–£26 net of VAT and excise duty) then it's probably worthwhile, but if you take typical DPD (duty paid, delivered) prices paid by wine merchants of £12–£15 (£9.23–£12.23 net of excise duty) then the maths is more questionable. Still, vineyard owners are eternally optimistic and without their positive attitude Britain wouldn't have a home-grown wine industry. The massive 2018 harvest will put a huge strain in producers' cash flows, since in order to stay in the sparkling wine business, they have to find the funds to make, bottle and store the larger than average quantities of wine. One producer with a (for the year) modest 10 tonnes per hectare crop said she needed to find £100,000 to bottle and store the wine from her 2-hectare vineyard.

25 The CIVC is the body that governs the complete production process in Champagne, from specifying where and how vines are to be grown and which clones are to be used, through to setting yields, pressing percentages, stock levels and many other things besides.

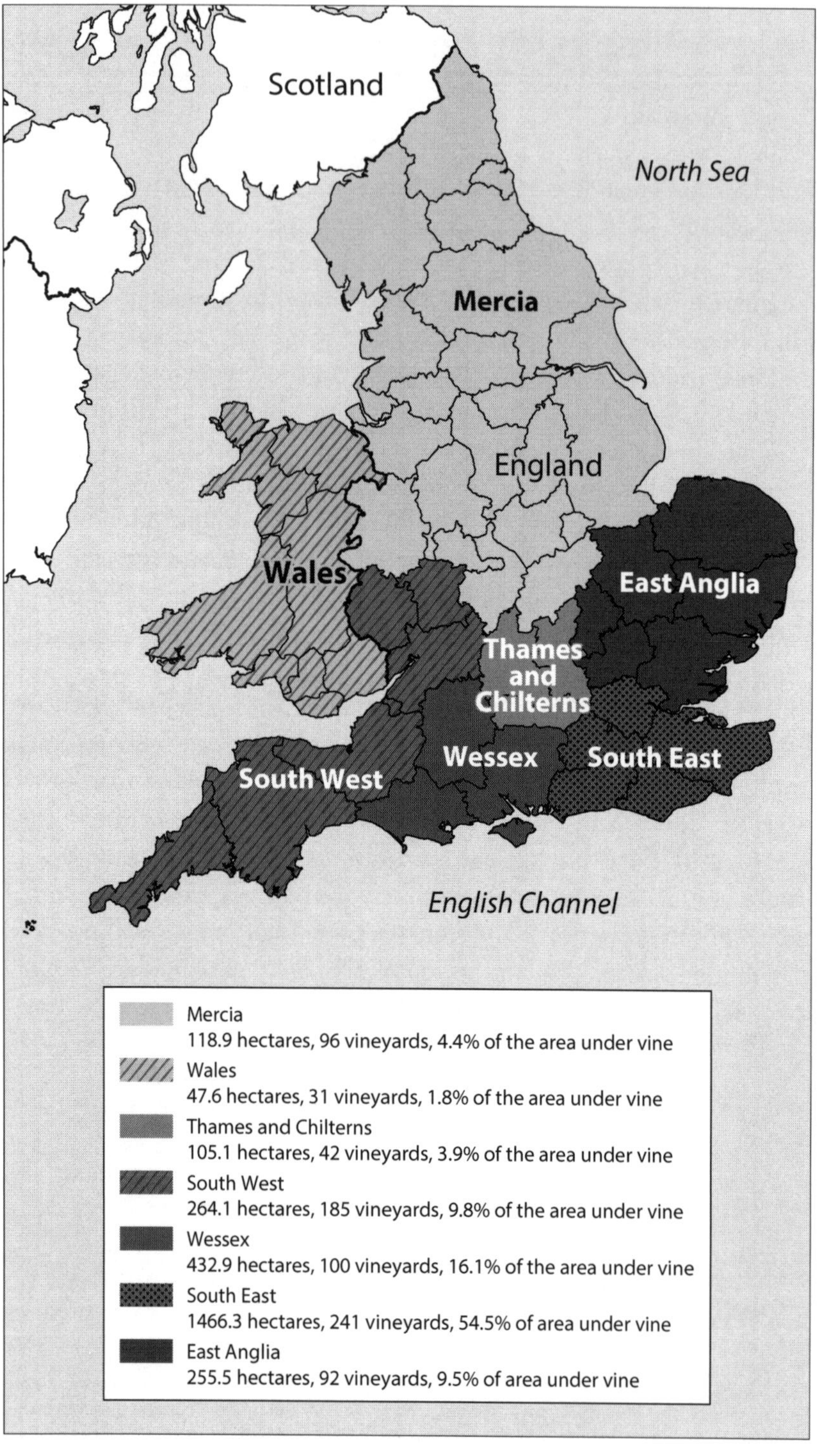

Area planted to vines in England and Wales

4

VITICULTURE AND WINEMAKING

From a single 0.4-hectare (1-acre) vineyard planted in 1952 to today's almost 3,000-hectare industry with several vineyards of 40 hectares or more, each employing staff numbered in the dozens, is a remarkable journey, in just over 65 years. Mistakes have been made and lessons (sometimes) learned in every aspect of production and there is no doubt that many of Britain's growers, winemakers and wine marketeers are today world class. This is not to say that every vineyard is planted in a perfect spot, with the right varieties, clones and rootstocks and managed expertly – but then this could be said of almost any winegrowing region. The best vineyards in Britain are certainly up there with the best from around the world.

TRAINING AND EXPERIENCE

There is no doubt that many of those who planted vineyards in the past were rank amateurs when it came to growing vines (or for that matter, growing anything). They seemed to think that vines were an undemanding crop, farmed by generations of peasant growers overseas who seemed to muddle by without much bother, and therefore it couldn't be that difficult – could it? Many also took the view that vinegrowing was an occupation they could fit into their spare time, weekends and summer evenings, forgetting that sometimes a week is a long time in a vine's life, especially if rain disrupts the spraying or weed control programme. This fairly casual approach to the process resulted in some very poorly established vineyards, with inadequate site preparation, inadequate trellising and some unusual pruning techniques. It also resulted in high levels of disease, which meant poor crops in terms both of quantity and quality. A lack of quantity only impinges on one's own finances; a lack of quality affects the whole of the English and Welsh wine fraternity. Most vineyards were also fairly small, too small to make employing anyone (with or without experience in growing vines) possible and this too gave rise to problems.

Very few of the early growers had anything approaching a formal training in vinegrowing. Several were farmers. This helped, but they were usually large-scale arable farmers and not growers used to looking after fruit crops. Ken Barlow, who owned Adgestone Vineyard on the Isle of Wight, had spent some time in Germany learning what he could about viticulture, as well as having spent over 20 years in agricultural research. This experience showed and he won the Gore-Browne Trophy twice in the mid-1970s. (I too was lucky enough to spend almost two years working in a vineyard and winery and attending lectures at Geisenheim in Germany before I planted a vineyard and started making wine, a fact that seemed to go against me when I won the Gore-Browne Trophy with my second vintage. 'You've been trained,' a friend said, 'That's cheating!')

A few growers were large enough to employ specialists, the most notable being Kenneth McAlpine at Lamberhurst Vineyards. The scale of that enterprise meant that right from the start, before the first vines were planted, everything from site selection to winemaking was in the hands of trained professionals brought over from Germany. It helped that his farm manager, Bob Reeves (whose wife was German), spoke the language. When Lamberhurst started winning all the prizes, the reasons were not hard to find: a professional approach from the outset resulted in quality fruit which, using the right equipment and a talented winemaker, could be turned into good, even very good, wine. Although good wines had been made 'BL' (Before Lamberhurst) – Ken Barlow at Adgestone, Peter Cook at Pulham, Colin Gillespie at Wootton, and Nigel Godden at Pilton were all early Gore-Browne Trophy winners – everything changed once Karl-Heinz Johner arrived at Lamberhurst as winemaker and established himself as the man of the moment in English Wine. Since then, the realization that viticulture requires both investment and expertise if good wines are to be the end result has become lodged in the viticultural psyche of British winegrowers. Of course there will always be a few who think that the 'dog and stick' approach to farming will work with vines, but these are today very much in the minority.

Since those early days, the level of professionalism at all levels in the wine production chain has greatly improved. Plumpton College, which started in a very low-key way in 1988, has over the years expanded its range of courses and its alumni are to be found not only in British vineyards, but also in vineyards and wineries around the world. Their £1 million training facility, opened by Jancis Robinson in June 2007, is a testament to the change in attitudes and approaches to growing vines and making wine in Britain. Others in the business are graduates of viticulture and winemaking colleges in France, the USA, Australia and New Zealand. Some British vineyards are now being run by the very experienced sons and daughters of their founders and there are even third-generation family members involved in some places.

The advent of sparkling wine as a serious commercial product has also helped change attitudes. The level of investment required and the length of time from planting to first sales are both substantially higher and longer than for still wines and this tends to exclude all but the serious and those without access to capital. The average size of these new enterprises is considerable. Many are far too large to be owner-operated and must rely on good-quality, trained staff to make them function, which must augur well for the future of Britain's viticulture and winemaking and, eventually, its wines. Sparkling wine production is also benefiting (we hope that is the right word) from the mini-influx of Champagne houses. Both Taittinger and Vranken-Pommery have planted and will eventually be producing wines; Hambledon and Hundred Hills are both using the services of French consultant winemakers. That's not to say that Britain's home-grown winemakers are lagging behind; many of the best sparklers are being produced by local talent.

SITE SELECTION

Historically, poor site selection was probably one of the major reasons why many English and Welsh vineyards failed to last the course. The desire to own a vineyard and to have one's name on a label has led growers in the past to plant vineyards on sites of dubious quality – sites chosen on the 'because it was there' principle, rather than for the site's intrinsic quality for wine production. The usual errors were sites that were too exposed, at too high an altitude and too windswept and where no consideration was given to providing shelter; sites which were in frost pockets; and sites where the soil conditions required drainage and none was done. Add to this sites that are hidden from the view of their owners and therefore tend to get neglected on the 'out of sight, out of mind' principle and you have a fair recipe for disaster. Several vineyards come to mind as I write these words.

Highwayman's Vineyard near Bury St Edmunds in Suffolk (a vineyard of almost 10 hectares planted in 1974) was, according to the farm manager I spoke to (a man I am fairly sure was called Bonaparte), planted on the worst land on the farm as he'd heard that 'vines liked poor soil' and the land in question 'wouldn't grow sugar beet'. The fact that the site seemed to catch all the easterly winds going and consequently rarely produced worthwhile crops seemed to have escaped his notice. Take another – Barnsgate Manor near Crowborough in East Sussex. This grand enterprise, the subject of an ADAS[26] Farm Walk (back in the days when 90 per cent drainage grants were available to all), consisted of about 20 hectares of vines planted in a steep bowl which, at 50 metres above sea level, would have been perfect. Unfortunately it lay between 130 and 165 metres above sea level with wonderful views towards the Channel but far too exposed to be successful. Add to this the proximity of unfenced woodland teeming with rabbits and deer, and the idiosyncratic way in which the enthusiastic owner, a Mr William Ross, had planted the vines using a cabbage planter, and the recipe was not a good one. Unsurprisingly, the picking machine, which Ross confidently spoke of buying, never materialized and as far as I am aware, no bottle of wine was ever produced under his ownership. These two were, unfortunately, not rare and many other examples could have been chosen.

You can still ask vineyard owners the question, 'Why did you plant here?' and the answer is still often (depressingly) the same: 'Because it was there.' Many growers plant land that they already own, convinced for some reason that it will be good enough and ignoring what could be learnt from past growers' mistakes. Of course, site selection is not down simply to picking the most suitable piece of land in the neighbourhood and planting it. It has to be for sale, it has to be accessible and in many

26 The Agricultureal Development and Advisory Service (ADAS) was a free advisory service provided by MAFF.

instances it has to come with a house to live in and some buildings to make wine in. Compromises often have to be made and one of the surprising things about English and Welsh wines – given the degree of care that went into site selection – is that some of them are as good as they are.

Overseas, where vines have been growing in some regions for centuries, site selection is less of a problem. The Old World wine regions are mapped in the minutest detail and *appellation* boundaries are based on the suitability of certain sites to produce wines true to the ideals of the *appellation*. In any event, in climates warmer than Britain's, the pressure to find sites where vines can fruit and grapes can ripen is less as there are many more of them. It always has to be remembered that Britain is the coolest winegrowing region in the world bar none and it is essential to grasp whatever natural advantages there are by correct site selection. Lighter, sandy soils, with good natural drainage are to be favoured and soils that overlie even leaner sand and gravel deposits are best of all. MAFF used to publish an excellent booklet called *Soils and Manures for Fruit* (Bulletin 107) which listed all the suitable fruit soils in Britain, together with their attributes. The 1975 edition can still be picked up second hand, but prospective vine growers should ignore the advice given on page 14 which states that vines are 'less susceptible to drought or adverse drainage conditions than most fruit crops,' although they should take the advice which says that 'shallow or coarse sandy soils are acceptable'. The advice on page 2 that 'aspect is not of great importance except for vines which need a southerly slope,' and that 'land above 400' [122 metres] is not suitable,' should also be noted. Suffice it to say that one can drag a horse to water but making it drink is another matter.

Despite the availability of advice from both books and consultants, many vineyards in Britain, both past and present, have been planted on sites unlikely to allow vines to prosper and this, sadly, has been reflected in the quality of the wine produced. The importance of choosing south-facing slopes, rather than flat sites (the second choice if south-facing sites are not available) or sites facing in other directions, especially north, is set out by George Ordish in great detail in his book *Vineyards in England and Wales* (1977). Any prospective vineyard owner searching for a British site on which to grow vines should read it. In an appendix, Ordish quotes a thesis written by Nick Poulter of Cranmore Vineyards which accurately states: 'although the amount of sunshine reaching a 30° south facing slope compared to a level site will only be 8% more in midsummer (which is towards the beginning of the growing season), by October, when the grapes are struggling to amass sugars, it will be 70% more'. To owners of level sites, let alone those with east-, west- or – heaven forbid – north-facing sites, this is frightening information.

However, the tide in site selection appears to be turning with many of the newer, post-2003 vineyards planted on sites where considerable thought has gone into site selection. This is partly because of the size of the enterprises – it is, perversely, easier to buy 100 hectares containing the 20 hectares you would like to plant with vines, than just the 20 hectares you need – partly because many of the new *vignerons* are better financed and therefore more able to pick and choose land, and partly because as many of these vineyards are planted with Champagne varieties, growers have gone out looking for chalk-rich soils that resemble the Vallée de la Marne and the Côte de Blancs in order to give their wines a suitable home and heritage. 'Planted on soil similar to that found in the best Champagne vineyards' looks so much better on a back label than 'Planted on some of the toughest Wealden Clay it was possible to find'. The truth of course about Champagne and chalk is that, firstly, a lot of Champagne is not grown on chalk (especially in the southern Aube region of Champagne) and there is a fair bit of clay-rich terroir that produces excellent wines. Secondly, the reason that the Champenoise like their best Chardonnay to be sitting in chalk-rich soils is that the high water-holding capacity of these soils (one cubic metre can hold 300–400 litres of water) allows for high yields and good leaf cover, both of which keep acid levels nice and high. And as we all know, high acidity is required for great, long-lasting sparkling wines. The idea that growers in Britain require soils that retain acidity in the grapes is of course somewhat perverse given typical acid levels.

My concern in the hunt to find chalk-rich soil in Britain is that much of this land is at 100 metres or more above sea-level, or very exposed to prevailing winds. Rathfinny Estate, one of Britain's latest mega-vineyards, is 100 per cent on chalk and situated in a fairly exposed valley in the South Downs, just over 3 kilometres (less than 2 miles) from the sea and in a valley ideally placed to catch the south-westerlies that come up the Channel. With 71 hectares already planted and a further 91 hectares to be planted in the near future, this is set to be one of Britain's largest vineyards. Whether they will also be one of Britain's largest producers remains to be seen. One hopes that the massive rows of 4-metre-high plastic windbreaks and multiple lines of windbreak trees that have been planted will help get over the wind problem that the owner, Mark Driver, admits to in his blog:

> *Before we bought Rathfinny I thought long and hard about wind and I looked at historical weather statistics from the Met office. They seemed to be okay, the average wind speed during the summer growing months was 4.5 metres per second, which is less than 10 mph, and that is the average for the whole site ... the lower part of the slope at Rathfinny gives much greater protection from the south-westerly winds and we could plant wind breaks to slow it down further. How wrong could I be? Well as it turns out the average is the 24-hour average and the winds tend to be stronger during the afternoon, when the vines are meant to be growing. And the trees we planted as windbreaks are taking a lot longer to grow than I had expected.*

Time will tell if this multi-million-pound venture will be a financially viable enterprise. In truth though, better site selection is part of the realization, after over 65 years of commercial viticulture, that if you don't have a good site, you cannot grow many grapes and if you don't have many grapes, you cannot make much wine.

ROOTSTOCKS

The selection of the correct rootstock is something of a black art and wherever one goes throughout the winegrowing world, growers debate the matter endlessly. Most, but not all, rootstocks stem from crossings made in northern European nurseries. In France, Germany and Hungary, the great vinebreeders of the late nineteenth century developed many crosses using wild American *Vitis* species as crossing partners to produce phylloxera-tolerant rootstocks. Over the intervening 145 years since the aphid struck in Europe, the colleges and universities that specialize in vinebreeding have clonally selected and improved those original varieties, increasing their phylloxera tolerance, improving their resistance to drought, to calcium-rich soils and to nematodes (which spread viruses). There are hundreds of rootstocks available worldwide, with scores in regular use. When Britain had a list of permitted rootstocks there were 46 separate rootstock varieties, although probably no more than ten were in use.

Which ones should be used in British vineyards? This is a very debatable matter. Traditionally, since most of the vines were Germanic in origin, they came from German nurserymen and were only available on what would be, to a German grower, a standard rootstock. Whether these were the most appropriate for British varieties and soils is another matter altogether. Many of Britain's problems in growing and ripening grapes in sufficient quantity and quality stem from the fact that here vines suffer from excess vigour and shaded canopies and as many of the rootstocks in use in Britain – 5BB, SO4, 125AA and 5C – are classed as 'medium vigorous' to 'very vigorous', they may not be helping this situation. Rootstocks with less vigour such as *Riparia Gloire de Montpellier* (RGM), 420A, 41B, 101-14, 161-49 and 3309C, all of French origin, might just help in this battle. Luckily, since the increase in planting of the Champagne varieties, many more of the vines planted (although by no means all, as some British vine dealers still source from Germany) have come from French *pépiniéristes* (nurserymen) for whom these rootstocks are standard fare. Add on to this the chalk factor (rootstocks suitable for planting on land with a high active calcium carbonate content tend to be less vigorous than others) and the rootstock spectrum used in Britain starts to look more respectable. My only worry is over the continuing use by many of SO4 as a suitable rootstock in all situations. Although it is classed as a 'medium' vigour rootstock, on some soils (although not chalky soils) it still seems to make vines fairly pushy. Time will tell. The new chalk-tolerant rootstock Fercal appears to be quite growy in its youth (it is classed as 'medium' for vigour) and I just hope that once it gets its roots down into the subsoil, some of its energy will dissipate.

The number of British vineyards planted on their own roots is very small, largely because of the dangers from phylloxera. In England and Wales this is a notifiable pest – meaning that if present it must be disclosed to the plant health authorities, who can order the destruction of your vines, but are more likely to impose a movement order on you, your workers, machinery and any vines (or parts of the vine) you may wish to move. Having said that, the results from own-rooted vines can be encouraging. Vines on their own roots are usually less vigorous than their counterparts on rootstocks and in many situations appear to break bud earlier, leading to a longer growing season; they are also immune to chlorosis. If a complete *cordon sanitaire* can be guaranteed around one's vineyard, these benefits (and those of cheaper home-produced rooted cuttings) might be worth taking. In addition, some take the view that vines on their own roots, having neither a rootstock nor a graft, are two steps better off when it comes to what are known as 'trunk diseases'. These ailments live in the woody sections of the vine and will, in stressed vines, cause a decline in vigour and yield, and often death. My view is that the phylloxera threat is too great – I know of three outbreaks in the South East in recent years – and any grower with aspirations to be around to see his or her vines into their old age would not risk planting on anything else but good phylloxera-tolerant rootstocks. More on rootstocks can be found at the end of Chapter 5 (see p. 134).

TRELLISING, TRAINING AND PRUNING SYSTEMS

Even now, more than 65 years since the first modern vineyard was planted in Britain, few in the business would claim that the question of how best to trellis, train and prune vines for British varieties and climate has been completely answered. However, over the last twenty years, some methods of trellising, training and pruning have fallen out of favour and growers appear to be reaching some sort of consensus that straightforward Vertically Shoot Positioned (VSP) Guyot-trained vines are best.

In the early days of the revival there was great debate between those predisposed towards the wide-planted, low-density, spur-pruned GDC system and those who favoured a more European approach with more intensively planted, Guyot (cane) pruned vines. Did GDC offer all the benefits its proponents suggested were there for the taking? Was it as cheap to establish as they said? Was the manpower required to manage a hectare of GDC-trained vines really that low? Were crops really that large? The intensively planted Guyot growers claimed much earlier cropping (in year two to three, rather than year six to seven for GDC), better disease control and better wine quality. These benefits had to pay for the extra costs of establishing and growing cane-pruned vines planted relatively close together.

Since those early days, the debate over GDC versus Guyot seems to have quietened down, largely because many of the large GDC vineyards have disappeared. The original GDC vineyard, Bernard Theobald's at Westbury, went soon after his death, sometime in the early 1990s and many planted under the aegis of David Carr Taylor, another great GDC proponent, followed suit. Many of these were large vineyards beaten eventually by the sheer volume of work involved in managing vineyards in the British climate or beaten by dealing with (i.e. selling) the large volume of grapes, and therefore of wine, which was often produced. I have never felt that the quality of fruit coming from GDC-trained vines was as good as that coming from VSP Guyot vines, mainly I suspect because many GDC vineyards did not get the attention to detail in such matters as shoot positioning and leaf removal that are so much easier with upright-trained vines.

However, there is no doubt that in some years, GDC does work well in Britain. Whether this is because the vines are big and therefore individually stressed so that they fruit rather than grow excess canopy (known as the 'big vine' theory) is debatable. British GDC-trained vines seem just as vigorous as their Guyot-pruned counterparts. It may be, however, that the basal buds – which in a spur-pruned system are the only buds there are – are more fruitful because, being close to a large body of permanent wood, they are better supplied with reserves. These reserves (carbohydrates) also help the buds withstand spring frosts and in addition bring about a slightly earlier bud-burst, leading to a marginally longer growing season. Disease control is still a problem in GDC vines, partly because there tends to be a lot of crossing-over of canes leading to much of the fruit getting covered up, but also because many growers do not possess sprayers of sufficient power capable of putting spray onto the target. When these two problems are addressed – by canopy management and by using more powerful air-blast sprayers – results do seem to improve.

I like to think that when I started growing vines, I adopted a more technical approach to the problem of trellising and training, having had the good fortune to spend a considerable time studying the subject while at Geisenheim. I came back from Germany in 1976/7, having worked in the densely planted vineyards in the Rheingau, convinced that a 2-metre row width, with vines planted at 1.2 to 1.4 metres in the row, was right for British conditions, and essentially have not changed my mind over the 30 years since then. A new science of 'canopy management', a term invented by Dr Richard Smart and Mike Robinson, formed the basis for their seminal work *Sunlight into Wine – A Handbook for Winegrape Canopy Management* (published in 1991), which became essential bedtime reading for modern viticulturalists worldwide, myself included. Whether all of its advice was suited to British conditions is open to debate. British average yields are so much lower than those in many other countries (especially compared to New Zealand and Australia where much of the research work that led to *Sunlight* was done) that some of the 'Golden Rules' advocated by Smart and Robinson in the book and by Richard during several canopy management workshops that he has held in British vineyards, do not really apply. However, the basic philosophy that underperforming vines with low yields can be helped both by leaving more fruiting wood per metre run of vine and by opening up the canopy to allow in as much light, heat and air as possible, still holds good, albeit to a lesser degree. Despite the extra growing costs involved, the yields from Guyot-trained vines are higher, more consistent and of better quality. The additional capital costs of establishing a closely spaced, intensively planted vineyard are a reality, but taken over the upwards of 25-year life of a vineyard, these do not add significantly to annual overheads. (Even GDC growers will admit that a cheaply established vineyard, where the quality and quantity of posts and end-anchors have been skimped, is a false economy.) Growing costs in closely planted Guyot vineyards can be lowered with the mechanization of some vineyard operations – summer pruning in particular – and a more relaxed view of how often, and how severely, vines should be tucked in.

In *The Wines of Britain and Ireland* (2001) I noted that Nyetimber, using advice from Épernay, had:

> *... planted narrow 1.6-metre wide rows with single Guyot trained vines at 1 metre apart – a planting density of 6,250 vines/hectare (2,530 vines/acre). This is very near the original planting scheme that Hambledon adopted when they planted in 1951 and was followed by many others at the time. Most decided that it was an unmanageable system for British conditions – the costs of summer pruning and training were too high – and very few vineyards survived with vines trained in this way.*

I speculated that Nyetimber's high quality of product would soon lead to others using similar planting schemes if they could be confident of correct yields. Since then, much has happened. A lot of vineyards have been planted and many, while perhaps not adopting quite such tight spacing as Nyetimber's original plantings (even Nyetimber themselves plant at 2.2 metres now), have planted with a row width of between 2 and 2.4 metres, with VSP-trained, Guyot-pruned vines. Most of the bigger, new, Champagne-variety vineyards have been planted like this, although Didier Pierson from Avizes in Champagne who planted a vineyard in Hampshire (Meonhill) stuck to the 1.2- by 1-metres planting that he uses in Champagne.

Of the many other growing systems available, very few have found much favour in British vineyards. There are a handful of Scott Henry growers in Britain, but, like the many ex-Scott Henry growers I met on a visit to Adelaide and Melbourne's winegrowing regions, there are even more that have tried and given up on the system. Why? Too much work and not enough benefit over VSP Guyot-trained vines. There are the odd one or two growers who use the Lyre system, but it shows no distinct advantage over either GDC or Guyot and establishment costs are higher. Following a three-week visit to New Zealand in 1998, a trip sponsored by the Canterbury Farmers Club (Canterbury in England, not the NZ one) in order for me to study the rootstocks and viticultural systems used there, I came back convinced that vines trained onto a single high wire (which could be called a high Sylvoz system, but which I dubbed the Blondin system after Charles 'The Great' Blondin, the first man to cross the Niagara Falls on a tightrope) could achieve as much yield and as good a quality as other systems, yet both establishment and growing costs are lower. This system does have several advantages over both GDC and Guyot and with experience can be made to perform well. It seems to incorporate some of the advantages of GDC (lower capital costs, more fruitful buds, better frost resistance and lower growing costs) with the better yields and more effective disease control associated with Guyot-trained vineyards. Weed control is also easier (or less demanding which comes to much the same thing) and the ability to vary the bud-count by leaving longer or shorter spurs could be an advantage. I trialled this system on four rows of Seyval Blanc in my old Scott's Hall vineyard and Chapel Down adopted a version of the system when they planted their Pinot Noir vineyard at Tenterden – the vines have produced a Bernard Theobald Trophy winning red wine. However, on all their more recent plantings they have kept to a 2-metre or 2.2-metre by 1.2-metre VSP Guyot system, exactly the one I used when first planting vines at Tenterden in 1977. Sam Lintner at Bolney Estate also trellised quite a few hectares to this system, but has reverted to VSP.

Whether training and trellising in British vineyards will change in the future is open to debate. Growers tend to get used to the systems they initially adopt, partly one suspects because change is either impossible or prohibitively expensive and also because no one likes to admit that they were wrong. Given that they are stuck with their chosen system, they tend to adapt and modify it to suit their individual circumstances and equipment and put up with its imperfections. Whether this attitude can be sustained is one that ultimately comes down to economics – few can support really low yields for ever. I suspect however, given that the largest and most high-profile vineyards – Chapel Down, Nyetimber, Rathfinny, Ridgeview – are all planted on more or less the same VSP Guyot system, this will remain the *de facto* system for growing vines in Britain.

VITICULTURAL EQUIPMENT

The viticultural equipment used in British vineyards has not changed that much since the early days and in any event, there is nothing very different about British vineyards that means they require specialist equipment not seen overseas. Tractors have got more powerful and four-wheel drive tractors, with Q-cabs (quiet and air-conditioned), are now universal. Sprayers are more efficient with low and ultra-low volume nozzles widespread (although not always very effective for controlling diseases such as powdery mildew) with quite a few vineyards now using four- and even six-row sprayers as vineyards get ever larger. Recirculation sprayers, which capture any excess spray that passes right through the row (which is then filtered and returned to the spray tank), are also used in several vineyards. These sprayers are said to reduce the volume (and therefore the cost) of the chemicals used by up to 50 per cent. Some vineyards with these only use them for the first half of the growing season, preferring to revert to high-volume, high-airflow sprayers for their post-flowering spraying. Many vineyards now mechanize their summer pruning with tractor-mounted trimmers and leaf strippers, both mechanical and air-driven. We have yet to see any automatic tucking-in machines, but I feel one cannot be far away. Many growers now use electric secateurs, a boon when pruning older vines with their thicker trunks and arms.

Traditionally, most vineyards in Britain controlled weeds in the under-vine area with herbicides, the practice favoured (and still preferred) by most soft- and top-fruit growers. Given the right weather conditions and the right materials for the weeds to be controlled, herbicides used twice (or at most three times) a year will result in a fairly weed-free zone beneath the vines. However, with recent scares about the use of glyphosate (Roundup being the best known product containing this active ingredient) many growers have investigated, and some have taken to, using under-vine ploughs and cultivators as an alternative (sometimes in conjunction with herbicides). Whilst under-vine cultivating is a great idea in theory, many growers find that the window between when the soil is too wet to attack and too dry to shake the weeds loose is sometimes very small in Britain's rainy summers. This results in them needing to be in their tractors ploughing up and down their rows (each row needing to be ploughed down each side) for days on end, costing them time, fuel and wear-and-tear on their equipment. In November 2017, the EU voted in favour of giving glyphosate a 5-year extension to its use, so maybe this will temporarily halt the spread of mechanical weed control, although long-term the trend is undoubtedly away from herbicides. Organic and biodynamic farming are even more challenging in Great Britain than conventional methods.

As far as harvesting goes, almost all grapes are still hand-harvested, that being an essential part of the *méthode Champenoise*, and the picking machines at Denbies and Buzzard's Valley are the only ones in use in Britain.

WINEMAKING

Again, as with viticulture, there is little in the production of wine in England and Wales that differs from winemaking in other cool wine regions of the world. While grapes grown in Britain do have natural sugar levels that some winemakers might find discouragingly low and acid levels that would have winemakers from warmer climes rushing for their text books, in essence the task of turning home-grown grapes into wine is much the same as it is in wineries worldwide.

When the first few vineyards of the revival started cropping, the level of winemaking knowledge was, by all accounts, fairly basic. Jack Ward at Merrydown had some technical expertise to draw on, but his staff had little experience of making wine from grapes at this time – cider and fruit wines were their specialities. Dr Alfred Pollard and Fred Beech, who ran the Cider Department at Long Ashton Research Station, near Bristol, helped Ray Brock with his winemaking. However, from what Pollard wrote in the winemaking section of the 1953 book *Vineyards in England*, he too had had little experience of working with grapes. Sir Guy Salisbury-Jones had help from a Monsieur Chardon (a friend of Allan Sichel's from Bordeaux) for the first Hambledon vintage (in 1955) and the results were described as 'encouraging'. What this meant in terms of wine quality one can only hazard a guess at. About the only person who professed to know anything about the job was Anton Massel. He quite quickly became involved with the fledgling wine industry and supplied both advice and equipment to Salisbury-Jones, the Gore-Brownes at Beaulieu, Major Rook at Stragglethorpe Hall, as well as a number of others. Nigel Godden at Pilton Manor took a different tack: he employed a cousin of the famous opera singer Mario Lanza to help in the vineyard and winery. Since Pilton Manor won the Gore-Browne Trophy two years running (1975 and 1976) he must have been doing something right.

From all accounts, the early English and Welsh wines were, at their best, 'interesting', at their worst, fairly thin and austere. Vineyards tended to suffer from bird damage which forced growers to pick early and rely upon chemicals to remove excess acidity rather than allowing the grapes to ripen naturally. Without today's modern anti-botrytis and anti-mildew sprays, the grapes suffered badly from disease which again led growers to pick early. The equipment found in many wineries was also fairly primitive and in some cases, very unsuitable for the production of the fresh, fruity wines which today's producers are able to produce with regularity. There were almost no stainless steel tanks in the early wineries and up until the mid-1970s, most wineries were equipped with second-hand fibreglass tanks, many of which had already seen 20 years' service in the cellars and railway arches of the wine companies that used to bottle wines in Britain. Many wineries had small vertical screw presses, more suited to red wine production than white, although Massel did persuade Salisbury-Jones to import a Willmes airbag press in 1965, which greatly improved both the efficiency of the operation and the quality of the wines. In 1969, Ward started the Merrydown Co-operative Scheme which gave smaller growers the chance to have their wine made by professionals and greatly helped raise the general standard of British-produced wines. Ward employed Kit Lindlar, already mentioned in relation to Nyetimber and their first few vintages, who had worked on the Mosel and spoke German, to work in the winery from 1976 until the last vintage under this scheme in 1979.

Until Lamberhurst started producing wine in 1974, very few English and Welsh wines had been produced (intentionally) with noticeable residual sugar. Up until then, wines tended to be fairly dry and crisp, relying on time in the bottle to soften the acidity, rather than any added sweetness. The arrival of two German-trained winemakers (Ernst Abel and Karl-Heinz Schmitt) to make the first Lamberhurst wines marked the start of a new era. Their first wines were naturally – for they were Geisenheim trained – sweetened slightly with sterile grape juice (*süss-reserve* as it is usually known by winemakers in Britain) and bottled through sterile filters. The results were something of a revelation. The sweetness balanced the acidity and the fruity grape juice gave the wines an added dimension which pleased, if not some purists, then at least the public who were becoming increasingly interested in English and Welsh wines. With hindsight, it is easy to say that the wholesale addition of grape juice – much of it imported from Germany – was perhaps overdone and in some cases used as a mask to cover excess acidity and unripe phenolic flavours. However, at the time, when the wines were being appreciated by ordinary customers, many winemakers saw the technique as a very valuable one.

As the size and importance of Lamberhurst, both as an individual wine producer and as a contract winemaker for many different vineyards in Britain, grew, so did the influence of their style of wine. Karl-Heinz Johner, another Geisenheim graduate, who took over winemaking in September 1976 and was there for 12 vintages until 1988, continued to make many wines in what one might call a German style – then extremely popular. It has to be remembered that at this time, brands such as Blue Nun, Golden Oktober and Black Tower, as well as a large number of generic Hocks, Mosels and Liebfraumilches dominated the entry-level and mid-markets in wine retailing in Britain. More and more wine was being sold through the rapidly growing national supermarket chains, and their wine-buying customers – many of them female

– found this style suited their palates. Many of the newer, larger British vineyards opened shops to sell wines directly to the public and it was very evident that when buyers had the chance to taste them first, wines with residual sugar found greater favour.

The years since Lamberhurst was the major player in the English and Welsh wine industry have seen many changes. Several other large vineyards and wineries have been established, with even more impressive facilities and capable of producing wines of equal technical quality. Growers have, through a combination of better vineyard management, better chemical sprays to control botrytis and mildews and an appreciation that quality really does start (and often end) in the vineyard, been delivering higher quality grapes to their winery doors. Winemakers such as John Worontschak, then based at Valley Vineyards (now called Stanlake Park), but who also worked as a consultant to many other wineries, and David Cowderoy, at Chapel Down until 1999, both of whom graduated from Australian winemaking universities, brought with them new ideas and new techniques which have resulted in more approachable wines – much more in the New World style. The fact is that while some would like to believe that English and Welsh wines are somehow immune from market forces, the truth is that they are not. The domination of the lower and middle market by the big German and German-style brands has ended and been replaced by more attractive New World styles. Old-fashioned English and Welsh wines, packaged as they almost always were, in brown Hock or green Mosel bottles, with their funny-sounding varietal names have largely – thank goodness – disappeared.

While many of the smaller wineries still retain simple equipment and use techniques suited to their scale, there are now a number of wineries – over twenty – of considerable size and complexity that would not look out of place in any winemaking region. They are equipped with 100 per cent stainless steel tanks (most refrigerated), airbag presses, modern filtration equipment and good bottling lines, including some with screw-capping facilities. Those vineyards specializing in sparkling wines have presses with Champagne programmes, gyro-pallets and modern disgorging and corking machinery. Hambledon, Rathfinny, Ridgeview, and Nyetimber all have Coquard PAI Champagne presses, considered by many to be the Rolls-Royce of sparkling wine presses.

In the winery, too, practices have changed. Winemakers have come to appreciate the benefits of gentler handling techniques, whole-bunch pressing, cold maceration of fruity varieties to extract more flavour, cold settling to produce clearer juice at the point of fermentation and the use of certain yeast strains to enhance flavours or add complexity. Until 1986, the use of oak barrels for the maturation of white wines was unheard of in British wineries, whereas today, while not perhaps to be found in every winery, they are quite widely distributed. As winemakers have gained experience with barrels, learning which of the different oaks suit their wines and how long to leave them on the yeast lees, so the quality of these wines has risen. A number of wineries also now produce 'oaked' wines, a term used to denote that the oaking is carried out with oak chips or oak staves, and that the wines have generally only fleetingly seen a barrel or often not seen a barrel at all. The use of oak chips and staves, made from the same wood and treated (toasted) in the same way as the wood used for making barrels, is nothing new and while it may not be openly admitted as such on labels, it is a common practice in wineries throughout the world. Both chips and staves can be introduced into tanks of juice or wine at any stage and the amount used and the length of time they are left in contact will determine the degree of 'oakiness' imparted. While these techniques do not give the same effect as using barrels, they can be very effective and impart an oaked character at a lesser cost. The use of the malolactic fermentation (the conversion of the harsher malic acid to the softer lactic acid by bacteria) to soften both white and red wines and add complexity during lees ageing – until the late 1980s unheard of – is also a practice that some winemakers in Britain have now taken to. In most cases, pH levels were too low, indicating that acid levels were too high for a spontaneous secondary fermentation (as it is often known) to take place. Now, by picking later, pH levels are higher and acid levels lower, and malolactic cultures can be used to induce the secondary fermentation, a technique seen very much more often.

WINE STYLES

Red and rosé wines, which once accounted for a very small percentage of the total wine produced, are increasing in quantity and together account for around 15–20 per cent of all wines made. Whilst true red wines of any quality are few and far between, although the warm and ripe 2018 vintage might produce a few better examples, English and

Welsh rosé wines, both still and sparkling, are gaining in quality and popularity. Still rosés made from Pinot Noir can be very attractive and sell for up to £15 a bottle, much more profitable than turning these grapes into sparkling wine and waiting three to four years.

Red vine varieties such as Acolon, Pinot Noir Précoce, Regent, Rondo and Dornfelder (which together occupy just over 6 per cent of Britain's vineyard area), have definitely helped to produce much deeper coloured and fuller bodied red wines, and the increasing use of oak for ageing is a significant factor in their improvement in quality. However, wines made from Pinot Noir have won the Bernard Theobald Trophy for the Best Red Wine in the national competition for fifteen out of the last seventeen years (since 2002). With Pinot Noir now officially the most planted vine variety and with the increase in average summer temperatures, it would seem likely that even more reds from this variety will be produced. Growers such as Chapel Down and Gusbourne have worked out which are their best plots of Pinot Noir and by some hefty thinning and careful viticultural attention, are both producing very good reds year in, year out.

A very few British growers have produced successful sweet wines and while this is an even smaller category than red wines, it is certainly one where value can be added. Early ripening varieties such as Ortega, Optima and Siegerrebe, together with botrytis-prone varieties such as Bacchus and Huxelrebe, which can all produce high sugars if allowed to ripen fully, have been used to make some excellent late-harvest style wines. Using Ortega, Denbies make an amazingly powerful dessert wine called 'Noble Harvest' (which in 1992, had a potential alcohol at picking of 22 per cent) and this wine continues to be the best British sweet wine. Jim Dowling at Pilton Manor won the Gore-Browne Trophy in 1994 with his 1992 Westholme Late Harvest, made from Huxelrebe which had succumbed to botrytis. Northbrook Springs made a gold medal winning wine called 'Noble Dessert' in 1994 from botrytis-infected Bacchus, Huxelrebe and Schönburger. Today, these wines are but a memory, brought about I suspect by better vineyard management and better anti-botrytis sprays, which prevent noble rot appearing. However, Tony Skuriat at Eglantine Vineyard in Nottinghamshire consistently (and completely legally) produces a *faux* icewine by freezing Madeleine x Angevine 7672 grapes, which quite often wins medals in the WineGB Competition, as well as overseas. Three Choirs usually make a semi-sweet dessert wine using the early ripening Siegerrebe which can be good. In general though, this is not a burgeoning category for English and Welsh wines.

Sparkling wines of course now dominate English and Welsh wine production and with around 65 per cent of Britain's vineyard area planted with Champagne varieties, and more and more being planted each year, this product is here to stay. Almost all sparkling wine produced in Britain is bottle-fermented and almost all carried out according to the strict *méthode Champenoise* as laid down by the CIVC. A few producers in the past have used carbonation to produce sparkling wines: Barton Manor won a gold medal with their Sparkling Rosé in 1984 and Chris Hartley at Meon Valley Vineyard produced many carbonated sparkling wines under contract. Today, however, the story that sells best is that Great Britain's sparkling wines 'are as good as Champagne', and to back that up serious producers are concentrating on using the three standard grape varieties (Chardonnay, Pinot Noir and Meunier) and using the officially approved CIVC equipment and techniques. Growers and winemakers making sparkling wines from non-Champagne varieties and adopting techniques not CIVC approved will, I feel sure, never reach the quality heights that have been shown to be possible.[27] Perhaps more importantly, those not using the classic varieties and processes will be viewed by the wine trade and consumers – at least by those that care about such things – as country-cousins who are not really trying hard enough. In 2017, two producers started to make Charmat (tank-method) sparkling wines using a blend of varieties including Bacchus, Chardonnay, Reichensteiner, Seyval Blanc and Madeleine Angevine, selling it for around £20–22 a bottle. If it really sells at this price, then it is probably quite a profitable product given the production process, the speed of production and the lack of ageing. It may well be that the bountiful 2018 harvest will give other producers ideas about what to do with the extra wine they have to deal with and rather than bottle it and wait 3–5 years, they might consider making it into a lower-priced Charmat-method sparkler and seeing what happens. One thing is for certain, most of the wine-buying public will not know what the

27 Having said that, both Camel Valley and Chapel Down make perfectly respectable – even award-winning – wines using other suitable varieties such as Seyval Blanc, Pinot Blanc, Auxerrois, Müller-Thurgau and Reichensteiner. In time, however, I feel sure these will be replaced with the more 'noble' varieties.

Charmat method is and when told 'it's the Prosecco or Asti' method will be quite happy to buy it and drink it.

There is no doubt that winegrowing and winemaking will continue to change and develop, to the benefit of British-grown wines. Huge advances have been made in every aspect of wine production in Britain and there is no reason not to suppose that similar changes will happen over the next few decades. In sparkling wine production winemakers have really only just started to understand how to grow and make good wines and as the large number of new vineyards planted with Champagne varieties start cropping and their grapes are made into wines, much experience will be gained for producers to learn from. Most vineyards make vintage sparkling wines and true non-vintage (i.e. made from a blend of three to four vintages, plus reserve wines) are very much in the minority. Nyetimber have produced a *Classic Cuvée MV* (multi-vintage) wine which sits at the bottom of their quality ladder – yet still sells for quite high prices – and other vineyards are also starting to produce true non-vintage (NV) wines. For most new vineyards, however, the additional wait whilst you grow, pick, process and make three vintages before you even bottle your first release (and then wait two to three years before it is ready to disgorge and sell) is too long and they prefer to bottle their first small harvest as a vintage and get something to show for all their time, trouble and investment as soon as possible. Taittinger have stated that they will be making a true non-vintage, using wines from their first three vintages, so maybe this will start a more pronounced trend towards NV wines.

5

VINE VARIETIES AND ROOTSTOCKS

The selection of a vine variety, a clone or a rootstock, for planting in Britain or in any other part of the world, can only be taken with reference to three principal factors: the climate, which dictates the spectrum of varieties which can be grown; the quality of the site on which the vines are to be grown; and the type of wine to be produced. In cool climates, such as Britain's, which many would consider marginal for sustainable viticulture, the choice of varieties is limited to those which will ripen sufficiently to produce good quality wine and which will produce yields which are high enough to make the considerable investment in a vineyard worthwhile.

In cool climates, growers are limited in the types of wine that can be produced successfully and their choice of varieties must be made on the basis of those varieties which will produce respectable wines year in and year out. Whilst it might be possible in some very favourable (warm) years to produce acceptable red wines using suitable varieties, in most years it will be a struggle, especially if top-quality red wines are required. British growers also have to be realistic about the limitations imposed by the climate and attempts to date to grow classic cool climate varieties such as Chenin Blanc, Riesling and Sauvignon Blanc have yet to produce acceptable wines on a regular basis. However, cool climates are ideal for producing light, fruity white wines, excellent rosés and light reds and of course superb bottle-fermented sparkling wines: *blancs de blancs*, classic cuvées, rosés and even some *blancs de noirs*. Chardonnay, today Britain's most widely planted variety, has a distinct advantage, being an important constituent in sparkling wines and a reliable producer of useable crops year in and year out, yet in favourable years it can be harvested – perhaps after some judicious thinning, and only on the best sites – for still wines. Pinot Noir, Britain's second most widely planted variety, is again an important component in sparkling wines and can also, given the right clones, good husbandry and a favourable year, be made into excellent rosés and (very) occasionally, respectable light reds. Whether it is really capable of making red wines that match those from other 'cool' regions such as Burgundy, New Zealand, Tasmania and Oregon is (in my opinion) questionable, but with the possibility of warmer years ahead, who knows?

The question of site quality is also critical in cool climates, far more so than in warmer regions, where the opposite problem – too much heat – may be more of an issue. In cool, marginal climates, those sites that are elevated, exposed to cooling winds and facing away from the south will be less able to ripen certain varieties and it goes without saying that in general terms, the further north you are (in the northern hemisphere) the lower will be the average temperatures and the more difficult will be the task of having good crops and fully ripening grapes. Site specifics are important as the quality of the site will dictate not only the quality of the wine, but also the quantity of wine. Being able to harvest ripe grapes is one thing; harvesting enough of them to make the enterprise financially viable is another. This is necessary if a sustainable enterprise, an enterprise that will outlive the enthusiasm (and possibly deep pockets) of its creator, is to be established.

VINE VARIETIES FOR BRITISH VINEYARDS

Although vines have been grown in Britain for many centuries, true commercial viticulture, where vineyards were established to produce grapes which could be made into wine for sale, is a relatively new phenomenon. Ignoring the efforts of the third Marquess of Bute in his Castle Coch vineyards in South Wales between 1875 and 1920, the modern revival started with the 0.4 hectares (1 acre) of vines established at Hambledon in Hampshire in 1952 (see p. 43). Since then, Britain's vineyard area has grown, slowly at first, to an official figure of 2,328 hectares (5,752 acres) as of November 2018, although the actual area is probably nearer to 2,750 hectares (6,795 acres).

Vine varieties in Britain, 2018

Variety	hectares planted	Proportion of planted area (%)
Chardonnay	637.52	27.38
Pinot Noir	617.56	26.53
Bacchus	196.69	8.45
Meunier	182.56	7.84
Seyval Blanc	101.34	4.35
Reichensteiner	67.90	2.92
Rondo	53.55	2.30
Solaris	47.27	2.03
Müller-Thurgau	43.15	1.85
Pinot Noir Précoce	39.22	1.68
Madeleine x Angevine 7672	38.64	1.66
Ortega	38.59	1.66
Pinot Blanc	29.03	1.25
Pinot Gris	28.76	1.24
Regent	28.64	1.23
Phoenix	24.63	1.06
Schönburger	21.63	0.93
Siegerrebe	19.37	0.83
Dornfelder	18.71	0.80
Other varieties	90.35	3.88
TOTAL	2328.11	100.00

In the early days of the re-establishment of viticulture in Britain, most growers planted just two varieties: the German cross-breed Müller-Thurgau (MT) and the French-American hybrid Seyval Blanc. As vineyards developed and spread, growers started experimenting with other varieties, almost all modern German cross-bred varieties, and by 1984, when Britain's planted area totalled 430 hectares (1,063 acres), the eight most widely planted varieties (accounting for 76 per cent of the vineyard area), were (listed in alphabetical order): Bacchus, Huxelrebe, Madeleine x Angevine 7672 (MA), Müller-Thurgau, Pinot Noir, Reichensteiner, Schönburger and Seyval Blanc. Thirty-five years later, the varietal spectrum has changed greatly. Climate change has meant that varieties such as Chardonnay and Pinot Noir, which up until the mid-1990s would not have ripened well enough to produce viable crops of grapes, now dominate. These top two varieties, together with the other classic Champagne variety, Meunier, account for 62 per cent of the planted area; Bacchus, Madeleine x Angevine 7672, Müller-Thurgau, Ortega, Pinot Noir Précoce (Frühburgunder), Reichensteiner, Rondo, Seyval Blanc, and Solaris (listed in alphabetical order) account for another 27 per cent. So together these twelve varieties account for a fraction under 89 per cent of the planted area. The next seven most planted varieties – Dornfelder, Phoenix, Pinot Blanc, Pinot Gris, Regent, Schönburger and Siegerrebe – account for a further 7 per cent, meaning that the 19 varieties detailed in this chapter account for 96 per cent of the planted area.

OTHER VARIETIES GROWN IN BRITAIN

Wine Standards lists an additional 23 varieties being grown in Britain on 0.1 hectares or more, all of which are planted on a small scale and in only a few vineyards. Together they account for 90.35 hectares, occupying 3.88 per cent of the planted area, and very few are worth mentioning. Since 2009, plantings of the following varieties have increased very modestly: Acolon, Albariño, Bolero, Cabernet Cortis, Cabernet Dorsa, Cabernet Franc, Merlot, Sauvignon Blanc and Villaris. All the other minor varieties are declining in area.

VINE VARIETIES – THE LEGAL SITUATION

Until Britain reached a total of 500 hectares of planted vines, MAFF (now DEFRA) was reluctant to get involved with the vine varieties growers had in their vineyards, although in theory growers were only meant to plant those varieties on the 'Recommended' and 'Authorized' lists. These lists, which had been drawn up prior to Britain's entry into the Common Market in 1973, were subsequently updated by the 'Vine Varieties Classification Committee' and brought into line with the varieties actually in the ground. Once a planted area of 500 hectares was reached, in 1987, growers in Britain were restricted to planting varieties on the lists, but while Britain's wine production remained under 5,000 hectolitres in any one year, restrictions on planted areas, and planting bans, were avoided (see p. 243). The production limit now sits at 50,000 hectolitres average annual production over 5 years. The most recent (2014–18) 5-year average annual production figure is 47,079 hectolitres but the EU confirmed that a planting ban would not be introduced, even were Britain to breach this limit. Following Brexit, Great Britain will (presumably) be in charge of its own wine regulations and vine planting will be something to put on the table at the first post-Brexit meeting with DEFRA.

The current British vine planting situation is that except for six old American and/or hybrid varieties – Clinton, Herbemont, Isabella, Jacquez, Noah and Othello (which are not permitted to be planted anywhere in the EU) – there are now no restrictions on the vine varieties one may plant, any variety may be used for winemaking and the variety name may be used on the labels of almost all wines. Not all vine varieties can be made into Protected Designation of Origin (PDO) wines.

INDIVIDUAL VARIETY DESCRIPTIONS

Notes to variety descriptions

- **Madeleine x Angevine 7672**: I have used the name Madeleine x Angevine 7672 and the abbreviation MA in the following pages, even though this name is not strictly correct. Please refer to the entry on this variety for the reasons why.
- **Meunier:** I have used Meunier, the name that INRA and ENTAV agree is the correct name for the variety often called Pinot Meunier or even Wrotham Pinot.
- **Müller-Thurgau:** When referring to Müller-Thurgau in the individual variety descriptions I have used the abbreviation MT.
- **German vine-breeding establishments:** References are made in the variety descriptions to the following vine-breeding establishments, all of them in Germany:

Alzey, Rheinpfalz	Geilweilerhof, Rheinpfalz
Freiburg, Baden-Württemberg	Geisenheim, Rheingau

Oppenheim, Rheinhessen
Würzburg, Bayern
Weinsberg, Baden-Württemberg

- **Sugar and acid levels:** Sugar levels are usually given in per cent potential alcohol. Most English and Welsh winegrowers and winemakers use degrees Oechsle (ºOE). As in almost all other countries – France and French-influenced regions being the exception, where levels in sulphuric acid are used – total acid levels in Britain are expressed in grams per litre of acidity as tartaric. To convert, multiply tartaric by 0.66 or multiply sulphuric by 1.52.

Bacchus

- Type: *vinifera*
- Colour: white
- Origin: (Silvaner x Riesling) x Müller-Thurgau

Bacchus, a crossing made by Peter Morio and Professor Husfeld at Geilweilerhof in 1933, was first registered in 1972 and was known in the Rheinpfalz as the 'Early Scheurebe'. Its parentage is the same as Optima. Bacchus is the second most popular white *neuzüchtung* (new-crossing) in Germany (after Kerner). It first appeared in Britain in the Wye College vineyard in 1973 as an experimental variety and was upgraded to 'Recommended' in 1998. Bacchus, as a variety for Britain, is here to stay and the area under cultivation has risen from 76 hectares in 1990 to 197 hectares in 2018. Bacchus is the best white variety being grown in Britain today for the production of still wines and it regularly wins many of the major prizes. In growth habit it is similar to MT, although perhaps not quite as vigorous, but just as prone to botrytis. It appears to ripen readily in most vineyards, although acids can be high and care needs to be taken that they are not too high in the bottle, especially with wine made from grapes harvested at lower sugar levels. A little residual sugar often helps.

In the bottle, Bacchus falls into two camps: what one might term the Sauvignon de Touraine or pretend Sancerre camp, where the wine is light, fruity, with a modest spiciness, but of no great weight; and the full-on Marlborough Sauvignon style with luscious, spicy, even catty, fruit with enough body and weight to carry the flavour. These tend to be the riper (higher natural sugar) examples and are best when they are bottled with perhaps a few grams of residual sweetness (as are many

Marlborough wines). Chapel Down's Bacchus Reserve is often a fine example of this latter (and to me, more preferable), style. With top Bacchus wines selling for £12–15, this is a variety that can make money. The one *really* good thing about Bacchus is the name – free from the umlauts and unfortunate prejudices associated with Germanic names – just a name everyone recognizes and thinks has something to do with wine. Who was that Bacchus fellow anyway, some sort of god?

Chardonnay

- Type: *vinifera*
- Colour: white
- Origin: original variety

With its origins lost in the mists of viticultural time, Chardonnay is now found in virtually every grape-growing region in the world, from the hottest parts of Australia, South Africa and California to the coolest of all growing regions, Britain. As the dominant (often the only) variety in white wines from Burgundy and of course of major importance in Champagne, it is not surprising that early vineyard owners in Britain were seduced into thinking that it would do well there. Brock had it in his collection at Oxted, but could never get it to ripen properly. Salisbury-Jones planted it at Hambledon and had the same problems, as did others who made early attempts: excessively high acid levels and low natural sugars in all but the most exceptionally hot summers.

In the mid-1980s, some growers – New Hall, Surrenden and Nyetimber – started to plant Chardonnay for the production of bottle-fermented sparkling wines. In the 2001 edition of my *UK Vineyards Guide* I wrote: 'through a combination of good site selection and traditional training systems (aided by a degree of global warming) they have started to produce some interesting results. While acids are still high at harvest (15 g/l is not uncommon) the combination of a full malolactic fermentation and the traditional secondary bottle fermentation, renders them manageable'. Well, the 'interesting results' turned out to be more than interesting and since then some extremely good wines, almost all sparkling, and occasionally on suitable sites, as well as some respectable still wines, have been produced. High acids are a problem and growers, especially those with less than perfect sites, need to make sure they select the right clones and rootstocks, plus prune and canopy manage, to get acids down. Chardonnay plantings in 2018 are 638 hectares, making it

Britain's most widely planted variety, accounting for over 27 per cent of the planted area. Given the way the British climate seems to be heading and the quality of the *blanc de blancs* sparkling wines and occasional still wines being produced, I can only see Chardonnay going from strength to strength.

Viticulturally, Chardonnay is no more demanding to grow than most varieties. It buds up quite early and in frost-prone sites this can be a problem. It is susceptible to powdery and downy mildew and botrytis, and vines almost always need spraying in their year of planting. Until it can be demonstrated otherwise, single or two-cane Guyot pruning appears to work best. British growers still do not get the very high yields found in Champagne (where 15–20 tonnes per hectare is not uncommon), so it would seem that Cordon pruning is not required. Chardonnay benefits from an open canopy and deleafing both after flowering and pre-*véraison*. Late-season downy mildew will affect the ripening process, so protection needs to be maintained until the bitter end.

Chardonnay ripens late and is usually not harvested until the third or even fourth week of October. In a very late year – such as 2013 – it was still being picked on 20 November, which must be the latest British harvesting date ever. Of course, 'late' is subjective – I was rarely able to enjoy sharing Guy Fawkes night (5 November) with my children in the late 1970s and 1980s, as I was always pressing Seyval Blanc, so perhaps today's Chardonnay growers shouldn't complain too much. Potential alcohol levels are usually in the 8–10 per cent region – ideal for sparkling wine – although in cool years and late sites 7–8 per cent is quite common. Acid levels are typically 12–15 g/l, with the cool year/late site figure commonly reaching 16–17 g/l – even higher not unheard of. British vineyards are using a mixture of clones of Chardonnay for sparkling wine and none is especially dominant. Many growers use the CIVC recommended clones 75, 78, 95, 96, 118, 121, 124 and 131. Other clones used include 119, 277 and 548 and in some vineyards one can also find German clones, although they do not appear to show any advantages over French ones.

For sparkling wines made in Britain, Chardonnay is an indispensable component and no serious grower can be without it. Ridgeview produces some great Chardonnay wines and their 100 per cent Chardonnay Grosvenor Blanc de Blancs is very often their best wine. Their 2006 Grosvenor Blanc de Blancs will surely go down as one of their best wines and its winning of the International Sparkling Wine Trophy at the Decanter World Wine Awards (beating four very prestigious Champagnes in the process) was a real affirmation of the quality of British sparkling wines. There are today many other British growers making very good *blanc de blancs* sparkling wines, Gusbourne and Nyetimber being worthy of a mention, and this can only enhance its reputation as a must-have variety.

For the production of still wines, Chardonnay has shown that with a suitable site, correct canopy management and, most importantly, the right level of crop, very good wines can be produced in Britain. If growers can make still wines from Chardonnay that sell at the same sort of prices as middling Chablis and entry-level white Burgundy, then we will see even more Chardonnay planted in years and decades to come. For still wines, I regard clones 75, 76, 95 and 548 as suitable for Britain. Clones 121 and 131 have also been recommended for still wine, but acids are said to be higher. However, given that in France alone, thirty-one clones of Chardonnay are registered for use and in other countries there are tens of dozens more (some of them duplicates admittedly), it is likely that there are other clones suitable for British vineyards yet to be trialled and proved.

The combination of a classic name, its Champagne heritage and many excellent sparkling (and a few still) wines, have made Chardonnay indispensable for any British vineyard with pretensions to seriousness. Whether it suits all the sites it has been planted on remains to be seen and some growers may yet struggle to ripen it and/or find that their wines need five years or more in the bottle to come round – not usually a recipe for guaranteed financial success.

Dornfelder

- Type: *vinifera*
- Colour: red
- Origin: Helfensteiner x Heroldrebe

Dornfelder is one of the new(ish) wave of German crossings, bred at Weinsberg in the heart of Germany's red wine producing region, Württemberg. Here, the traditional varieties – Trollinger (Black Hamburg) and Limberger – suffer from a lack of colour and substance and Dornfelder was bred to produce more of both. Dornfelder's parents are two other Weinsberg varieties: Helfensteiner (which is Blauer Frühburgunder x Black Hamburg) and Heroldrebe (which is Portugieser x Limberger). The crossing was made in 1955 by August Herold and released to growers in 1980 and it is now the most widely grown 'new variety' in Germany. It is capable of producing some good wines, albeit in a spicy Rhône style rather than a classic Bordeaux style, although some German examples can be fairly light and insubstantial, probably due in part to high yields: 120–150 hectolitres per hectare is not unknown.

Dornfelder first appeared in Britain in the late 1980s and is able to produce tolerable red wines, especially in blends with other varieties. It is no more difficult to grow than other *vinifera* varieties and in good years can produce quite heavy crops. Very few 100 per cent Dornfelder wines have been produced in Britain; it is mainly blended. Plantings have expanded modestly over the years, but it is not a variety that will ever become widely planted in Britain.

Madeleine x Angevine 7672

- Type: *vinifera*
- Colour: white
- Origin: freely pollinated seedling of Madeleine Angevine

The variety we loosely call 'Madeleine Angevine' comes from a cutting sent by the Alzey Institute to Ray Brock and planted at Oxted in 1957 and is more properly called Madeleine x Angevine 7672, for the reasons explained on page 35. Just when the crossing was made is not known, although the timing would suggest that it was while Georg Scheu – responsible for varieties such as Faberrebe, Huxelrebe, Kanzler, Regner, Scheurebe, Septimer, Siegerrebe and Würzer – was the Alzey Institute's Director.

The shortening of the name was unfortunate as another variety already existed under this name. There is also another variety, to cause further confusion, called Madeleine Angevine Oberlin, a crossing between Madeleine Angevine and Bouquettraube.

The true Madeleine Angevine (also sometimes called Madeleine d'Angevine) is a female-only table grape variety, for many decades said to be a crossing of Madeleine Royale[28] and Précoce de Malingre made by Pierre Vibert at the Moreau-Robert nurseries in Angers in 1857 (some reports say 1859), but described in *Wine Grapes* to be a crossing of a

28 Madeleine Royale, a table grape vine variety once thought to be a Chasselas seedling, but now shown to be a Pinot x Black Hamburg cross, has been 'outed' by the gene-jockeys as the father of Müller-Thurgau, with Riesling being the mother.

Chasselas-based table grape variety called Circé and Madeleine Royale. It is one of the earliest table grape varieties for open cultivation in France and named after St Madeleine's Day (22 July), said to be the date on which it can be picked. Having only female flowers and being very early, it has been used by plant breeders in a number of crosses over the years. Morio and Husfeld used it for Forta and Noblessa and it is one grandparent of Reichensteiner. Scheu himself used it to produce Siegerrebe and interestingly, this variety, which at one time was credited with being a Madeleine Angevine x Gewürztraminer crossing, was unmasked by Heinz Scheu, Georg's son, as also being a freely pollinated Madeleine Angevine seedling. It is conceivable that the variety we now grow in Britain as Madeleine x Angevine 7672 comes from the same crossing programme that produced Siegerrebe. In 1992, I asked Professor Alleweldt (or Professor Dr Dr h.c. Diplomlandwirt Gerhardt Erich Alleweldt to give him his full title), then head of the Geilweilerhof State Institute for Grapevine Breeding, to see if he could discover more about our Mad Angie (as it is often known). He located Georg Scheu's old breeding books in the Alzey archives and found that 'Sämling 7672' was – as Brock was originally told – an 'open pollinated progeny of Madeleine Angevine'.

Madeleine x Angevine 7672 found favour with many of the early British growers and became fairly widespread. At one time it was the third most popular variety (after MT and Seyval Blanc) and Gillian Pearkes, one of the pioneers of British grape growing who was an influential character in the West Country, thought highly of it. Unfortunately, owing to the confusion over the name and the fact that this variety was not available from any source other than Brock's original stock or vineyards planted with vines obtained from Brock, some growers were sold vines of the true table grape variety Madeleine Angevine, which was barely suitable for Britain, except in the very best years. Unless it was being grown in proximity to other early varieties for pollination, it seldom set a good crop and in some years ripened at the end of August. The wines from this variety were flabby and never really acceptable except for blending. The confusion over this variety – foreseen by the EU Commission in 1973 when MAFF submitted vine varieties for classification – has meant that it gained something of a chequered reputation.

Madeleine x Angevine 7672 is easy to grow, ripens early, can give good crops and produces wines with a light Muscat tone and low acidity. Despite these advantages, except in less-favoured regions, it is unlikely to be planted very much and the planted area will slowly decline over time.

Meunier

- Synonym: Pinot Meunier, Schwarzriesling, Müllerrebe and – in Britain only – Wrotham Pinot
- Type: *vinifera*
- Colour: red
- Origin: original variety

Meunier, one of the numerous mutations that go to make up the Pinot family, accounts for around one-third of the plantings in Champagne (although a larger percentage of the production as it yields more than either Chardonnay or Pinot Noir). Whilst it is seldom spoken about in the same breath as its two nobler companions and is not allowed in *Grand Cru* wines, it is used in some of the finest cuvées (Krug for example). In Champagne it is favoured for its acidity which can be higher than in Pinot Noir, its ability to withstand spring frosts and its higher yields, and is often found in the cooler sites. It is characterized by its white-tipped shoots and its hairy leaves, especially on the underside, which give it the 'dusty' look from which the name – which means 'miller' in French – stems. Like many of the Pinots, it can show reversions back to the true Pinot Noir and it is quite possible to have, on the same vine, both hairy and non-hairy leaves on different shoots in one year, which disappear in another year.

In the early 1950s, Edward Hyams, one of the early pioneers of British grape growing, discovered a vine growing on a cottage wall at Wrotham which he named Wrotham Pinot and which he gave to Ray Brock at Oxted. Given that this foundling had the classic dusty and red-edged leaves of Meunier, Brock assumed, wrongly or rightly, that it probably was a Meunier, although he reported that it had 'a higher natural sugar content and ripened two weeks earlier' than supplies of Meunier obtained from overseas. Brock sold cuttings and it became quite popular with some of the early vineyards. It is doubtful now whether any cuttings from Hyams or Oxted still survive in British vineyards and all plantings of Meunier stem from France or Germany (where it is known as Schwarzriesling or Müllerrebe). However, the name Wrotham Pinot is still a permitted synonym for Meunier in Britain.

Although it has been grown for more than 50 years in British vineyards, Meunier has never really shone as a variety capable of making interesting wines on its own and most of it has been blended with other varieties. However, the rise in the planting of Champagne varieties has meant a resurgence of interest in the variety and my experiences to date, despite my former misgivings about its suitability for the British climate, have been favourable. The quality of the Nyetimber 2003 Blanc de Noirs Meunier, which won a gold medal in both the 2006 and 2008 EWOTYC and which for me (and for Tom Stevenson) was the best wine in the *Decanter* March 2008 mega-tasting of British sparkling wines, opened my eyes to its possibilities. There is no doubt today that it is seen as an indispensable part of many classic cuvée sparkling wines and often accounts for 15–20 per cent of Champagne variety plantings in British vineyards. The planted area has grown by 73 per cent since 2009 so that today Meunier is Britain's fourth most widely planted variety and will soon overtake Bacchus and rise into third place.

Müller-Thurgau

- Synonym: Rivaner, Riesling Sylvaner
- Type: *vinifera*
- Colour: white
- Origin: Riesling x Madeleine Royale

Professor Dr Hermann Müller, a Swiss from the canton of Thurgau near Zurich, produced this crossing while working at Geisenheim in 1882. Returning to Switzerland in 1891 to become Director of the Wädenswil Research Institute, Professor Müller asked for 150 of his best crossings to be sent to him at Wädenswil, including No. 58, which was eventually to become MT. Owing to some confusion with the labelling when the crossings were delivered, the true parentage of No. 58 was never discovered and it eventually became known as 'Riesling Sylvaner' on account of its wine style, said to resemble a blend of Riesling and Sylvaner. Professor Becker, head of Geisenheim in the 1970s and 1980s, attempted to recreate the variety by making multiple Riesling and Sylvaner crossings, but failed. He was, however, of the opinion that MT resembled a Riesling x Riesling crossing more than any other.

In 1996 Dr Regner, an Austrian from the viticulture school in Klosterneuburg, proved that the crossing was between Riesling and a member of the Chasselas family, a table grape vine variety that (he thought) was called Admirable de Courtiller. It was then discovered that the reference vine of this variety in Klosterneuburg's collection was in fact another variety altogether – it turned out to be Madeleine Royale (a

Chasselas seedling variety). In 2001, two researchers in Germany, Erika Dettweiler and Andreas Jung, were able to unravel the DNA in MT and prove that it was indeed a crossing between Riesling and Madeleine Royale: after 119 years MT's parents were finally found. Madeleine Royale is itself Pinot x Black Hamburg.

In 1912, wet-sugaring (the use of sugar in solution to chaptalize wines) was forbidden in Switzerland and MT started to replace Elbling, up until then a widely grown variety, but high in acid. It then began to find favour in Germany and, in the early 1920s, was taken up by Georg Scheu, then at Alzey in the Rheinland-Pfalz. He subjected it to clonal selection and helped improve its yield. Following the Second World War, when many vineyards were suffering from phylloxera as well as the ravages of the war, MT was widely planted and its large yields, early ripening and soft wines, lower in acidity than either Riesling or Sylvaner, were much appreciated. It was once Germany's second most widely planted variety (after Riesling) but is today much diminished in popularity.

Its introduction into Britain stems from Ray Brock's visit to Switzerland in 1946 when he met Mr Leyvraz at the Swiss Federal Vine Testing Station at Caudoz-sur-Pully. In 1947 vines of various varieties were sent by Leyvraz to Brock, including 'Riesling Sylvaner'. Brock gave cuttings to Edward Hyams in 1949 and they both trialled it for a number of years. Brock first harvested grapes from MT on 14 October 1950. In Hyams' 1953 book *Vineyards in England* Brock wrote in his chapter on vine varieties: 'Riesling Sylvaner is known to give an outstandingly fine wine in cool climates.'

When Jack Ward was looking for vines for the Horam Manor vineyard, planted in 1954, he was recommended MT, and it became a staple of all the early British vineyards. Ward was a very influential figure in the early days of the revival (the EVA's first Chairman) and undoubtedly did much to persuade growers to plant MT. Ward's company – the Merrydown Wine Company – sold vines and gave advice and ran a winemaking cooperative between 1969 and 1979 to which many of the early growers belonged. When I selected varieties for planting in 1976–7 MT was top of my list; at that time it was almost unthinkable to plant a vineyard in Britain without it. Most German wine and viticulture experts considered England to be a country of mists and not-very-mellow fruitfulness and thought that a high-cropping, early-ripening, low-acid variety (which is what MT is in Germany) was just what its vine growers needed.

MT is a vigorous variety, especially in its early years, and it will grow thick canes and large leaves, leading to excess shading. This often results in poor cropping, especially in years with low light and heat levels in the previous season. It suffers from botrytis, powdery and downy mildew, requires regular spraying and must be deleafed after flowering and then again around *véraison*. In heavy-yielding years, stem-rot can be a problem. The wood often ripens poorly and does not over-winter well, often showing active botrytis in mild winters. It is probably a variety best avoided by organic growers. Since the advent of better anti-botrytis chemicals such as Scala, Teldor and Switch, disease control has become easier (if more costly) and clean crops of MT are the norm, rather than the exception they were in the 1970s and 1980s.

The grapes of MT can have good fruity flavours with light Muscat hints, and at their best the wines made from them can be very good. However, when less than fully ripe, they tend towards the herbaceous and catty. The acidity is usually average to low and with some balancing residual sugar, the wine can be very attractive and fresh when young and will keep well, although is probably best drunk within two to three years after bottling. Picked early, with sufficient acidity and when the fruit flavours are more neutral, it can be used for sparkling wine and Chapel Down have used it in the entry-level Vintage Brut Reserve, although over the years, the percentage in the blend has come down, to be replaced with pressings from Chardonnay and Pinot Noir.

In 1984, MT was by far the largest single variety being grown in Britain with 149 hectares, accounting for 35 per cent of the planted area, but today it is down to 43.2 hectares and 1.85 per cent and no one is planting it anymore. With hindsight, it was a variety that Britain could probably have done without, although one must not forget that the most popular wine style at the time it was being planted was light, fruity Liebfraumilch, for which MT is very well suited. Its extreme vigour, especially in the early years, coupled with its on–off cropping pattern and disease problems, made it a difficult variety for British conditions.

Ortega

- Type: *vinifera*
- Colour: white
- Origin: Müller-Thurgau x Siegerrebe

Ortega is a crossing made by Dr H. Breider at Würzburg between MT and Siegerrebe. Siegerrebe is a freely pollinated Madeleine Angevine seedling with Gewürztraminer the most likely culprit as father. Ortega was first registered in 1971 and is named (somewhat curiously) after the Spanish philosopher José Ortega y Gasset.

In Britain, Ortega was introduced by Jack Ward, who planted it at Horam Manor in 1971, and it has slowly grown in popularity. It is one the earliest varieties to ripen in Britain – just after Siegerrebe and Optima – has high sugars, low acids and plenty of flavour. An early bud burst makes it susceptible to spring frost damage, it is sensitive to poor flowering conditions and will suffer from coulure in poor years. It can be quite vigorous and canopy management needs to be good to get the best fruit. It will also get botrytis towards the end of ripening which will turn to noble rot if sugar levels are high enough. Given good canopy management and timely attention to spraying, this variety can provide high-quality grapes, useful for both normal still wines and dessert wines. Growers report that its bunches tend to get tangled up with each other and with the canes and wires, and picking can take twice as long as for other varieties.

When fully ripe, wines made from Ortega are rich and zesty with good balance, although warm years may result in wines with rather low acidity; care needs to be taken to pick at the correct time. Biddenden Vineyards have won numerous gold and silver medals with Ortega wines, winning the Gore-Browne Trophy with one in 1987, and Denbies use it for their multi-award-winning Noble Harvest. Growers of Ortega seem to like the variety and the area has risen from 29.5 hectares in 1990 to 39 hectares in 2018, which must be seen as a vote in its favour. Expect to see more of it in the future.

Phoenix

- Type: *vinifera* (complex hybrid)
- Colour: white
- Origin: Bacchus x Seyve Villard 12-375

Phoenix (and not Phönix) is another of the many complex hybrid crossings made by Professor Dr Alleweldt at Geilweilerhof and is Bacchus x Seyve Villard 12-375 (Villard Blanc). It was first registered in 1984 and listed for general growing in 1992.

Phoenix first appeared in Britain in the late 1990s. There were only 1.9 hectares planted in 1999 but the area has risen very slowly, to cover

24.6 hectares in 2018, which, all things considered, is relatively respectable. Although only planted on a few sites in Britain, the wine can be good quality (Three Choirs' is usually the best), with higher sugars and lower acids than MT, and is Bacchus-like, although not as powerful. It is one of the several complex hybrids that can be made into Quality Wine in Britain. It will probably never be widely planted, but could be useful in climatically less-favoured vineyards.

Pinot Blanc

- Synonym: Weißer Burgunder
- Type: *vinifera*
- Colour: white
- Origin: original variety

Pinot Blanc is one of the most widely distributed varieties across Europe and comes from the vast family of Pinots. It is often confused (one suspects mostly deliberately) with Chardonnay. The style of wine they produce can be similar but in general terms it is less demanding than Chardonnay, will ripen more easily and has a higher yield. It is to be found in France, Alsace especially, Germany, in many Italian regions in great quantity and in many other cooler regions.

In Britain it is a fairly new introduction (since 1990) and has grown steadily from 6.2 hectares in 2006 to 29 hectares in 2018, which must be seen as positive. It is mainly used for the production of sparkling base-wine and very few 100 per cent varietal wines exist, although Chapel Down's version (made from grapes grown in Hampshire, Essex and Kent) is one of their best wines and more growers should follow their example. Like Chardonnay, it requires a good site and careful management to ripen it fully and get the acids down. It will find a good home in sparkling wine blends and it deserves to be planted a bit more for still wines. Another important, but minor, variety.

Pinot Gris

- Synonym: Ruländer
- Type: *vinifera*
- Colour: white
- Origin: original variety

Pinot Gris is another variety from the large Pinot family and appears to have almost as many clones as there are winegrowing regions using it. In Alsace, its most respected home (where it was known as Tokay d'Alsace), it is capable of producing exceptionally fine late-harvest dessert wines. In Germany – where it is known as Ruländer for wines with residual sugar and Grauer Burgunder or Pinot Gris for dry wines – it is the fourth most widely planted white vine variety and makes an easy-drinking soft wine. In Italy (as Pinot Grigio) it makes a very neutral, quite crisp wine, ideal with food. It seems to be able to change its style to suit the region. It is, of course, also one of the six varieties permitted to be used in Champagne, although seldom found.

In Britain, where it has been grown since the late 1970s, it is making slow progress, from 6 hectares in 2007 to 28.8 hectares in 2018, and is gaining in popularity as a quality still wine variety. It is not the easiest variety to grow and requires a good site and careful canopy management to make the best of it. Yields are not the highest and need to be kept under control to produce the best wines. Some reports talk of a prolonged flowering, resulting in picking in two or more passes. Assuming that the climate continues to improve Pinot Gris should make steady progress and become a minor, but useful, still wine variety for British growers.

Pinot Noir

- Synonym: Blauer Spätburgunder
- Type: *vinifera*
- Colour: red
- Origin: original variety

Pinot Noir is one of the most ancient of varieties and probably has more clones and variants than any other variety. While its home is often thought of as Burgundy, where undoubtedly many of the finest examples can be found, it seems to thrive in both very warm and very cool climates and good examples can be found in Australia, California, Canada, Chile, Germany, New Zealand, Oregon, South Africa and Spain. It is of course not only used for still red wines, but is also one of the classic sparkling wine grapes, found not only in Champagne, but wherever good sparkling wines are made.

In Britain it was one of the earliest varieties to be grown. Brock trialled it at Oxted, but was not pleased with it and by 1961, when he issued *Report No. 3 – Progress with Vines and Wines*, he stated that Pinot Noir: 'appears to be very much later [than on the continent] in this climate ... and has been discontinued'. His lack of success was probably due to the fact that, at the vineyard's elevation of 125–137 metres above sea level, the site was just too cool. In addition, Brock was not, at least not in the early years, looking to make sparkling wines, although he did make some later on. Jack Ward was likewise somewhat dismissive of the variety and also thought it too late.

Despite the reservations of these pioneers, it seems to have been planted quite widely, if not in any great quantity. Many of the early growers seem to have limited their investigation of continental vineyards to a quick visit to Champagne, returning enthused with the idea that Pinot Noir, and for that matter Chardonnay, were naturals for the British climate. The truth of the matter is that in those early days they were not, and good wines made from them were *very* few in number. Whatever Bernard Theobald at Westbury Vineyard claimed in the 1970s and 1980s, Pinot Noir was *not* the best variety to be growing then. What I wrote in 2001 (I hope) bears repeating:

> *There are a number of factors which might make Pinot noir a more acceptable variety for Britain. There is no doubt that vine breeders have done much to change Pinot over the last 50 years. Clones are available now that ripen earlier, are more consistent, produce better quality wines and are more disease resistant. The upsurge in interest in making bottle-fermented sparkling wines seems set to continue and Pinot noir must be considered as a major variety in this respect. Today's fungicides, especially for the control of botrytis are markedly better than they were only a decade ago and this undoubtedly allows growers to leave their grapes to hang for longer and to ripen more fully.*
>
> *... Most winegrowers sense that weather patterns are changing and we are now experiencing earlier budbursts (although this is coupled with a higher incidence of spring frost damage) and therefore longer growing seasons. This does mean that the more marginal varieties – of which group the Pinots and Chardonnay are members – may fare better in the next decade than the last ... There is no doubt that the public will buy wines bearing names that they recognise and Pinot noir is one that has its devotees.*

The upsurge in plantings since 1984, when 11 hectares were recorded as being planted in British vineyards, to today's 618 hectares, occupying 26.5 per cent of the planted area, is impressive and speaks volumes about the ease with which it can be grown, its relatively good crops and its suitability for being turned into fine sparkling wines. It is also a name which almost every wine-drinker will know.

I am also more convinced now than I used to be about its suitability to make good red wines in Britain. The consistent winning by wines from Pinot Noir of the Bernard Theobald Trophy for the Best Red Wine is significant. However, these trophy-winning wines are very few and far between. Too many British red Pinot Noir wines are just thin, acidic and very poor value for money. The best are generally quite light in colour (although no lighter than many top-class Burgundies) and have simple red-fruit bouquets, perhaps with a touch of oak, adequate tannins and a fresh, fruity crispness about them that says 'attractive' rather than 'serious'. They are not usually very substantial wines and must be put in context with Pinot Noirs from other cooler growing regions: the Loire (Sancerre especially), Burgundy and even Alsace. Against wines from warmer climes they stand no chance. Many British-grown Pinot Noirs would be much better presented as light, fruity rosés with a touch of sweetness and a very light *pétillance*. However, in recent high-sugar years, producers such as Chapel Down and Gusbourne have managed, by selecting their best sites, restricting yields and careful canopy management, to grow some excellent grapes, which have been turned into some very acceptable still reds. This may indicate that we are turning a corner for still red wines from this variety.

Viticulturally, Pinot Noir presents no great problems to the seasoned grower. It buds up quite early, making it susceptible to damage on frost-prone sites, but will shoot from secondary buds. It gets all the usual ailments and requires good management to keep it botrytis free if the fruit is needed for whole-bunch pressing or for fermenting on the skins as a red wine. With a good spray regime and deleafing at the appropriate times, 100 per cent clean fruit is achievable in almost every year. On the cropping front, I have been very impressed by the level of the yields and whilst years such as 2007, 2011 and 2012 might set the averages back, 10 tonnes per hectare (4 tonnes per acre) would appear to be achievable in 'normal' years, with even higher yields in better years, fine for sparkling wine. For still red wine production, the quality of the site and the year will play a major role in fruit quality, but it is probably wiser to aim for nearer half this figure if good wines are to be made.

As with Chardonnay, British vineyards are using a mixture of Pinot Noir clones for sparkling wine and none is especially dominant. Many growers use the CIVC recommended clones 292, 375, 386, 521, 779, 870, 871, 872 and 927. You will also find clones 114, 115 and 459 being used, plus quite a wide range of German clones (and even some northern Italian ones). There is also a French 'loose-bunch' (*grappes lâche*) clone being used by some growers. For still wines, red and rosé, Pinot clones such as 113, 114, 115, 667 and 777 are being used, the last two probably being the best. There are also quite a few German clones being used for still reds, plus the occasional *teinturier* clone (a clone with both red skin and red flesh). Of course, with the 85:15 rule applying to labelling i.e. if the wine is at least 85 per cent of one variety, it can carry the name of that variety, there is ample scope to add a wine made from one of the better colour red varieties in order to beef up the colour of a Pinot Noir varietal.

Pinot Noir Précoce

- Synonym: Blauer Frühburgunder
- Type: *vinifera*
- Colour: red
- Origin: original variety

Blauer Frühburgunder is a relatively old variety, planted in the 1800s in the Ahr wine region, Germany's most northerly winegrowing area. The region is named after a tributary of the Rhine which joins the main river just south of Bonn. By the 1900s the variety had migrated to the town of Ingelheim am Rhein,[29] '*Die Rotweinstadt*' (the red wine town) and it became that town's dominant variety, for which they became very well known. Geisenheim has done some work on it, cleaned it up (the old clones had Leaf Roll and cropped very poorly) and today there are five clones listed that are worth growing (in Germany).

When growers started planting Pinot Noir in earnest in Britain, those searching for the earliest ripening clones were offered Frühburgunder, believing it to be a clone of Pinot Noir. This was all very well until they started labelling wine 'Early Pinot Noir' and Wine Standards realized that this variety was not on the list of permitted vine varieties for Britain and therefore any wine made from it could only be sold as UK Table Wine. After some discussion with the industry, it was agreed that the synonym Pinot Noir Précoce (PNP) would be a permitted name (as it

29 Ingelheim, situated on the southern side of the Rhine, about halfway between Mainz and Bingen, is where Charlemagne built a palace (in about 800). According to legend, he noticed that the snows melted first on the south-facing slopes opposite and could see that the area had a unique microclimate. His son, Ludwig the Pious, started growing grapes there and the slopes eventually became the site for what is today Schloss Johannisberg.

is already called this in other EU member states and was better liked as a name than Blauer Frühburgunder). Growers with this variety were asked to confess their misdeeds and re-register their vineyard parcels that contained this 'clone'. This explains why it has suddenly appeared from nowhere on the variety lists and the area has gone from 8.2 hectares in 2007 to 39.2 hectares in 2018. As a variety for the future, I suspect that it will find favour in some more marginal vineyards but not where true Pinot Noir can be successfully grown.

Regent

- Type: *vinifera* (complex hybrid)
- Colour: red
- Origin: Diana x Chambourcin

Regent (pronounced in German *Ray-ghent* with a hard g as in Ghent, not as in Regent Street) is another of Professor Dr Alleweldt's Geilweilerhof crossings (see Orion and Phoenix). Its parents are Diana, a Silvaner x Müller-Thurgau crossing (and not the native Catawba variety of the same name grown in the US) and Chambourcin, a Joannès Seyve crossing of Seyve Villard 12-417 and Chancellor. Made in 1967, the crossing was released in 1995 in Germany and has become popular with growers. It has very good colour, is more disease resistant than *viniferas* and the wine quality is usually quite good (always a help). In 1996, despite not being 100 per cent *vinifera*, it was authorized for the production of quality wines in Germany, the first modern interspecific-cross to be allowed to do so. According to *Wine Grapes* it is named after *Le Régent*, the 140.5 carat diamond found by a slave in the Golkonda mine in India and eventually placed in the crown of the French King Louis XV when he was crowned in 1722.

In Britain, Regent has only been around since the 1990s. By 2006 there were 12.6 hectares. Today the area has increased to 28.6 hectares, making it the second most widely planted purely red wine producing variety (i.e. ignoring Pinot Noir and Meunier) after Rondo. It requires a good site, good management and deleafing at the right times, but no more so than other red varieties. It is certainly less disease prone than Dornfelder and Rondo, so on that score alone, it could be a better bet for a deep red wine variety, but is susceptible to downy mildew. It usually yields quite well and 7.5–10 tonnes per hectare (3–4 tonnes per acre) are achievable on a good site. For deep red wines, it has a higher quality than wines made from Dornfelder or Rondo, although is probably best used in a blend of all three. It takes oak well, has great colour and soft tannins, and acids are manageable. Its continuing expansion would suggest that it is a valuable variety for those wanting to produce deep-coloured blended red wines.

Reichensteiner

- Type: *vinifera*
- Colour: white
- Origin: Müller-Thurgau x (Madeleine Angevine x Calabreser-Froelich)

Reichensteiner is a Geisenheim cross produced by Professor Henrich Birk in 1939 by crossing Müller-Thurgau with a cross between two other varieties: Madeleine Angevine, the female French table grape used by Scheu (among others) for a number of his crossings, and Calabreser-Froelich, an early white Italian table grape. Together, these have combined to produce an early ripening variety, capable of producing large crops of relatively neutral grapes, high in natural sugars and low(ish) in acidity.

In Germany, Reichensteiner was seen as a substitute to the practice of 'wet-sugaring' (where up to 20 per cent by volume of water could be added to the must during the enrichment process in order to lower the acidity) – a practice that only came to an end in the late 1970s. In Germany, the area has fallen from 257 hectares in 1999 to less than 50 hectares today and it is undoubtedly on its way out there. In warm climates it is capable of producing massive crops – up to 30 tonnes per hectare (12 tonnes per acre) is not uncommon – and it is used as a blending partner for varieties with more acidity. It can be found in New Zealand, Canada, Belgium and the Netherlands, as well as Britain.

Reichensteiner was introduced into Britain by Jack Ward when he extended his Brickyard vineyard in Horam in 1971. Early results showed that it was a consistent cropper, with good yields and high sugars. Although it can be vigorous in its youth, it settles down after a few years and is less vigorous than MT at the same age. It has a good open habit and a leaf-wall that is less crowded and better ventilated than MT, both of which help disease control.

As a varietal wine, it does not have the character of fruitier varieties, but has lower acid levels, more body and extract and higher natural sugars. It is probably best used in a blend. It has been used for sparkling wine (Camel Valley, Carr Taylor, Chapel Down, Davenport, Meopham), as well as for the production of *süssreserve.* Although it has fallen in area, from 113.9 hectares in 1990 to 67.9 hectares in 2018, it still has a valuable part to play in Britain's wine industry on account of its reliable cropping record. Vines are difficult to obtain as no one is grafting them except to order.

Rondo

- Synonym: Gm 6494/5
- Type: *vinifera* (complex hybrid)
- Colour: red
- Origin: Zarya Severa x St Laurent

Of all the varieties with complicated histories attached, Rondo must have one of the most complex. The original *Vitis amurensis* vines from which Rondo is derived were wild vines from Manchuria, in the north of China, where the River Amur marks the border between China and Russia. Here, on account of the early onset and severity of the winters, wild vines need to be able to withstand deep winter temperatures and colour up and ripen early. In 1910, a Russian vine breeder, Ivan Vladimirovich Michurin (1855–1935) selected an open-pollinated seedling of Précoce de Malingre, which was probably pollinated by a *Vitis amurensis* in Michurin's vine collection, which he called Seyanets Malengra. Michurin was a famous plant breeder whose work was recognized by Lenin and whose private research station at Tambov, about 435 kilometres south-east of Moscow, became the Michurin Central Genetic Laboratory in 1934. Seyanets Malengra is a female vine used in Russia and Ukraine as a table grape variety. In 1936, two Russian plant breeders, Yakov Potapenko and E. Zakharova, working at the All-Russia Research Institute of Viticulture and Winemaking (later called the Potapenko All-Russia Research Institute of Viticulture and Winemaking), situated at Novocherkassk in Rostov Province, crossed Seyanets Malengra with another *amurensis* vine to produce a variety called Zarya Severa. This crossing then found its way to Lednice in Moravia, Czechoslavakia where Professor Dr Vilém Kraus crossed it, in 1964, with St Laurent, an old Austrian wine variety. This crossing then travelled to Geisenheim where Professor Helmut Becker improved it and gave it a breeding number Gm 6494/5. It was then trialled at Geisenheim and proved capable of producing good crops of early ripening, deeply coloured grapes.

In 1983 Professor Becker gave me 50 vines to plant at Tenterden (today's Chapel Down) as well as giving 50 to both Ken Barlow at Adgestone and Karl-Heinz Johner at Lamberhurst, to see what the results would be. From the first harvests it showed itself well adapted to British conditions and plantings have been increasing since then. From 2 hectares in 1990, it has continued to grow in popularity, is the seventh most widely planted variety and stands at 53.6 hectares in 2018 with 2.3 per cent of the planted area. Ignoring Pinot Noir and Meunier (from which little truly red wine is made) Rondo is the most widely planted red variety in Britain, with almost double the area of the next most widely planted red variety, Regent. In Germany there is very little grown although in other cool climates such as Belgium, Denmark, the Netherlands and Sweden it is one of the most important varieties. For the first decade of its life in Britain it was called Gm 6494/5, but eventually it was given a name – Rondo – and growers persuaded DEFRA to classify it as a *vinifera* (as the Germans had done five years earlier).

Initially, Rondo had all the makings of a good variety for Britain: early to ripen, with a good crop of deep red grapes with low(ish) acidity and wine quality that was certainly better than anything else seen in the mid-1980s – Léon Millot, Maréchal Foch and Triomphe d'Alsace (as it was then called) – being the alternatives. Chapel Down made two versions: a straightforward wine and a Reserve, both from grapes from Anthony Pilcher's Chapel Farm vineyard on the Isle of Wight. The Reserve, with enough oak and some time, could be very good, although the flavour was always very slightly unusual. I always likened it to a Syrah–Tempranillo blend – they used American oak which helped – and tried to persuade myself for years that it had a future. However, reluctantly, and in the face of the onslaught from Pinot Noir and Regent, I concede that the wine quality is not high enough for it to succeed in the long term.

It is a very vigorous variety, with big leaves (almost like the leaves of kiwi fruit) and canes that can stretch for several metres if allowed to run. Consequently, canopies tend to be crowded and shaded and although an interspecific cross, it is still fairly susceptible to botrytis. The wine colour is excellent, deeper than Dornfelder and Regent, and the quality is passable, but not of the first order and certainly not what the consumer expects of a wine of that appearance. Although the area planted in Britain has expanded, most of this additional planting is in vineyards in the more challenging parts of Britain and it is unlikely that any mainstream vineyards view it as a serious variety for the future.

Schönburger

- Type: *vinifera*
- Colour: white
- Origin: Pinot Noir x IP1

Schönburger is a crossing made at Geisenheim by Professor Dr Heinrich Birk in 1939 and first registered for use in 1980. Like many of the crosses from this era, it combines a classic winemaking variety, Pinot Noir, with an early ripening table grape variety, in this case a crossing from an Italian, which I. Pirovano called IP1, which is Chasselas Rosa x Muscat Hamburg. The hope was that a unique German table grape could be produced. There is very little Schönburger planted in Germany and countries such as Canada, New Zealand and Britain have more. Some can even be found in Australia and South Africa.

It has been grown in Britain since the late 1970s, and on account of its high-quality, award-winning grapes, low acidity and regular crops, it has become quite widely planted. Colin Gillespie at Wootton Vineyard made it his speciality and won the Gore-Browne Trophy with it in 1982 and Lamberhurst won the same trophy with Schönburger wines in 1982 and 1990. By 1990 there were 75.3 hectares, making it then the fifth most planted variety. It is an undemanding variety, more disease resistant than MT and not so on–off in its cropping habits. Yields are never large, but what is picked is almost always of excellent quality, with high sugars and low acids. As they ripen, the grapes change colour from a light lime-green to, at first, light pink and then, when fully ripe, an almost tawny brown colour. This gives a very good visual indication to the pickers as to which bunches are ripe and allows for some selective picking, which can only aid wine quality. The wines are almost always light and very fruity, with some good Muscat tones (some resemble a less powerful version of Gewürztraminer) that are best balanced with a slight amount of residual sugar. Wines age well and have been known to keep for up to seven years. Schönburger is one of the few varieties grown for wine that can be eaten with pleasure and although the berries are small, they are packed with flavour. Despite all these attributes, the area has fallen to 21.6 hectares in 2018 and it is likely that this decline will continue. Why? The name is tricky – an umlaut and -burger on the end never helped any vine variety become popular – and in style it's just a bit too weak and wishy-washy.

Seyval Blanc

- Synonym: Seyve Villard 5276
- Type: hybrid
- Colour: white
- Origin: Seibel 5656 x Seibel 4986

Seyval Blanc, a crossing made in 1921 by Bertille Seyve (the younger) at the nursery of his father-in-law, Victor Villard, in St Vallier on the Rhône, was originally known as Seyve Villard 5276. In some references, the crossing is given as Seibel 4996 x Seibel 4986, but Pierre Galet (probably the most famous ampelographer in the world) assured me that Bertille Seyve's son stated in the *Viticulture Nouvelle* of 1961 that the crossing was Seibel 5656 x Seibel 4986. Seibel 4986 is known as *Rayon d'Or*. In 1958 there were 1,309 hectares in France, but plantings have declined since then and are now down to below 50 hectares. It can also be found in many different parts of North America, most notably in New York State and Ontario, and is also grown in Switzerland.

It was first grown in Britain by Edward Hyams who, in 1947, obtained vines directly from the Seyve Villard nurseries (as they had become known by then) and planted them in his small vineyard at Molash near Canterbury, Kent. Brock also imported the variety from the Swiss Federal Vine Testing Station at Caudoz-sur-Pully a year later in 1948. These two pioneers tested it and soon found that it was a very suitable variety for the British climate and together with MT, it became the standard variety for almost all the early vineyards. When Sir Guy Salisbury-Jones planted his vineyard at Hambledon in 1952 he chose Seyval Blanc on the advice of a helpful Burgundian grower whom he sat next to at a Confrérie des Chevaliers du Tastevin dinner.

Seyval Blanc has many attributes. It sets good crops even in cool years, is not vigorous and has a good open habit with small leaves and only a few side-shoots. It is unusual in that the flowers appear and are very prominent before many of the leaves really develop. It is very resistant to disease, although botrytis has become more of an issue as sugars have increased since 2000, and it yields well – in some years very well. Although the grapes are never very high in natural sugar (I remember plenty of years in the 1970s and 1980s when only 5–6 per cent natural alcohol was reached), wine quality can be good *if* the winery knows what it is doing. On the downside, apart from the low natural sugars, the wine can be very neutral, high in acidity and if not pressed with care, can get a rather grassy herbaceous tone. However, it takes to oak-ageing well, is a good foil for lees-ageing and battonage and is great for sparkling wine. Wines made from Seyval have won their share of medals and awards: I won the Gore-Browne Trophy twice (in 1981 and 1991) with the variety and Colin Gillespie at Wootton won it in 1986 with a Seyval Blanc – all still wines of course. It can also be found in some very good sparkling wines (Bluebell, Breaky Bottom, Camel Valley, Denbies, Sixteen Ridges and Stanlake Park for instance). Many growers like it and although the area fell from a high of 122.7 hectares in 1990 to 88.9 hectares in 2000, it has now staged a very modest comeback to 101.3 hectares in 2018 and is Britain's fifth most widely planted variety.

Having seen a fair few Seyval vineyards, both in Britain and overseas, I am convinced that there is quite a bit of clonal variation and some of Britain's vineyards are planted with inferior clones. This might account for the grassy, herbaceous notes that are sometimes seen, although that could just be harsh pressing. In 2013, I travelled to Switzerland to see an excellent mother-block of Seyval and have been selling vines using scion wood from this block since then. As the increased plantings show, there are growers who respect it for its qualities and it is likely to remain a 'top ten' variety for decades to come.

Siegerrebe

- Type: *vinifera*
- Colour: white
- Origin: freely pollinated seedling of Madeleine Angevine

Siegerrebe is another Georg Scheu crossing from Alzey, made in 1929 and released to growers in 1958. In the *Taschenbuch der Rebsorten* (2010 edition) the breeding details are given as follows. It was originally said to be Madeleine Angevine x Gewürztraminer, but it was later revealed by Scheu's son, Heinz, to be a freely pollinated seedling of Madeleine Angevine (which is the same as Britain's Madeleine x Angevine 7672). However, in *Wine Grapes* it is given as Madeleine Angevine x Savagnin Rose. Savagnin Rose (without an é) is a 'non-aromatic version of Gewürztraminer', which, in Germany, is often called Roter Traminer (Red Traminer). In Germany, where a small area is grown, the variety reaches very high natural sugar levels and is used for making sweet dessert wines, although the acid levels are often very low. The grapes have a strong Muscat character and when ripe, can be very concentrated and almost overpowering. It is more often used for blending with other, less distinctive, varieties.

It has been in Britain since 1957, when Brock was sent cuttings from Alzey. By 1960 he was able to report that it was 'exceptionally early and the grapes have a strong bouquet,' and he highly recommended it as suitable for both the table and winemaking. Despite its attributes of early ripening, low acidity and strongly flavoured grapes, it has really failed to be planted in anything like serious amounts and although one or two vineyards do make interesting varietal wines from it, it mainly gets lost in blends. It is possible that because it ripens very early and falls so far outside what most growers consider their normal harvest time it is rather disruptive. Wasps are a particular problem and good wasp nest control needs to be practised if real damage is to be avoided. Birds, likewise, tend to be a nuisance. Three Choirs consistently make an interesting semi-sweet wine with the variety (it's usually one of their better wines) and their 2006 Estate Reserve Siegerrebe won the Gore-Browne Trophy in 2008, their 2007 Three Choirs Siegerrebe won a gold medal in 2009 and their 2010, 2011 and 2012 all won silver medals. Siegerrebe can add a nice piquancy to an otherwise dull blend and is probably worth considering as a minor variety. The area planted in Britain has risen slowly from 9.3 hectares in 1990 to 19.4 hectares in 2018 which would suggest there is some interest in the variety and plantings are likely to continue to increase, if slowly.

Solaris

- Type: *vinifera* (complex hybrid)
- Colour: white
- Origin: Merzling x Gm 6493

Solaris is a Freiburg interspecific-cross, once known as Fr. 240-75, bred by Dr Norbert Becker in 1975 and released in 2001. In 2012 there were 101 hectares planted in Germany, mainly in the south, and it is also found in Belgium, the Netherlands and Switzerland, and is by far the most widely planted white variety in Denmark. Its parents are Merzling and Gm 6493. Merzling is a crossing between our old friend Seyval Blanc and a (Riesling x Pinot Gris) crossing. Gm 6493 is a Geisenheim

Vitis amurensis influenced crossing and is Zarya Severa x Muscat Ottonel, Zarya Severa being one of the parents of Rondo. Complicated indeed. The *Taschenbuch der Rebsorten* says that it is very vigorous, with very large leaves, and that it ripens early with very high sugars, usually over 100ºOe (13.8 per cent potential alcohol) and often nearer 130ºOe (18.4 per cent potential alcohol). It also states that the acidity is lower than that of Ruländer (Pinot Gris) – which would mean that its acidity is towards the bottom of the acid spectrum, i.e. 5–6 g/l as tartaric acid. Being a hybrid, it has a good resistance against the major diseases, especially botrytis, to which high-sugared varieties are usually prone, and its loose bunches help in this respect. It sounds very similar in many ways to Reichensteiner, but with better disease resistance.

In Britain it is planted on 47.3 hectares, up from 4.7 hectares in 2009, which is a greater rate of expansion than any other variety, Chardonnay and Pinot Noir included, and has found favour in vineyards in the more challenged, northerly counties. To date, little single-variety wine has been made from Solaris and the jury is still out regarding its long-term potential. However, as vineyards spread ever further north in Britain – a vineyard in Scotland can surely be only just around the corner – perhaps Solaris will fill a small, but useful, niche. Early reports suggest it is a vigorous variety, with loose bunches and good disease resistance. A variety to watch.

ROOTSTOCKS FOR BRITAIN

With the exception of a few growers who obtained their vines from France, the bulk of vines planted in Britain up until the early 1990s were German varieties, of German origin and consequently, on German rootstock: 125AA, 5BB, 5C and SO4 being the four standard German rootstocks with Teleki 8B and Börner bringing up the rear. All of these are classified as 'high' to 'medium-high' in terms of vigour and coupled with already vigorous varieties such as Bacchus, Huxelrebe, Kerner, Müller-Thurgau, Ortega, Reichensteiner and Schönburger, they tended to produce, in Britain's cool climate, with its fresh, loam-rich, well-watered soils, some exceptionally large, leaf-endowed canopies which did little to help the problems associated with shading and over-vigorous canopies. Of the 'old' varieties, only Seyval Blanc, being a naturally low-vigour variety, avoided the curse of over-vigorous canopies, one of the reasons why, of the varieties popular in the early days, it has maintained its position in the list of British vine varieties.

The arrival in Britain of the Champagne varieties has somewhat altered the rootstock situation and made a significant impact upon the vigour of the canopies. In France, the origin of the majority (but by no means all) of the Chardonnay, Pinot Noir and Meunier vines now being grown in Britain, the most popular rootstocks for these varieties are 41B, SO4 and Fercal in high active calcium carbonate ($CaCO_3$) soils (with 161-49 as another option) and 101-14, 3309C and 420A in soils with 20 per cent or less active $CaCO_3$. With the exception of SO4 and Fercal (both classified as having 'medium' vigour') all of the others are classified as 'low' or 'low medium' in terms of vigour. On paper, this may seem a very marginal difference, but experience shows that these marginal differences in the vineyard make an appreciable difference to vigour of shoot-growth and therefore to the density of the canopy.

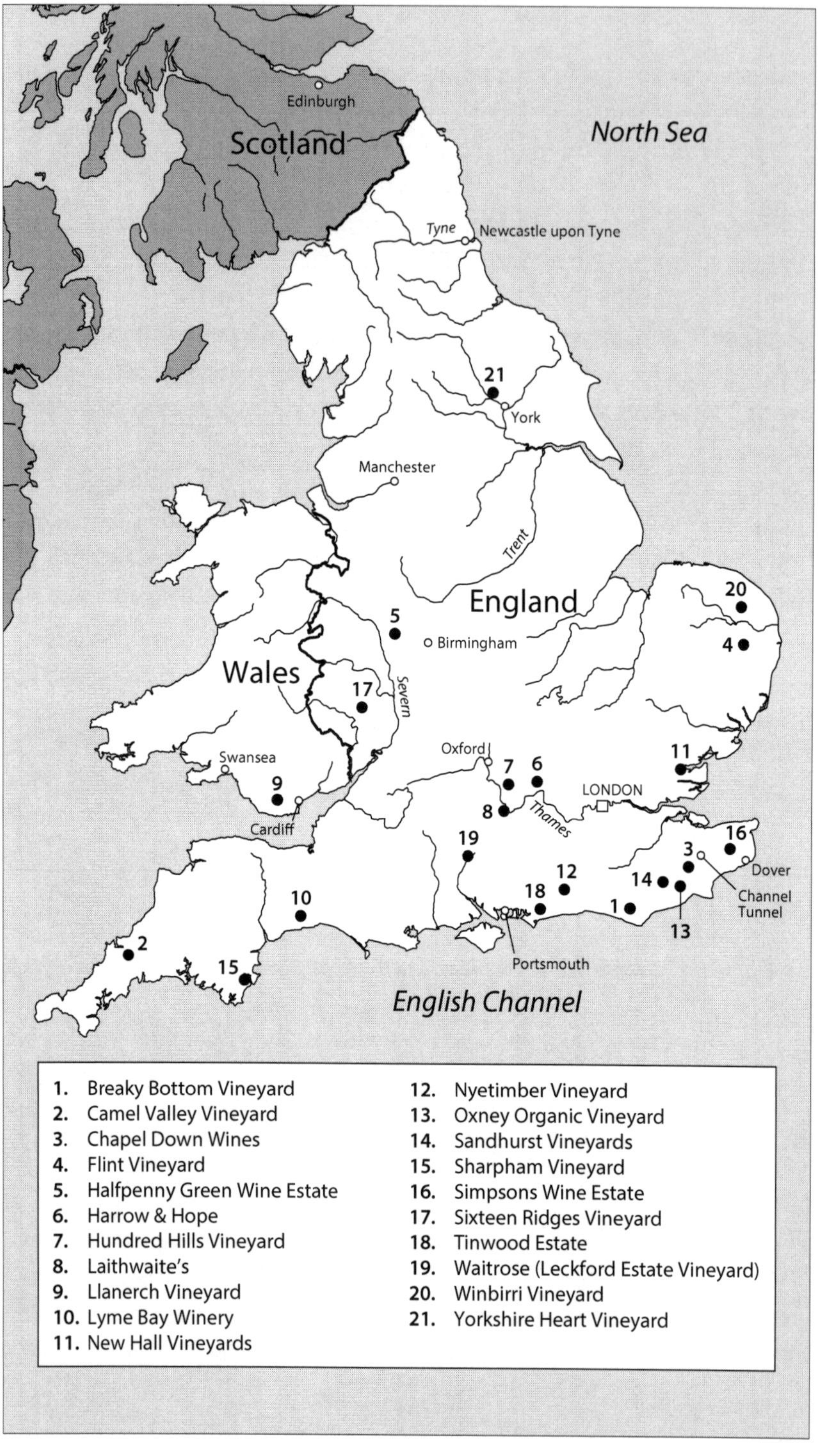

Locations of the producers

6

PRODUCER PROFILES

INTRODUCTION

The producers who feature in the twenty-one profiles in this chapter have been chosen for several reasons, the principal one being that taken together they cover the complete spectrum of those owning vineyards in Britain today. The aim of these profiles is to get behind the usual copy found on websites, back labels and in publicity material and inform the reader about what it's really like to own a vineyard in Britain today. There are producers who have very successful farm-gate outlets from which they sell 60 per cent (or more) of their output and there are producers who sell almost all their wines through wholesalers and retailers and in on-trade outlets. There are producers that buy some (or even most) of the grapes they use to make their wines and there is one grower who only grows grapes, selling them all to producers around the country. Taken together, these profiles give what I believe is a unique insight into the business of growing vines and making wine in Britain today and in selling that wine at home and abroad.

Geographically the producers come from the four corners of England – from Cornwall to Norfolk and from Yorkshire to Kent – plus Wales' oldest vineyard. I have included the two largest producers, Chapel Down and Nyetimber, who between them either own or take grapes from around 550 hectares (1,359 acres) of vineyards and who are at opposite ends of the business model in terms of financing, Chapel Down being one of only two publicly quoted companies involved in vineyards in Britain (Gusbourne being the other one) and Nyetimber very much privately funded with well over £100 million invested to date. There are also some smaller ones, Breaky Bottom and Sharpham with 2.43 hectares (6 acres) and 3.4 hectares (8.4 acres) respectively, both of whom have been around for a good few years, forty-five and thirty-seven respectively. The profiles include one of the oldest vineyards in the country too. New Hall in Essex, originally planted in 1969, was the first to grow Bacchus commercially and the first to make a sparkling wine using Champagne varieties, and is today run by the third generation of the family. I have included two of the newest producers, Hundred Hills (planted in 2014) and Flint Vineyard (planted in 2016); both have yet to market wine from their own grapes but have very different approaches to their businesses. One of the producers, Simpsons Wine Estate, comes into the English Sparkling Wine business having successfully taken over and brought into profit a 40-hectare producer in the Languedoc over the last sixteen years, selling the 400,000 bottles of wine it produces each year outside of France. They bring to Britain their skills as wine producers, marketers, brand-builders and wine exporters – skills which some say producers in Britain could do with developing.

All of the vineyards in these profiles are conventionally farmed, with the exception of Oxney Organic, which is Britain's largest organic vineyard and winery. I had arranged to include a Welsh biodynamic producer too but unfortunately he changed his mind and was ultimately unwilling to discuss his business with me.

I have included one grower-only operation, Sandhurst Vineyards, where they have been growing grapes as a crop to sell to others since 1986. They now farm 29.95 hectares (74 acres) of vines (from whose mature 25.9 hectares in 2018 they picked 400 tonnes of grapes) and also look after another 14.97 hectares (37 acres) of vines for Chapel Down. Having been picking grapes over thirty vintages and with the fourth generation on the farm now taking over, they say with some confidence: 'we are doing it off the bank, there's no private wealth going in year after year. It has to pay.' Finally, I have included two commercial concerns who make their living selling wines of all sorts, but who each have a serious interest in a vineyard or vineyards in Britain. The first is Laithwaite's, one of Britain's largest and most successful wine sellers, operating on-line, via mail order and through bricks and mortar retail, who through various members of the family have an interest in three separate vineyards: Harrow & Hope (which has a separate producer profile), the

Mezel Hill vineyard planted in Windsor Great Park, and Wyfold Vineyard, in total covering almost 12 hectares (29.4 acres). The second of these commercial concerns is Waitrose, the supermarket owned by the John Lewis Partnership, which operates the 6.75-hectare (16.68-acre) Leckford Vineyard on the partnership's 1,620-hectare (4,000-acre) Leckford Estate in Hampshire. According to industry data, Waitrose through its retail outlets and on-line sales is responsible for selling 60–70 per cent of all English and Welsh wine sold by British multiple retailers and multiple wine merchants. This gives it a unique insight into the marketing of wines from Britain, who buys them, what sells and what prices they achieve. Of course the twenty-one producers featured in this chapter are but a snapshot of the industry and there are many other excellent producers with interesting stories I could have chosen in their place. Sadly, however, I could not include every producer of note.

Growing grapes and making wine, and deriving an income from either or both, is an economic activity and most (but oddly not all) people who find land, plant vineyards and produce grapes or wine hope, one day, to make money out of their enterprise. In writing these producer profiles I have attempted to get behind the businesses, looking at where the money for the enterprise has come from, where it has gone and whether they are getting (or hope to get) a return on their investment. Some of the producers are old friends, some clients, and some I met for the first time when interviewing them for this book. All of those featured have been generous with their time and information.

Breaky Bottom Vineyard

Rodmell, Lewes, East Sussex, BN7 3EX
www.breakybottom.co.uk
2.43 hectares (6 acres)

Boutique vineyard, planted in 1974, in a magical setting tucked into a downland 'bottom'. Still owned and operated by the founder and making excellent sparkling wines from both Seyval Blanc and Champagne varieties.

'Turn off the main road, through the farm yard and follow the track. It's a mile or so, but don't give up – we are there!' Thus were my instructions on making my first visit, in 1976, to Breaky Bottom: 'bottom' because it's a deep downland valley and 'breaky' because it's full of chalk and flints and a hard place to survive. In many ways Breaky Bottom is the archetypal English vineyard of the pioneer years: the name is slightly quirky, the site is very picturesque, it is situated down the end of a long, rough, very English car-busting track, and it appears small in a compact, cosy sort of way. Oh – and I almost forgot – it manages to produce sparkling wines of genuine interest and quality. However, as ever, there is more behind the image than meets the eye.

Peter Hall first discovered the valley in late 1960s when, as an agricultural student at Newcastle University, he got a relief-shepherd's job on the farm which then encompassed what is today Breaky Bottom. He was told that he could use the half-derelict cottage at the bottom of the furthest valley on the estate. Whilst working in the valley he was soon introduced to the farmer's daughter, who after a suitable interval became his wife and then mother of his four children. Peter's mother came from Normandy and her father owned a well-known restaurant in Greek Street, Soho, called Au Petit Savoyard. Wine, therefore, was nothing new to Hall and in April 1974, having found a great site and secured a tenancy from his father-in-law, he set about planting a vineyard. In the early years, in order to get some cash flowing, he established a small sow unit, fattening weaners (piglets) for the market. Eventually, as the vines started bearing and wines were made and ready for sale, the pigs and their unlovely sheds (and the flies that I remember so well) departed and 'BB' became a fully-fledged member of the then tiny English wine industry.

As with most British vineyard owners of the early '70s, the vine varieties planted were the two staples, Müller-Thurgau (MT) and Seyval Blanc, to which Hall added a third, Reichensteiner, then an up-and-coming variety, which ripened earlier than MT and promised sweeter grapes and higher yields. He also experimented with some Würzer, which didn't fare well, staying hard and green until the end.

The site consists of one south-facing side of an east–west running valley and the valley floor. The westerly facing slopes are too steep and too shaded. The land rises from the vineyards to about 120 metres above sea level, before descending to the sea between Newhaven and Brighton. Although the farm is just 4 kilometres (2.5 miles) from the coast, it is protected from the worst of the sea breezes by this barrier of rising land. Neighbouring Rathfinny Estate has no such barrier of rising ground and has suffered greatly from wind, despite huge windbreak fences and natural windbreaks. This isn't to say that Breaky Bottom hasn't had its share of problems with cool temperatures, and in the still wine era very poor crops (and occasionally no crops at all) were experienced. Since the general rise in temperatures and the planting of Champagne varieties, yields have improved, although quite large variations in yields still happen across vintages (as they do in most British vineyards). Yields at Breaky Bottom have been between 0 bottles and 20,000 a year – with the average at around 10,000 bottles. In the days of still wines, this was a problem, with some vintages running out before the next one was bottled. Today, with the stocks of maturing sparkling wines buffering the process from picking to sale, things are steadier, although larger stocks – Breaky Bottom are still selling 2009 wines – have a huge impact on cash flow. In 2018 they picked just over 18 tonnes, not their largest ever, but excellent quality and enough to keep the cellars topped up. Chardonnay cropped at a very respectable 10.63 tonnes per hectare (4.3 tonnes per acre).

Hall's first vintage was in the endlessly warm year of 1976 but sadly, despite producing grapes that year which the winemaker said were the best he'd seen, the wine was ruined by the contract winery into whose hands he had delivered his crop. Post-fermentation sulphur dioxide had been added and a decimal point shifted in the calculations, resulting in ten times too much being added. Efforts were made to remove the offending chemical but it was too late and the damage had been done. After considerable negotiations, Hall was paid compensation based upon the full retail value. Following this first vintage debacle, Hall has always made his own wines. The winery is housed in a lovely old Sussex flint barn (built in 1827) that sits square in the middle of his vines, waiting for the harvest. Today, there are stainless steel tanks, a 1.5-tonne Vaslin press, a seven-head filler and all the other paraphernalia required in a small winery. In recent years, improvements have been made to the storage facilities and there is now a temperature-controlled wine store to hold maturing stocks of sparkling wine. Riddling, disgorging and dosage is done off-site by another winery.

The series of calamities that have struck Breaky Bottom over the years seem to have induced in Hall a Job-like patience, and he doggedly refuses to give in or give up: herbicide spray-drift (from his father-in-law) ruined one harvest; damage from supposedly beneficial chemical sprays ruined another; an underground fungus attacked the roots of some young vines, destroying them; infestations of grape-eating badgers and pheasants took their share of the crop; extensive flooding and soil deposits from further up the valley brought damage and destruction on an unimaginable scale (at one stage Peter and family had to move into a mobile home for two years); and small, conical snails managed to eat their way through hundreds of young vines. However, all of these have been endured, insurance claims have been made and won, grapes have been harvested and wines made. In recent years some vines have succumbed to what are known as 'trunk diseases' and Hall is fighting an ongoing battle with these. Many of the replacement vines (all on rootstocks) that have been planted in recent years have failed to perform consistently well and Hall is experimenting with own-rooted cuttings, which appear to be doing better.

Hall's approach to winemaking has changed little over the more than forty years that he has been making wine. In essence, it is to let the grapes speak for themselves. In the first two decades, when only still wines were made, the vineyard would be netted against birds and the grapes allowed to ripen at their own pace. The grapes were harvested by a loyal band of friends (as they still are today), carefully pressed, allowed to ferment with the minimum of physical disturbance and left on the lees to gain some extra character. After that they were bottled in as calm a way as possible. Both deacidification and the use of *süssreserve* were avoided. Occasionally wines were oaked with chips, which added another layer of complexity. This style of winemaking brought individual results and the wines, austere in their youth, gradually developed as they matured and often turned from ugly ducklings into quite nice swans. His best (still) wines had an austere, Loire-like quality, with plenty of body and character. Many Breaky Bottom wines aged exceptionally well and could even be better after ten years in bottle – they were often compared to the wines from Savennières. Those made from Seyval Blanc had a *goût de terroir* not found in other wines from this variety and we often joked that it was due to the volumes of Old Holborn that were consumed in their making. In 1995, the first bottle-fermented sparkling wine was made and since then sparkling wines have become a larger and larger part of the output, so that today only sparkling wines are made. Every vintage and every cuvée is labelled after someone important in the lives of the Hall family: Cuvée Maman Mercier; Gerard Hoffnung (a family friend); Koizumi Yakumo (Hall's great uncle); Reynolds Stone (the famous engraver who did the lettering and picture for the first label); Sir Harry Kroto (Nobel Prize-winner, Lewes resident and family friend); Cornelis Hendriksen (another dear friend).

Over the years, Breaky Bottom has built up a loyal clientele and today around 40 per cent is sold direct to the consumer with the balance going to local outlets – independent wine shops, pubs, hotels and restaurants – to Waitrose, their biggest single customer, and since mid-2018 to City wine merchants Corney & Barrow. Hall used to sell a larger percentage directly to the consumer, around 60 per cent, but this has tailed off in recent years as the competition from other vineyards, of which there are a considerable number in this part of Sussex, has increased. The access to the farm, as has already been mentioned, is not ideal for even modestly slung private cars (let alone low-slung ones) and most taxi, private hire and coach drivers wouldn't entertain going down the lane. With better access and better visitor facilities, more could be made of cellar-door sales, but there have been substantial problems with the freeholder of the track and a great deal has already been spent on legal fees.

In the more than forty years since his first vintage, Hall has entered competitions and notched up an impressive list of medals, trophies and awards. Although he is not one to set great store by winning these, they are a very real recognition that his wines have commercial appeal, and his sparkling wines are regularly ordered by Government Hospitality for serving at official functions. In the last decade, as all of the older Müller-Thurgau and Reichensteiner vines have been grubbed-up and replaced with Chardonnay, Pinot Noir and Meunier, the style of the wines has changed and (dare I say it) improved. Hall is still loyal to the old stalwart Seyval Blanc and whether alone or in a blend with Champagne varieties, it finds a home here.

Over the years, with much hard work and help from friends and family, the Halls have managed to keep going and one has to admire their tenacity. In 1994, Peter and his (second) wife Christina managed to buy the farm – he was previously a tenant – and thus make the future much more certain. Although Peter has cut back on the Old Holborn and his intake of hard spirits seems to have lessened somewhat, he shows no signs of giving up the wine business yet and whenever I am down there, there is always talk of what should be done in the future. There are almost no other British vineyards of over forty years of age still run by their original owners (I am racking my brain to think of another), and it is a great testament to Peter's (and Chris') stamina that Breaky Bottom is one of them. I hope to be able to share a glass or two with them for many years to come.

Camel Valley Vineyard

Little Denby Farm, Nanstallon, Bodmin, Cornwall, PL30 5LG.
www.camelvalley.com
6.3 hectares (15.56 acres)

Family-owned, family-run vineyard and one of Britain's top wine producers, making excellent still and sparkling, white and rosé wines, from several different varieties. Well worth a visit.

I guess when you have just had a mid-air collision at 600–700 mph, activated the ejector seat and are hanging there from a parachute with a spine broken in two places, the thought of relaxing on the terrace of your own vineyard and winery, with a glass of award-winning sparkling wine in your hand, is probably the last thing on your mind. Thus it was that Bob Lindo ended his career in the Royal Air Force, leaving in 1987. After spending two years recovering, he then, aged 38, felt able to embark on the second phase of his life. Some years earlier, in 1982, he and his wife Annie had bought a small 33-hectare (81.5-acre) farm in the valley of the river Camel, about halfway between Bodmin and Padstow, for £100,000 (reduced from £120,000 because nobody was interested in it). Bob had intended to do a bit of livestock farming whilst finishing his time in the RAF, but the accident had put paid to that plan.

Farms in this part of the world are small and generally unprofitable, not suited to either large-scale arable or multiple-cow dairy production, and if you want to try and earn a living from the land, you need to specialize. Bob and Annie knew their farm was warm – they had witnessed the grass drying out in summer and had needed to feed their cattle and sheep with precious winter forage. They remembered from a camping holiday that they had taken (on a motorbike) to Burgundy that they had seen vines flourishing there despite the same dried-out conditions. They decided to investigate vines. The farm and surrounding area had several things going for them. It was in a good tourist region (even then and this was before this area became the huge tourist magnet it is today), the fields faced mainly south and vines didn't need a lot of land. Vines it had to be. In 1989 the Lindos planted 8,000 vines – Seyval Blanc, Reichensteiner and Triomphe – and got ready for their first crop. Bob spent a vintage in Germany, gleaned what he could from winemaking books and a short course put on by Gillian Pearkes, an early English wine pioneer, and made sure that he understood the machinery he was using. Since those very early days, their vineyards and wines have never been out of the news. Whether it's awards for their wines, awards for their business, orders for their wines, the first vineyard to have its own personalized *appellation controlée* or the first winery in Britain to get the Royal Warrant – Camel Valley is there.

Today, Camel Valley is the largest Cornish vineyard and wine producer by far and in just under thirty years has established itself amongst the best in Britain. The haul of trophies, awards and medals, for both their wines and their tourism and business achievements, is impressive, but they are only the just rewards of hard work, innovation and attention to detail. The vineyards have grown from the original 2 hectares (5 acres) to 6.3 hectares (15.56 acres), with plantings of Pinot Noir, Pinot Noir Précoce, Dornfelder and Bacchus but the removal of Triomphe. In 2010 they planted Chardonnay and swapped the Pinot Noir Précoce for more Pinot Noir. As their production expanded and as their sales grew, they soon realized that they could sell more than they could grow themselves and started to look for growers in other parts of Britain to supply them with grapes, parts perhaps where yields were a bit bigger and a bit more certain than can always be achieved in what can be a rain-swept county. Today, of the average 150,000 bottles of wine, both still and sparkling, that they produce a year, around one-third comes from their own vineyards, and the rest from two vineyards that they rent, one in Essex and the other in East Sussex. Having this diversity of supply is a form of insurance against poor harvests, which can strike any vineyard at any time, but hopefully not every vineyard in the same year. Bob says that one day 'he is sure that all 33 hectares will be planted with vines' as the business expands over the generations.

The winery, much bigger than it was in 1992, when the first commercial vintage was produced (their 1991 harvest only produced 200 litres), has recently been enlarged yet further and can now produce 250,000 bottles a year, with a new £250,000 temperature-controlled wine store for 1 million bottles and an additional four-station *gyropalette* enabling them to riddle 4,000 bottles at once. They bought four new 10,000 litre tanks to cope with the 2018 harvest, which amounted to over 300 tonnes. Both still and sparkling wines are made, with the first 400–450 litres of juice per tonne of grapes reserved for sparkling (a significantly smaller amount than many other sparkling producers). Bob says, 'if you make just fizz, the temptation is to put too many pressings in the fizz.'

They use the rest of the juice for still wines, Pinot Noir red and rosé, which 'usually win gold medals'. Their output is around one quarter still wine and three-quarters sparkling, with farm-gate and direct sales accounting for 40 per cent of the turnover. 'Our bottle sales of still wine haven't changed in 15 years,' says winemaker (Bob's son) Sam Lindo, 'what's changed is the sparkling.' Which underlines the importance of sparkling wine to both their business and the rest of Britain's wine producers. All of their sparkling wines are vintage wines as the Lindos like the variation of style (but not quality) that each vintage gives. They also do not want to slavishly copy the Champenoise model.

In addition to new buildings, they have also built a new service road to keep delivery and collection vehicles away from the areas to which tourists have access. The roofs of the new storage buildings are lined with PV cells (solar panels), supplying Camel Valley with all the power it needs, with the excess sold to the National Grid. Tourists are very much part of the business mix at Camel Valley, with around 35,000 a year, many taking the 'grand tour and tasting' which takes place every Wednesday evening between April and October, with an extra tour on Thursday evenings during August. This is usually hosted by Bob or Sam, probably one of the reasons why TripAdvisor gives them a 94 per cent 'Excellent–Very Good' rating. Annie is also very much part of the business with her own vineyard – the original Seyval Blanc plantings – which she, and only she, gets to prune, and from which, in 2014, Sam made a special Annie's Anniversary Brut to celebrate the vineyard's twentieth vintage.

In 2012, the Lindos had the idea to apply for PDO status on Darnibole vineyard for the production of still wine from Bacchus. Quality standards were set – no chaptalization, acidification or deacidification and all grapes to be hand-picked – and an application sent to DEFRA, from where it was forwarded on to the EU. Five years later, with the area having been extended from an initial 2.83 hectares (7 acres) to 11.33 hectares (28 acres), PDO status was granted – the first single-estate *appellation* granted in Great Britain. Apart from the Darnibole Bacchus and Annie's Anniversary, Camel Valley makes three other estate-grown wines: Darnibole Sparkling Brut, Cuvée Raymond Blanc Sparkling and Pinot Noir White Sparkling.

The list of awards, medals and trophies that Camel Valley wines have won since their first wine, the 1992 Seyval Blanc, won an EWOTYC bronze medal, is far too long and repetitive to list here, but it includes almost every top award given to wines made from grapes grown in Britain. Sam Lindo was Winemaker of the Year in 2007, 2010 and 2011. Their wines have been served to royalty, both domestic and foreign, to presidents and premiers, and at prestigious events including those held at Buckingham Palace and 10 Downing Street. In 2018 they became the first wine producer in Britain to be welcomed into the Royal Warrant Holders Association, for supplying wine for five years to HRH The Prince of Wales. In 2017 they won the *Best Managed Small Business* Trophy at the Cornwall Sustainability Awards. On the sales side, their turnover has grown from around £500,000 a year when Sam joined the company and took over winemaking in 2005, to around £3 million today. Their largest order to date has been from British Airways for their 2013 Camel Valley Brut, which was served in First Class. Like others, they have tried exporting, selling to twenty-three US states and becoming the first English and Welsh wine producer to enter the Japanese market. However, they find exporting expensive, requiring too much input from them, and Bob says, 'We have more or less pulled out of America. It's pointless when we can sell it here.' Exports account for only 2–3 per cent of their wine sales. Latest accounts (for 2017–2018) show just over a million pounds' worth of wine in stock, almost £1.25 million in the bank and net assets of just over £2.50 million, results which, Bob points out, have been achieved, 'without banks, investors or crowdfunding'. In the context of making a decent living and creating a sustainable business on a small area of land, this is a business masterclass. Bob also says, 'we have the capacity to grow and we have had many [financial] offers to help us do that, but we prefer a natural evolution and hope to maintain a family business for generations to come.' In 2017, Bob was awarded the International Wine Challenge (IWC) Lifetime Achievement Award in recognition of the part he has played in the success of wines from Great Britain, and in 2018 picked up a second lifetime achievement award, this time in the Western Morning News Business Awards for 'putting Cornish and UK wine on the global stage'.

Camel Valley is without doubt one of the leading wine producers in Great Britain. They make a wide and attractive range of wines – something for everyone you might say – and don't mind reaping the returns. Opening to the public does not suit everyone and it can be hard work and sometimes wearing. In one sense their business seems quite old-fashioned – they are not like the new sparkling-wine-only producers who appear to be ruling the English wine roost. However, with their devotion to visitors, tourists and local trade, as well as selling to the wider trade, they are the ideal template for what can be achieved with a vineyard in Britain. There are very, very few vineyards and wine producers in Great Britain who have created viable, sustainable businesses that will outlive their originators and will serve their owners well into the second and third generations and beyond. To have done this with little initial experience, without vast wealth or external investment and (it has to be said) in a region not always best-suited to growing and ripening economic crops of grapes, is a testament to the Lindo family. Bob, Annie and Sam are to be congratulated.

Chapel Down Wines

Tenterden Vineyard, Small Hythe, Tenterden, Kent, TN30 7NG.
www.chapeldown.com
216 hectares (533 acres) owned, leased and under contract

Britain's largest wine producer and second largest vineyard owner. Makes very wide range of wines using both Champagne and other varieties which regularly win top medals and awards. Excellent visitor facilities, including a restaurant.

Chapel Down Wines traces its origins back to a vineyard on the Isle of Wight called Chapel Farm. This vineyard had been planted in the 1980s and managed by Ken Barlow of nearby Adgestone Vineyard, who used the grapes in his wines. However, owing to a drop in Adgestone's sales, this arrangement had ended and the owner, Anthony Pilcher, was contemplating what to do with his grapes. Jan Trzebski, owner of nearby Morton Manor vineyard (now grubbed), suggested that a close friend of his, David Cowderoy, with whom he had been at Wye Agricultural College, might be interested in taking the grapes. David, son of Norman Cowderoy, who had been growing grapes at Rock Lodge Vineyard since 1965, had recently returned from Australia, where he had been studying winemaking at Roseworthy College. Cowderoy's idea was to create what today we might call a 'virtual vineyard', by contracting out the grape growing to others and concentrating on the two aspects of the wine business that required the most expertise: winemaking and marketing. By sourcing grapes from a number of different vineyards spread about Britain in order to minimize weather-related supply problems, and by making wines on a much larger scale than would normally (in Britain at least) be the case, economies of scale in production would be achieved which would enable the wines to be marketed at a competitive price. A company was formed in 1992 with Pilcher as chairman, Nicky Branch, an accountant and financier, as managing director, Carl Koenen, whose family had been in Britain's wine trade since 1925 as sales director and Cowderoy as winemaker. They would concentrate on making a new style of English wine in sufficient volumes to be attractive to supermarkets and multiple off-licence chains and would also specialize in making sparkling wines, a product they felt was very suited to the British climate. They would also offer contract winemaking services for making both still and sparkling wines. That, at least, was the plan.

For the 1992 vintage, the winery at Rock Lodge vineyards was used as a base and grapes from both Chapel Farm and other vineyards were purchased and made into wine. They quickly realized that this winery was far too small and in 1993 a building on a factory estate in nearby Burgess Hill was rented and speedily transformed into a winery. For the next two vintages this was home to the fledgling enterprise. As volumes grew and as stocks of maturing wines, especially sparkling, became larger, it was obvious that another move would have to be made. A chance conversation between Koenen and me in February 1995 about the search for new premises led eventually to the company buying Tenterden Vineyards (the vineyard I had planted in 1977 and subsequently sold) from the bank. The 25-hectare farm, vineyards, winery, business and stock were purchased for £500,000. Nicky Branch, in his characteristically flamboyant style and with his flair for financial engineering, managed to persuade Dunbar Bank (the owners) to give the company a five-year loan covering 100 per cent of the purchase price at a 0 per cent interest rate for the first 12 months, rising (as I recall) by 1 per cent a year for the next five years. In September 1995, with the harvest already under way, the complete winery was shipped the nearly fifty miles from Burgess Hill to Tenterden and reassembled as best it could be, in between loads of grapes arriving to be pressed. I became a director of the company, making the wines coming from the vineyards at Tenterden itself and negotiating a deal whereby I could use the facilities to make and bottle wine for my contract winemaking customers.

Much wine has flowed under the bridge since those early days. The original company got into financial problems in 2000 once the full interest rate (to say nothing of capital repayments) kicked in and merged with Carr Taylor Vineyards and Lamberhurst Vineyards to form English Wines Group plc. However, the big personalities involved in the merger never got on and in November 2001 a full-time managing director, Frazer Thompson (then aged 42), was appointed to bring both common sense and business sense to the company. Thompson had spent many years in the brewing world, first at Whitbread where he led the team behind the relaunch of Boddingtons and latterly as Global Brand Director at Heineken. It was therefore something of a culture shock when on his first day at Chapel Down he had to persuade the company that leased the photocopier not to repossess it as their invoices hadn't been paid for months. The biggest customer then was British Airways (BA), for whom a brand called Horizon had been created to be sold in single-serve bottles on almost all BA short-haul flights. This accounted for 44 per cent of Chapel Down's turnover. When the (second) Gulf War started in early 2003 and nobody wanted to fly, BA tore up the contract ('sue us' they said) and 'the company almost went under'. Thompson vowed never again to let any single customer take more than 15 per cent of sales.

From that inauspicious start, Chapel Down Group plc has blossomed into the biggest English Wine producer in the world with a market capitalization of £120 million, and around 4,500 mainly small shareholders who act as ambassadors for the wine and beer brands. The directors of the company include Nigel Wray, best known for his investments in Saracens Rugby Club, the Prestbury property company and Domino's Pizza, who has been an investor since the company was formed in 2001. One of the largest (and newest) investors is IPGL, the private investment company of Michael Spencer, wine lover and very successful businessman, who has been a shareholder since 2014, but who sold his company NEX Group in 2018 and now owns just over 25 per cent of Chapel Down. There are also a few institutional investors such as the world's largest asset manager BlackRock, which owns 9.77 per cent, Lombard Odier with 12.37 per cent and Henderson Global with 3.56 per cent. Chairman since 2013 is John Dunsmore, ex-CEO of Scottish & Newcastle brewers and C&C (Magners Ciders) and currently a non-Executive Director at brewers Fuller, Smith & Turner.

Fundraising in recent years has been both spectacular and innovative. In July 2013 £3.95 million was raised via crowdfunding from 1,470 new shareholders for Chapel Down Wines. This was the first time that shares in a plc had been sold via crowdfunding and was one of the largest and fastest ever crowdfunded fundraisings. In April 2016 £1.74 million was raised, again by crowdfunding, this time from 895 investors for the beer company Curious Drinks (which now operates as a separate company, but part of the group). This latter fundraising enabled the company to buy a 0.65-hectare (1.6-acre) freehold site across the road from the Ashford International Station to build a brewery (its beers to date have been brewed under contract) designed to brew 8 million litres a year and where it will open a shop, bar and 'visitor experience'. By 2025 the brewery hopes to be employing 160 full-time staff. In 2018, they opened the 'Chapel Down Gin Works', a restaurant, wine and gin bar, and micro-distillery in the new canalside Gas Works development at Kings Cross. Here they will be serving their full range of products, as well as distilling their Bacchus-based gin and Chardonnay-based vodka. In 2017, a massive new fundraising scheme was launched and £18.53 million was raised by issuing 37 million new shares plus another £2.35 million from existing shareholders. The company's cash reserves stood at almost £20 million at the end of 2017. Sales of wines, beers and, since 2017, gin and vodka, have seen a mainly upward progression from £981,000 when Thompson joined in 2001 to an impressive £11.8 million in 2017. Profits have been up and down due to a variety of factors and in 2017 were £253,115 (before tax). The business currently has around 70 employees, including MD Mark Harvey who is ex-LVMH and on the beer side Gareth Bath who is ex-Brew Dog. As Thompson says, it all shows 'that you don't have to be a millionaire to be successful in English wine,' which – coming from someone whose shares in the company are worth almost £4 million – is an interesting comment. He also says that the company's growth of 'seven consecutive years of twenty per-cent compound annual growth shows that English wine isn't just a flash in the pan.' He states somewhat intriguingly that, 'we've been quite open and public about saying we are the natural consolidators of the industry. Cash and quoted paper etc. I'll let you guess who'd be a complementary match!' I think that's a case of 'watch this space'.

Chapel Down Group is undoubtedly the market leader in English wines, taking grapes from 23 vineyards – owned, leased or contracted

– in Essex, Dorset, Hampshire, Kent and East and West Sussex. Together, these cover 216 hectares (533 acres). As with all wineries, the number of bottles produced annually is a closely guarded secret, but in an average year it has to be approaching 1 million bottles. The company reported that in 2018 the harvest was '125 per cent more than the previous record,' which by my reckoning means around 2.25 million bottles. That's more wine than the whole country used to produce but a few years ago. Winemaking is in the talented hands of Josh Donaghy-Spire, who has probably clocked up more medals than any other winemaker in Britain given the number of different wines that come out of the winery each year. Stocks at the end of 2017 were worth £4.56 million, which probably represents near to five or six million bottles. Sales of sparkling wines for 2017 were around the 350,000-bottle mark, representing 60 per cent of sales, with around 235,000 bottles of still wine taking up the other 40 per cent. Exports – touted by many producers as the way they hope to sell up to 25 per cent of their production – have started slowly for Chapel Down. They have a five-year plan to sell in the USA, or more specifically in certain cities of the USA, and have a partner in New York (ABCK Corp.) who handles their wines. Currently they sell around 10,000 bottles of mainly sparkling and 'as long as the price per glass is below $20 it sells'. Their 2011 Three Graces sparkling got 95 points from *Wine Enthusiast Magazine* and sells for $55 which, as Thompson points out, is the same price as Veuve Clicquot, 'and that's not a vintage and doesn't get 95 points'. Exporting is not about 'sending pallets to Kazakhstan and hoping it will sell,' says Thompson, 'you have to build your market slowly but surely'.

Chapel Down's wines are certainly amongst the top ten English and Welsh wine brands for quality. While the sparklers may not always be as good as the very best, their still wines certainly take a lot of beating. The wines from their Kit's Coty site near Maidstone are starting to shine and it may be that this 40-hectare (100-acre) site still has a way to go in terms of wine quality. The 2016 Kit's Coty Estate Bacchus, which retails at £25, and the sparkling Kits Coty Coeur De Cuvée, £100, are certainly impressive wines. Chapel Down's home base at Tenterden offers one of the best British vineyard visitor experiences, with a well-designed and laid-out shop, which prides itself on service by people that know about their wines. Guided tours, a fine restaurant and good facilities for corporate and personal entertaining are taken for granted. Thompson says that visitor numbers are around 55,000 a year. The shop's turnover is £1.5 million (2017) which must represent a lot of wine – 50,000 bottles a year maybe? It's a far cry from 1980 when I sold the first bottle of 'Spots Farm' – as the vineyard we had planted there was then called – for £3.00 a bottle. They also operate a 'Vine Lease' scheme on their Tenterden Bacchus vineyard – similar to the rent-a-vine schemes elsewhere – which (as an example) for £900 a year (£600 if you are a shareholder) gives you 48 bottles of wine, free of excise duty and VAT, for your own consumption. You also get a ticket to the annual Vine Lease Holder's Event.

Even though Chapel Down has more than 200 hectares (500 acres) under vine they are not stopping planting. In September 2018 it was announced that they had secured the lease to 157 hectares (388 acres) on the North Downs in Kent, adjacent to their existing vineyards (beating another wine producer who also wanted to lease the land) and will develop around 130 hectares (321 acres) of vines there over the next three years. Thompson said they are still on the lookout for land 'to lease or buy' and have earmarked £12 million for vineyard development. He has pencilled in £37,000 per hectare (£15,000 per acre) for purchasing land, with the rest for planting and establishment costs to first fruit. Given that they paid £11,860 per hectare (£4,800 per acre) for their Kit's Coty land in 2007, that's an impressive leap in land costs (and values). The 40 hectares (100 acres) of vineyard established there must be worth at least £3.5–£4 million, maybe more. Thompson will consider anywhere in the South East (including Essex) but favours Kent and specifically the North Downs. 'It is without doubt the best place in Britain to grow grapes. It's got the infrastructure, the fruit farmers, the labour and great sites'. He also says that he needs to have sites separated from each other 'to minimize risk' which as a plc they have to take into account. On the question about an industry-agreed brand name for sparkling wines, Frazer is quite adamant. 'We don't need one and we already have one. It's four syllables long. It's English Sparkling Wine.' (It's actually five syllables, but I didn't like to correct him!)

As their productive capacity increases they will gain the advantages of scale both in production costs and in distribution. There is no other producer of English and Welsh wines who can match them for volume and that position doesn't look like being challenged any time soon. Chapel Down is one of the two English sparkling wines served at Downing

Street, they sponsor the Oxford and Cambridge Boat Race, support the Donmar Warehouse Theatre and their wines are to be found at the Royal Opera House and Royal Ascot amongst other prestigious venues. In 2016 they became members of the Walpole Group of luxury brands and are officially one of Britain's 'Cool Brands'. It all seems a long way from almost having the photocopier repossessed.

The future for Chapel Down – and for that matter for the whole English and Welsh wine sector – is as unpredictable as the English and Welsh weather. However, one has to admire the way this publicly listed and traded company has marketed itself and its products. With a sizeable number of loyal shareholders, both large and small, and a diverse offering of products which, as the new brewery comes on stream, will expand, and with spirits just starting to appear (they will soon have their own distillery in Kings Cross), Chapel Down seems well set for the future. One wonders how long it will be before someone decides to make a takeover bid?

Flint Vineyard

Camphill Farm, Earsham, Norfolk, NR35 2AH.
www.flintvineyard.com
5.83 hectares (14.41 acres)

Very young vineyard, first plantings in 2016. Making excellent quality and inventive wines from both home-grown and bought-in grapes. One of Britain's vineyards to watch.

Enthusiasm is always infectious and within minutes of meeting the Witchells, Hannah and Ben, one realizes that here are two relatively young people who have sold their souls to English wine and intend it to be their lives. For these two, this isn't a money-fuelled ego-trip, or something to brag about at the golf club, but a lifelong commitment to something they obviously love and for which they have a great passion. Surprisingly also, in these days of large, mainly sparkling wine enterprises, it is still wines and specifically still wines made from Bacchus, that are at the heart of their operation, although their business plan would not be complete without some sparkling wine as well.

After taking a degree in music (trombone and piano) and working in the IT industry, Ben was ready for a new challenge. In 2007 he and Hannah got interested in the possibility of making winegrowing and winemaking a career and after a year travelling, during which time they visited vineyards and wineries in the southern hemisphere, Ben realized he 'just wanted to make wine'. They sold their flat in London and moved to East Sussex so that Ben could embark on a three-year Viticulture and Oenology course at Plumpton College with Hannah working for British Airways at nearby Gatwick to keep bread on the table. With the wisdom of youth – Ben was 35 and Hannah 30 at the time – this seemed like a sensible thing to do. English wine had got over its dependence on still wines based upon old-fashioned German varieties and outdated hybrids and the broad sunlit uplands of Champagne variety sparkling wine loomed large. After three years spent in the company of fellow students, during which time Ben worked at Davenport and Sussex Vineyards, and with winemaking *stages* in Greece and California under his belt, he graduated with a first-class degree and awards for 'best research project' and 'top winemaking student'. Ben felt fitted to embark on his new career. His first winemaking job in fact took him and Hannah to Beaujolais where for two years he learnt the practicalities of running a winery (owned by a Brit) and where their first child, Rosie, was born in 2013. Whilst in France they toyed briefly with the idea of setting up shop there and considered buying a small vineyard in Burgundy in St Veran. However, England was where they really wanted to be. What they needed was some land, some buildings, some equipment, some grapes and some money (in other words almost everything) in order to turn their long-nurtured dreams into reality.

Hannah's parents had retired to south Norfolk and this seemed as good a place as any to start their quest, especially as Ben had undertaken a climate project whilst at Plumpton and had identified the area as one of the driest and warmest places in Britain. An email to a local farmer, Adrian Hipwell, asking whether he knew of any land that might be available to plant a vineyard resulted in a meeting at Christmas 2014. What were they doing here? Looking for land to establish a vineyard and winery. Would my land be any good? I don't know, maybe. Could we take a look? After visiting the farm, whose gentle, free-draining and south-facing slopes immediately suggested 'vineyard' and whose classic pan-tiled farm buildings and roadside access immediately suggested 'winery and tasting room', the Witchells knew they had found a possible home for their enterprise. Hipwell was in fact a second-generation tenant farmer, so his landlord, the nearby Earsham Estate, had to be consulted before things could proceed. Luckily they agreed to the idea and allowed the Witchells to rent the farmhouse which overlooks the valley in which the vines were to be established. Hipwell, who had spent his working life in the software industry and had recently sold his successful farm and crop management system (Gatekeeper) to the *Farmers Weekly* parent company, Reed Business Systems, was keen on local food and drink enterprises and decided to enter into a partnership with the Witchells.

The Witchells' business plan, by now many years in the making, was put into action. They made a start on establishing vineyards and in the meantime bought in grapes and began making wines for sale. In 2016 they planted 12,500 vines, followed by another 3,000 in 2017 and 11,000 in 2018. To date their vineyards, all planted at 2.2 metres row width by 1 metre between vines, total 5.83 hectares (14.41 acres). The varieties planted were (of course) Bacchus, plus all the Pinots – Noir, Blanc, Gris and Noir Précoce (Blauer Frühburgunder). As well as establishing their vineyards, they needed a winery, so a conversion programme was put in place to turn an old grain store into a winery. Initial funding came jointly from Hipwell and the sale of the Witchells' London flat.

Needing extra finance, the Witchells decided to try and obtain some grants to fund their winemaking and their winery. Ben's interest in Bacchus led him to develop a programme to analyse the variety's flavour profiles (and hopefully improve them) and in January 2016, they managed to get £23,000 from the Eastern Agri-Tech Growth Initiative to carry out scientific trials in order to do this. At much the same time they applied for a LEADER[30] grant from the Rural Development Programme for England (RDPE) to fit out and equip their winery and in April 2016 secured £42,000 in order to do so. Their winery programme could now go into first gear and a selection of mainly brand-new equipment was procured with Ben and Adrian installing the cooling and positive pressure systems to the tanks. Thus equipped, they were able to start making wine.

For their winemaking, grapes were sourced from three East Anglian vineyards: Great Whitmans, Martin's Lane and Humbleyard. For their

30 LEADER is a French acronym of '*Liaison Entre Actions de Développement de l'Économie Rurale*' which (according to the DEFRA website) 'roughly translates as "liaison among actors in rural economic development".'

first vintage in 2016, they bought 6 tonnes of Bacchus, 2 tonnes of Pinot Blanc and 1.5 tonnes of Pinot Noir and made 8,000 bottles. For 2017 they almost doubled this to 15,000 bottles. As sales grow, they intend to continue to buy in grapes as and when they are available and are already nurturing local vineyards for whom they can make wines and from whom they can buy grapes. Their own vineyards have started producing and in 2018, together with bought-in grapes, they pressed 40 tonnes, enough for around 30–32,000 bottles.

On the sales side, their first wines were available in spring of 2017 and got off to a great start when their inaugural wine, the Flint Bacchus 2016, won the East Anglian Vineyards Association's 'Wine of the Year' trophy. Within five months of starting selling wine, they had run out. Given that the wine was selling for around £15.99 that is pretty good going. Apart from Bacchus, they are also making some rosé using two PIWI[31] interspecific crosses, Rondo and Cabernet Cortis,[32] and a light red made from Pinot Noir Précoce. They also make a range of small-volume 'limited release' wines (such as a 2016 barrel-aged Bacchus and a 2017 Bacchus–Sauvignon Blanc blend) which are only available to their VENN club members, of whom there are currently 200. These lucky people – or 'mini-ambassadors' as Hannah calls them – pay £225 a year and in addition to 12 bottles of wine, get invited to special events, can take part in the harvest and have the opportunity to meet and taste wines with Ben and Hannah. As volumes increase, they are starting to sell wines further afield and have entered into a partnership with Berry Bros & Rudd (BBR), becoming the first English still wine BBR have sold on an exclusive basis. In June 2018 they released 4,000 bottles of a Charmat-method sparkling wine, being one of the first wineries in Great Britain to do so. This is made from a blend of Bacchus pressings (all their top-quality Bacchus is made from free-run juice from whole-bunch pressing), a little Rondo and Reichensteiner and four barrels of lees-aged and lees-stirred (*battonage*) Solaris. Ben made the base wine which was then shipped to David Cowderoy's BevTech winery in Burgess Hill for secondary fermentation in tank and bottling. The retail price was £21.99 and it had sold out by January 2019.

31 PIWI stands for *Pilzwiderstandsfähiger* which means fungus resistant.

32 Cabernet Cortis is a variety developed at Freiburg State Winegrowing Institute in Baden in 1982 and released in 2004. It is a crossing of Cabernet Sauvignon and Solaris. Solaris is a *Vitis amurensis* crossing.

Their long-term aim is to sell 70 per cent retail from the farm gate and 30 per cent through the trade in all its myriad forms. (As it happens, this is exactly the same percentage sales split that I aimed for in the early 1980s when I started selling my first vintage.) They have made some own-label Bacchus for Adnams, the local (Southwold) brewer, wine merchant and hotel owner, and would like to sell a fair proportion of their trade sales to premium hotels and restaurants in Norfolk, of which there are an increasing number. In 2018 they were taken on by FMV (Fields, Morris & Verdin – BBR's wholesale division) which will ensure their wines get good exposure to high-end on-trade and off-trade outlets. My guess is that their farm-gate enterprise with the tours and tastings, plus an expanded VENN club, will prove so popular that they will be able to pick and choose who they sell to away from the farm. However, they are in the fortunate position of being able to buy grapes when they are available and make wine at a cost they can be sure of, and in doing so, find ways of selling batches of wine at a profit. Reserve sparkling £35–40; 2016 sparkling £25? They have started to do tours and tastings of the vineyards and winery (£12 a head for a 2-hour tour) and offer their '15-mile lunch menu' featuring local breads, cheeses (including an unpasteurized brie made with milk from French Alpine Montbéliarde cows) and 'amazing' charcuterie from the area. It all sounds so tempting.

With their wine sales, tours, wine club and vineyard consultancy, the business is now cash-positive and generating an income (and there are not many British vineyards which can say that within barely three years of setting up) out of which they aim to fund their grape purchases. Their target is to produce (and eventually sell) 50,000 bottles a year. On the vineyards front, their landlords, the Earsham Estate, have several pieces of south-facing, free-draining land which are suitable for vines and these may become available in the future.

Taken altogether, the Witchells have made a great start in creating a long-term sustainable wine enterprise. Having met them now on several occasions and interviewed them for this book I feel the same sense of excitement that I had in the mid-1970s when I and my wife, then aged 27 and 29, and our two small children, planned and set up our vineyard and winery. Ben and Hannah are a committed couple, making the very best of their circumstances and with a bit of luck and a lot of hard work, have embarked upon a great voyage. Their vineyards, still yet to crop, look good and have been planted with a selection of today's varieties. They are building up relationships with other vineyards and grape suppliers with whom they can work and from whom they can get the raw materials they need to make the business flourish. In the winery they haven't been lavish, but practical and resourceful. Their wines are good, some excellent – as good as you can find from a British vineyard – but they are also inventive and different. With more vintages will come more experience and even better wines. At the moment they only have still wines, but the Charmat sparkling wine will expand their reach and their market. Flint Vineyard is undoubtedly a star in the firmament of English wine and I look forward to watching its progress.

Halfpenny Green Wine Estate

Tom Lane, Bobbington, Staffordshire, DY7 5EP.
www.halfpennygreenvineyards.co.uk
10.36 hectares (25.59 acres)

One of the few successful vineyards north of Birmingham. Makes a wide range of award-winning wines from 'old-school' varieties and has a good business making wines for others under contract. Excellent visitor facilities.

The Vickers family have been farming at Halfpenny Green since the 1930s. Situated just south-west of Wolverhampton in Staffordshire (and at almost exactly the same latitude as Berlin), the farm would not seem a natural place to establish a vineyard in Britain. Martin Vickers first planted a trial plot of vines, Huxelrebe, Reichensteiner and Seyval Blanc, in 1983 on what had, until then, been a wholly arable farm. To begin with, the enterprise was very much a hobby and there was no thought of it one day becoming a commercial enterprise. Tom Day, who then managed Three Choirs Vineyard, saw the site, was adamant that it had potential and supplied the vines. Martin 'didn't have a game plan' when he planted the first vines and wasn't worried about the risks as it was all 'a bit of fun'. Gradually, however, as he saw the vines grow and flourish and eventually bear fruit, he could see that indeed, there was the potential for an enterprise there.

To begin with, with quantities of grapes fairly small, they were taken to Three Choirs, one of the very few wineries in that region then offering contract winemaking services. The first vintage was 1986, when 200–300 bottles of wine were produced, all of which went to members of the family for their help over the establishment years. However, the wines were good enough for Martin to agree with Tom about the site's potential and he decided to expand plantings. Those initial trial vines were followed with plantings in 1987, 1988, 1990 and 1991, by which time they amounted to 6.59 hectares (16.28 acres). Varieties planted, in addition to more plantings of the initial three, included Bacchus, Faberrebe, Madeleine x Angevine 7672 and Pinot Noir. Since then, almost every piece of suitable land on the farm has been planted with vines and by 2017 there were 10.36 hectares (25.59 acres) of vineyard, making it one of the top 35 vineyards in the country for size and certainly one of the largest in this part of the world. Today, they have eighteen different varieties with Huxelrebe, Madeleine x Angevine 7672, Reichensteiner, Seyval Blanc and Rondo being the most plentiful. They have also recently signed a contract with a local grower for a further 3.2 hectares (8 acres) of Siegerrebe, Solaris, Pinot Noir and Pinot Noir Précoce. The business was handed over to Martin's son, Clive, in 2013 with Martin's stepson, Ben Hunt, as assistant winemaker. Martin is busier than ever, helping their contract customers grow better grapes and with the increasing numbers of people who want to plant in the region. Clive's wife Lisa, a trained chef, has been in charge of the catering and retail side since they married in 2000, and as Clive says 'we wouldn't be where we are without her'.

For the first eight vintages, the grapes went to Three Choirs, but with the area under vine rising, and the quantity of grapes increasing, it was decided that for the 1994 vintage, a winery would be constructed and the winemaking brought in-house. Whilst initially there was opposition from Three Choirs as they were losing their largest contract customer, they allowed Martin Fowke, then, as now, the Three Choirs winemaker, to help Clive with the first two vintages and set him on the right path. Today, with the help of Hunt, they manage the winemaking together.

In the early years, the winery was only used for making wines from their own grapes, but slowly and surely, as climate change improved the growing conditions for vines across the whole of the country and as the number of mainly small vineyards planted in counties which were once considered 'too far north' increased, Halfpenny Green's winemaking customers started to grow. From only three in 2010, today's total is sixty-five growers, forty-five of whom have wine made for commercial sale, with the others (with less than 1 tonne of grapes) putting their grapes into a collective blend for home consumption. The winery, upgraded and expanded, has three presses and more than 90 stainless steel tanks, many of them fairly small to cope with contract clients. A typical harvest would see around 300 tonnes of grapes being pressed, one-third Halfpenny Green's and two-thirds contract customers. They currently have a capacity for around 500 tonnes and with the number of contract growers rising, they will soon get to the point where the ratio is one-quarter their own grapes to three-quarters contract. The winery is continually being enlarged and improved with the latest addition to the equipment being an all-singing, all-dancing bottling line, plus a new disgorging line – total bill £300,000 – and a new bottle store under construction. The massive 2018 harvest saw them process 'about 100 tonnes' from their own vines and 'over 300 tonnes of contract work' including some for growers in the south who had run out of tank space.

Winning medals and awards has always been high on Martin and Clive's list of priorities and the wines were achieving medals in the EWOTYC as far back as 1990. Since 2011 they have won medals in all categories, gold, silver, bronze and highly commended in every year. The 2014 Tom Hill made from Huxelrebe won a gold medal in the 2016 EWOTYC. One of their most remarkable wines was a 15 per cent alcohol still red made in 2011 from Rondo, one of the highest alcohol wines ever made in Great Britain, which was awarded a silver medal at the 2012 DWWA. Sales of their wines, in common with most vineyards in Great Britain, are buoyant and increasing. Their most popular wine is their sparkling rosé, selling at £19.95. Halfpenny Green's wines can be found in twenty branches of Waitrose and thirty-five of Marks & Spencer (M&S).

Growing grapes at this latitude on a commercial basis is no easy task and Clive admits that in too many years, some of their varieties – Dornfelder, Faberrebe, Kernling, Reichensteiner, Triomphe and Schönburger – only produce around 2.5–3.75 tonnes per hectare (1–1.5 tonnes per acre). It's really only Huxelrebe, MA 7672, Rondo and Seyval Blanc that produce viable yields with any regularity. Clive reckons the average cost of production is around £1,600 a tonne which cannot be considered commercial, as this is barely what you would get for the grapes (of these varieties) if they were sold to another winery. It is only by maximizing returns from a high percentage of sales direct from the premises (through the catering outlets, to tours and through the busy shop) plus income from the other on-site activities such as the fishing lakes, rents from craft shops and last, but by no means least, the contract winemaking, that the enterprise flourishes. Typically, fifty per cent of sales are through the on-site catering and retail, fifteen to twenty per cent via external markets (farmers' markets, county shows, Christmas fairs etc.) and the balance through a limited number of wholesalers, plus Waitrose and M&S.

With the whole family engaged in the enterprise, plus five in the winery, three in the vineyard, and around 45 mostly full-time employees running the rest, Halfpenny Green is an extremely interesting example of how to prosper from viticulture in Britain. When I ask, 'wouldn't it be easier in the South East?', Clive quickly replies, 'three million customers live within half an hour of here, six million within an hour. We are open 362 days a year and this place never stops buzzing.' That's me put in my place. His two daughters help out at weekends: Imogen, the fifteen-year-old, wants to run the business and Emily, who is thirteen, is eyeing up the winemaker's job. The future of the place looks assured.

Harrow & Hope

Marlow Winery, Pump Lane North, Marlow, Buckinghamshire, SL7 3RD.
www.harrowandhope.com
6.4 hectares (15.81 acres)

Relatively young vineyard, first planted in 2010, that is starting to make excellent award-winning sparkling wines. A producer going places and one of the stars of the future.

Henry Laithwaite grew up in a family whose main business interest was wine. Henry's parents, Tony and Barbara, are the owners of Laithwaite's Wine, and it was therefore odds-on that he would end up in a wine-related occupation. As a child and a teenager he had been on numerous wine-buying and vineyard-visiting trips with his parents, and straight after leaving school worked as a cellar rat in a wine cooperative in the Ardeche, France, spending his eighteenth birthday there. After graduating from Durham University (where he met his wife, Kaye, who is today the other half of their enterprise) with a degree in biology, he became a flying winemaker, working in both Bordeaux and the McLaren Vale in Australia, helping run several winemaking projects for the family firm, and establishing the RedHeads Wine Studio – a sort of bring-your-own-grapes-and-we'll-supply-the-equipment winery – which Tony Laithwaite had founded to give small-scale grape growers and winemakers a facility they could use to make their own wines. Henry also found time to start his own wine label, Wilson Gunn (named after a Scottish ancestor) using the RedHeads facilities. These wines he sold himself around the world, allowing him to gain an insight into how the wine trade, in all its different variants, actually worked.

Henry and Kaye were married in 2008 and soon moved to France where they had bought a vineyard, Château Verniotte, in Castillon (paying €25,000 a hectare), intending to live there and make wine full time. However, the idea that Britain could make good wines, especially sparkling wines, was starting to interest Henry, perhaps influenced by the quality of wines starting to come out of Wyfold, a vineyard part-owned by his mother, Barbara, which had been planted in 2003. Henry and Kaye realized that perhaps France wasn't the place for them after all and so decided to look for land in Britain. In 2009 they came across a 6-hectare (14.83-acre) parcel of south-facing, gravelly, chalky, sloping land overlooking the village of Marlow (where they had rented a house), which was for sale. The location, the site and the soil all seemed perfect and they decided to buy it and plant some vines. In early 2010 Henry contacted me for my thoughts on it and I agreed that with the right soil preparation and the help of a few windbreaks, it would certainly make a good site. The main attractions were the soil, a lot of gravel and a high proportion of small flints in it, plus the chalk subsoil, the elevation – around 45–70 metres above sea level – and the south-facing aspect of much of it. Twenty thousand vines were ordered, 40 per cent each of Chardonnay and Pinot Noir and 20 per cent Meunier, enough to plant 4 hectares (9.88 acres).

An additional factor in the planting plans, which I knew would help the vineyard achieve both sustainable yields and very good quality grapes, was the high planting density. With his experience of working in France, Henry proposed a row width of 1.8 metres (and an intervine distance of 1 metre), giving a length of fruiting cane of 5,555 metres per hectare (2,248 metres per acre). Compare this to a vineyard planted at say 2.3 metres row width, a not uncommon row width found in Britain, and the length of fruiting cane is only 4,349 metres per hectare (1,760 metres per acre): 28 per cent less cropping potential. The high vine density is also important in giving both good yields and high sugars. Here there are 5,555 vines per hectare (2,248 vines per acre). At 2.3 by 1.3 metres you have 3,344 vines per hectare (1,353 vines per acre). Therefore, for an 8-tonne per hectare (3.24-tonne per acre) crop, each vine in the higher-density vineyard carries 1.44 kilograms of grapes whereas in the lower-density example, it needs to carry 2.39 kilos per vine, an increase of 66 per cent. No wonder the vines in the higher-density vineyard ripen their fruit more easily and retain more reserves for the following year. One can of course argue that the establishment costs are considerably higher in the higher-density vineyard, but that is an initial capital cost that can be amortized over the thirty to forty cropping years of the vineyard; good yield and good quality go on giving year after year.

The vines were machine planted in early May 2010, each vine protected with two wooden stakes, so that the hydraulic actuator arm of the intervine weeder, which would be used on the vines from day one, wouldn't harm the tender trunk of the developing vine. Having worked in France, where narrow rows and mechanical weed control were standard, Henry had no issues with these methods. After eight years, the vines are still kept weed-free with the same Clemens weeder, with the inter-row alleyways harrowed to keep them weed-free. Henry says that the acids are lower with clean alleyways and that it marginally lowers the frost risk. They did trial grassed-down alleyways, but felt that the vines were too stressed, although accepting that they were less vigorous.

Before they embarked on this project, Henry and Kaye had (of course) produced a business plan. Using production costs obtained from the published accounts of Ridgeview, taking a yield of 8 tonnes per hectare (3.24 tonnes per acre) and a retail price of £24.99 per bottle, they reckoned they had a viable enterprise. On the capital side, the initial 6 hectares (14.83 acres) of land cost them £200,000 (£33,333 per hectare or £13,490 an acre), which for Marlow, given that the land is within a stone's throw of a residential area of the town and in time might well become available for building on, they considered a reasonable price. In 2013 they expanded the original site by buying around 4.5 hectares (11.12 acres) of adjoining land to plant more vines and build a winery. This time round they had to pay £50,000 per hectare (£20,000 per acre). In total, they now have 6.4 hectares (15.81 acres) of cropping vines. They are looking for more land, but have decided that it must be in Marlow, they like the 'local' aspect of what they are doing, but say that anyone with land in what might broadly be called the 'town envelope' is 'sitting on their hands waiting for planning permission'. Although they are prepared to pay a decent price, and have looked into leasing, they would prefer to be owners rather than tenants, and no additional land to buy is on the horizon.

After planting their first vines, the next part of the project was establishing a winery in time for their first commercial vintage in 2013. (Although 2012 might have been their first vintage from the 2010 planted vines, it was, along with many other British vineyards, a write-off.) Being in an AONB (Area of Outstanding Natural Beauty) and being situated on a relatively quiet lane with neighbours who enthusiastically valued their peace and quiet, made obtaining planning permission harder than they had anticipated. Eventually, after promising to plant considerable screening trees and shrubs, sense prevailed and they were able to go ahead and build their winery ready for the 2013 harvest. The winery is equipped with all the main machinery, tanks and facilities needed to produce sparkling wines, apart from a bottling line. Bottling is carried out by IOC (L'Institut Œnologique de Champagne) whose travelling bottling line is used by many sparkling wine producers in Britain. Around 30 per cent of their wine is made in six-year-old 225-litre barriques which they source from the Laithwaite winery in Bordeaux. Barrels are expensive, time consuming and take up a lot of winery space, but the winemaker in Henry likes working with them and they certainly add some nuance and complexity to the final product.

Since producing their first wine, the quality of the site, in terms of both yields and wine, has been obvious. Yields since the 2014 harvest, the first one where all the vineyards were fully cropping, have averaged 7.08 tonnes per hectare (2.86 tonnes per acre) which included 2016 where they were hit hard by the April and May frosts. Had it not been for a poor 2016 crop (although it still came in at 2.66 tonnes per hectare, 1.08 tonnes per acre), the average yield would have been 8.55 tonnes per hectare (3.46 tonnes per acre). Their aim is to produce around 45,000 75 cl bottles of wine a year, a figure they are currently achieving. Henry is also now making the wine for Wyfold Vineyard. On the quality front, since the launch of their first wine in May 2016, medals and awards have been the norm. Their launch wine, the Harrow & Hope 2013 Brut Rosé, won a gold medal at the Sommelier Wine Awards and other awards have followed. They sell their wines through a mix of outlets including their own cellar door, into the British on-trade through wholesalers and to a small range of local shops and restaurants. They maintain a mailing list of around 2,500 customers, who get regular email updates, pre-release offers and invites to special events. The nearby brewery, Marlow's Rebellion Brewery, has a retail shop open six days a week, where they are firm supporters of the winery and sell more than their fair share of their wines. As volumes grow, other markets will be tackled. Harrow & Hope have already started to look at exports and won a three-year contract with Alko, the Finnish alcohol monopoly, which is taking 2,000 cases (of 9 litres) a year for three years. The Harrow & Hope Reserve Brut sells for €32.35 on the Alko website (which incidentally features thirteen English sparkling wines, ranging in price from €24.19 to €49.98 a bottle) and appears to be going down well with the Finns. They have also sold a few pallets to a Swedish on-trade distributor and made a start in selling to the USA in a small way, using an importer Henry used when selling his Wilson Gunn range of Australian wines. They know that the USA will be a tough market to gain a foothold in and know that it will take time, but they are prepared to wait. At the moment they only have a limited amount of stock but are hoping that by the time bigger volumes become available US sales will have started moving in the right direction.

All this selling takes up time and to run the vineyards they have three people on the books, in addition to a team of contract staff who do much of the canopy management under the supervision of one of their employees, an Italian who also speaks good enough Romanian to converse with the contract gang. Henry and Kaye would like to keep as much of the pruning as possible in-house to make sure it is done properly. A contractor is rarely going to take as much care as an owner-operator and pruning is the one job that has a huge impact on the long-term health of the vineyard.

Of course, being part of the Laithwaite's wine empire gives you certain advantages not open to others, but this independent couple want to prove that their wines can make their own way in the world, so have not relied very much on this sales channel. Yes you can find it on the Laithwaite's and Sunday Times Wine Club websites, but Henry says that 'volumes available to them are limited' and they would prefer to keep it that way. Harrow & Hope – the name derives of course from the harrowing of the vineyard and the hope that it would all turn out right in the end – has made an impressive start. Certainly, being brought up in a wine environment, having good friends such as (the late) Mike Roberts and his family at Ridgeview, being able to get Dr Tony Jordan who set up Moët & Chandon's sparkling wine facility in Australia, Domaine Chandon, to advise on blending and being able to persuade Oz Clarke to launch your first wine are all a great help. However, at the end of the day it's the vineyard, the vines, the grapes they produce, the yields, the winemaking, the presentation and the way the wines are sold that creates a viable, sustainable business – not who your family or friends are. Henry and Kaye have made a strong start and, given that they are only just getting into their second commercial vintage, still have a long way to go. But the foundations they have laid are good and there is no doubt that Harrow & Hope is a major British sparkling wine brand in the making.

Hundred Hills Vineyard

Patemoor Lane, Pishill and Stonor, Henley-on-Thames, Oxfordshire, RG9 6HS.
18.4 hectares (45.47 acres)

One of Britain's newest and most exciting wine producers, still several years away from releasing their first wine. The dramatic steep-valley site and award-winning winery create a stunning visual impact.

By any measure, Hundred Hills Vineyard, with its 83,000 vines spread over 17 hectares (42 acres) and its award-winning winery, is an ambitious project. The brainchild of Oxford couple Stephen and Fiona Duckett, the vineyard and its buildings have been created with impeccable taste and care and one can only look forward to the wines that will come from the project. The Ducketts, born in 1967 and 1968 respectively, met whilst studying at Oxford, both going on to pursue business careers. After getting his degree in engineering, economics and management, Stephen spent two years on a scholarship to Harvard Business School, and became involved with computers at the birth of the internet, before helping to run IT companies on both sides of the Atlantic. Fiona, whose doctorate was in applied linguistics, has also worked in industry as well as bringing up their four children. Stephen comes from a Somerset farming family but was the first to go to university and pursue a career outside farming – until now.

Always interested in wine, especially old Champagne, the Ducketts trace their enthusiasm for English sparkling wine back to a bottle of

Nyetimber they were introduced to in 2000. They remember it as being the Classic Cuvée, which vintage they don't recall, but they do recall it as being good, very good. They visited a few vineyards, Nyetimber and Ridgeview included, and in around 2008 decided that they would like to give up their other business interests and start their own sparkling wine enterprise. Their initial vision is one that hasn't changed. They want to create one of the best – if not *the* best – sparkling wines in Britain, and maybe one of the best in the world. They see this as a twenty-five-year project, family led and driven, with their four children – three daughters and a son aged between 21 and 15 – maybe involved at some stage. Their aim is for a project that will 'become both profitable in the medium term and create a valuable asset in the long term.' They cite Champagne houses such as Vilmart and Selosse as models in terms of wine style, range and quality, but see the enterprise styled on a 'Californian list-based model' where a relatively small number of customers are drawn into the 'Hundred Club' where they will gain access to some great wines. To do this they needed a site that would allow them to produce 'terroir-driven wines', wines that reflected the site, its geography and the differences that location and grape variety bring to a wine. Thus began the search for suitable land for the enterprise.

To bring their dream closer to reality they engaged the services of Frenchman turned Californian, Dr Michel Salgues, who for many years worked for Champagne Roederer, in 1982 setting up Roederer Estate, the sparkling wine operation in California's Anderson Valley. Here he was winemaker for 19 years, and in 1986 masterminded the establishment of vineyards in Tasmania that Roederer jointly owned with Jansz Tasmania (sold in 1997 to the Hill-Smith family). In 2009 the Ducketts started their search for suitable land, and in 2012 found 25 hectares (62 acres) of land in the Chilterns, high up in the Stonor Valley above Henley-on-Thames. At the time I was planting the nearby Fairmile Vineyard whose owner was also looking for additional land; he asked me to run my eye over it, so I drove up there. At 125–190 metres above sea level and with almost half the land facing north-east, my opinion was that it was 'too high and too cold' and I advised the owner of Fairmile to look elsewhere. This, however, didn't dissuade the Ducketts and they bought the land, then known as Bank Farm, in February 2013.

Soil samples were sent to the CIVC laboratories which pronounced the soils 'identical to those of the finest regions of Champagne' and in a letter attached to the winery planning application, Salgues pronounced that the 'soils and associated "terroir" across the property are of the highest quality for producing sparkling wine comparable to Champagne'. Salgues, who remained as their advisor throughout the process of both planting the vineyard and planning and building the winery, sadly died in October 2017. French viticulturalist Franck Mazy was also involved with the site, surveying it and carrying out soil analysis. He was also consulted with regard to clone selection. The Ducketts liked the site because the location fitted their plans for access and sales potential, right in the middle of the London–Oxford and Bicester Village–Bath triangle. The north–south valley offered them a variety of different aspects which, together with the different varieties and clones, would help create the different terroirs they wanted. And finally there was the soil – what's not to like about having high pH, chalk-rich soil if you are trying to create a Champagne lookalike? The site also had plentiful air drainage caused by both the steep slopes on most of the plots and the 65-metre difference in elevation between the highest and lowest parts of the site. This helps with air circulation both in spring, when frost might be an issue, and during the growing season as an aid to disease control.

Planting started in 2014 with 12.5 hectares (30.9 acres) and continued in 2015 and 2016 with the balance of 4.5 hectares (11.1 acres). Only Chardonnay and Pinot Noir were planted, the Meunier being considered by Salgues as a 'high-volume, low-quality clone of Pinot Noir – a filler,' and never used in any of the best Champagnes. Mainly CIVC clones were selected and the vines were sourced from Pépinières Guillaume (including some of their loose-bunch *grappes lâches* clone) all on Fercal rootstock and apart from a few of the very steepest banks, all planted with a GPS planting machine. The vines were trellised using treated timber posts, end-posts and intermediates, unusual for these days, when the vast majority of new vineyards in Britain (and indeed around the world) are trellised with galvanized steel posts. However, as with everything the Ducketts embark on, much research was done into the best type of timber and the best type of treatment and Stephen is sure that in their soil the posts will be fine. 'We chose wooden posts from a sales and marketing point of view' and they feel that they help form part of the 'vineyard experience' that people are expecting when they visit. I said that as long as Stephen didn't personally have to replace them when they started breaking, it was a wise decision.

One of the first things the Ducketts did after buying the farm and organizing the planting of their vineyards was to draw up plans for a winery, which had to be ready for their first vintage in 2016. Local architects were engaged, the Henley-on-Thames practice Nichols, Brown, Webber, and planning permission sought in June 2013 and obtained in March 2014. What has emerged has to be one of the best-looking small wineries, both externally and internally, certainly in Britain, if not further afield. With its use of natural materials, timber, stone, brick and tile, and its sympathetic barn-like appearance, it sits in the valley amongst the vines as if it grew there organically. It comes as no surprise that it won the Chiltern Society's 'Building of the Year' trophy in 2017. Inside, the wooden beams and Italian floor tiles give it a slightly domestic feel, although the two Coquard PAI presses, top-of-the-range Metalinox tanks, six 2,280-litre wooden tanks and fifty *barriques* are enough to show that this winery means business. There is both underground and above-ground bottle storage, enough space for up to 600,000 bottles, all stored in riddling cages. Much thought has gone into such things as the cooling and a 'night air' system designed to keep the winery cool without refrigeration is installed, although of course, refrigeration is available if needs be.

Whilst the Ducketts want to be heavily involved with winemaking decisions, they have the help of an assistant winemaker, Julie Feugier from France, who manages the winery on a day-to-day basis. During pressing, everyone keeps a watchful eye on how the juice is running, testing for acid, sugar and potassium and making decisions based upon data as well as taste. Pressing volumes are on the low side – in 2017 it was around 500 litres per tonne – and they may well sell off any pressings that they don't want in their own wines. Their Coquard presses are fitted with some 'unusual features' which were specified by Salgues, who had represented the company in California and knew the presses well. Exactly what these features are remains a secret. Rosé will be a significant part of their production, maybe up to one-third, but they will also aim to make a small volume of their very best wine into a prestige blend, maybe only three to four thousand bottles, much as Vilmart does with their Coeur de Cuvée. Their aim is to produce around 100,000 bottles a year – 125,000 maximum – and Stephen is confident that their site can do that. 'I may be proved wrong' he says 'but I am pretty confident that we can average 7.5 tonnes per hectare (3 tonnes per acre)'. In my experience that's a bold prediction; were they to achieve it their vineyard would be in the top ten per cent of producers by yield in Britain. Only time will tell.

The Ducketts aim to make a number of different wines each vintage, each reflecting different parts of the estate. There will be at least two different classic cuvées, a *blanc de blancs* made with the hillside-grown Chardonnay clone 95, and a rosé made from Pinot Noir and Chardonnay. Reserve wines will be kept back from each vintage and used in blends, especially in the rosé, which they see as a wine that requires less ageing. They want to avoid malolactic fermentation if possible, preferring the better purity of fruit that non-malolactic sparkling wines can have. All wines will see oak at some stage, whether spending some time in the large barrels, or in the *barriques* where the Ducketts would like to do some *battonage*, especially on their best Chardonnay. Ageing in bottle will be 'between three years and a decade' depending on the wine. The Ducketts are not going to be hurried if waiting will result in a better wine. Their aim is to 'try to get people to understand the link between terroir and taste'. Their range of wines will offer something for everyone, but with 'good wines that are genuinely scarce at the top of the range'.

The 2014 planted vines established well and the first small crop was taken in 2016 – enough for 5,500 bottles. Whether these wines are sold remains to be decided, but they will act as a test-bed for future vintages. With both their 2014 and 2015 plantings producing fruit, 2017 was a bigger vintage with 32 tonnes of grapes being processed. In 2018 they pressed a respectable 120 tonnes and were able to make individual base wines from each of the vineyard parcels. The vineyard is run by Enrico Cassinelli, an Italian from Piemonte, plus a Bulgarian family team who are in Britain for around six months of the year. The vineyard is well equipped with a new fully tracked New Holland tractor to cope with the steepest slopes and two Lipco tunnel (re-circulation) sprayers to keep the vines healthy. Frost can be a problem in the lower parts of the valley and the two 'tow and blow' frost machines they bought proved their worth during the frosts of April 2017.

The Ducketts' investment in the land, the vineyards, the winery and equipment is 'obviously into the many millions, with more to go'. It's all 'family money,' and whilst it is clear that this is no cheapskate operation, neither is it completely over the top or out of context with the impression that you need to make if wines of the anticipated quality (and anticipated price) are to be sold. Visitors, most of whom will hopefully become customers (if they can first get on the list), will definitely be impressed by the winery and its surroundings. Whilst the winery has facilities for private and corporate events, it is not planned to cater for weddings and large events and nor do they intend to do over-the-counter retail. I tell them that this is unrealistic and whether they like it or not, visitors will arrive expecting a tasting room and the opportunity to buy. The Ducketts are not so sure. Their plan is 'not to grow any larger, to generate a sensible return from our investment and to build a very beautiful family asset here.' They don't intend to grow by buying in grapes and, adds Fiona, 'workwise we feel that this is as much as we can manage together.'

At this stage, with the vines still establishing and no wines anywhere near ready to be sold, Stephen is keen to get to know the vineyard. He views it already as 'ten different parcels' delineated by variety, clone and location and in order to make sure he gives every bit of the vineyard his attention, has a 'walk generator' on his phone which generates a random walk through the vines each time he sets out to view the vineyard. Such is his attention to detail. Their aim is to create a 'list-driven business – building a list of people who are interested in us and our wines and buy from us regularly'. With their experience of living and working in the USA, they plan to sell in certain US cities from day one, although they know that building an export business 'takes a decade'. They see the wine business as three separate concerns: the farming of vines; the production of wines; and the sales, marketing and branding of the product. Each requires separate skills and experience.

The Ducketts are very bullish about the future and see neither the huge expansion of supplies of English sparkling wine that will take place over the next five to ten years, nor the advent of wines made by the Charmat method as a threat. The reason? They won't be selling wines in the same marketplace as larger expansion-led producers and will hopefully be able to keep their customers to themselves. 'If you ever see our wine in a supermarket,' says Stephen, 'then we have done something seriously wrong'. He feels that the market for English sparkling wine has only just started and that there is a huge potential in the 'English social season', Ascot, Glyndebourne, Henley – there are dozens of events, where Champagne is seen as the natural (traditional) drink. But times change, people change, teenagers become young adults and young adults become middle-aged wine buyers. By the time today's teenagers have enough income to celebrate their achievements, weddings, birthdays, Hundred Hills' wines (and the wines from the many other producers waiting in the wings) will be available for sale. The Ducketts feel that the overall market for English sparkling wines will expand and that 'all the marketing activity and money being spent' will help this happen. Stephen says that he has talked to several owners of boutique hotel and restaurant chains 'who are surprised by two things. Firstly by how much English sparkling wine they can sell and secondly by how much they can sell it for.' Both augur well for English sparkling wine in general. His aim is to have his wines in fifty to sixty high-end restaurants, bars and hotels around Henley.

Hundred Hills is an impressive project and one that has all the makings of a superstar in the wine galaxy. I have visited many wine producers both in Britain and overseas and seldom have come across one as meticulously planned and organized as this. Interviewing the Ducketts, I got the impression that nothing was done without a huge amount of research going on and the assembling of as many different views as possible in order to make the right decision. I have my reservations about the height of the site above sea level, but when it comes to advising others about where to plant I tend to be over-cautious, and the Ducketts have the luxury of making and standing by their own decisions. To be able to establish such an enterprise when still relatively young, with enough funds to invest at the right level and with the degree of certainty of a business model in order to make their investment pay, must be a hugely enjoyable experience. I am not sure the world of sparkling wines knows what will hit them in 2021–2022 when the first Hundred Hills wines are launched, but it's definitely a case of 'watch this space – the Ducketts are coming'.

Laithwaite's

One Waterside Drive, Arlington Business Centre, Theale, Reading, Berkshire, RG7 4PL.
www.laithwaites.co.uk
Wyfold Vineyard 2.23 hectares (5.51 acres); Windsor Great Park 3 hectares (7.41 acres)

One of Britain's largest wine companies, has sold English wines since 1975 but now has interests in several British vineyards and produces a wide range of English sparkling wines.

The Laithwaites have been firm supporters of English and Welsh wines for many decades. Founded in 1969 by Tony Laithwaite as Bordeaux Direct, under some railway arches in Windsor with five French wines, the business has expanded to become one of Britain's largest specialist retailers of wines, selling 1,500 wines to 750,000 customers in several countries and has over 1,000 employees worldwide. Turnover in 2017 was £307 million – that's an awful lot of wine – with an after-tax profit of £9.1 million. Since 1971, Tony's wife Barbara has been very much part of the business, and today their three sons, Henry, Thomas and William, are also on the board and poised to take over the business. One of the Laithwaites' early strokes of genius was founding the Sunday Times Wine Club, in 1973. Hugh Johnson, then the *Sunday Times* wine correspondent, was installed as its first (and to date only) president, 'to keep an eye on me,' says Tony. This club, the first of many, gave the company access to a large customer database of committed wine drinkers. Laithwaite's still run the club, plus wine clubs for other organizations such as the *Wall Street Journal*, British Airways, American Express, the National Trust and several banks. They also own the wine merchant Averys of Bristol.

Interest in English and Welsh wines started early for Laithwaite's, and in the mid-1970s they listed the wine from Adgestone Vineyard on the Isle of Wight, which was then probably the best still white (no sparkling in those days) available in commercial quantities. Adgestone – who only made one wine, a blend of Müller-Thurgau, Seyval Blanc and Reichensteiner – achieved early success in the annual English Vineyards Association's competition, runner up in the first competition ever held in 1974 and again in 1977, a gold medal in 1978 and finally the Gore-Browne Trophy for English Wine of the Year in 1979. For the very first edition of the Laithwaite's 'Wine Times', Tony went on a day trip to the Isle of Wight to interview its then owner, Ken Barlow, and came back full of praise. Barbara says 'we were in at the beginning of English wine,' and they are amazed at how it has progressed over the last four decades.

My first encounter with Tony Laithwaite was over the telephone. In 1981, a month or so after bottling my second vintage (the 1980) of wines from Spots Farm (now Chapel Down's Tenterden Vineyards), I was surprised to receive a telephone call from Tony. 'I hear you have a very good Seyval Blanc,' he said. 'Could I buy three cases?' To say I was surprised would be a significant understatement as I had barely started selling any wines to the trade and to receive a call from someone I had actually heard of, asking me (almost demanding) if he could buy some wine was nothing short of a miracle. I quickly dreamed up a trade price, I forget what it was, but I remember the retail price (at the time) was £3.75 a bottle. I vividly recall going back into our house (our business telephone was in a small office attached to the back of our house) and told my wife the good, if slightly surreal, news. Laithwaite's was going to stock our wines.

Quite soon afterwards, it may have been the same evening or perhaps the evening after, I received another call, this time from Colin Gillespie, then proprietor of Wootton Vineyards and, more importantly, Chairman of the English Vineyards Association. 'Good evening Stephen,' he said, 'I have some good news for you. Your 1980 Spots Farm Seyval Blanc has been awarded the Gore-Browne Trophy for English Wine of the Year!' Once again, a major surprise and one of the two vinous highlights of my life (the other one being passing the Master of Wine exams in 2003). It wasn't until a few days later that I started to put the two surprises together. The Chairman of the judges for that year was Hugh Johnson and he had clearly taken a peek at the label (or maybe in those days the judges were told what the wines were, hopefully after they had judged them) and had told Laithwaite about our wine. He probably said something like 'Tony, you had better give Skelton a call quickly and get an order in before he puts the price up,' which was precisely what we did – up to £4.75 – which didn't really slow down sales, but did bring a bit more income. Laithwaite of course got his wine at the agreed price.

Since those early days, Laithwaite's have always had English and Welsh wines on their list and today have around twelve sparkling and two still wines. Tony was always convinced that British vineyards should be 'following the Champagne model, not the German one,' and producing much more sparkling wine. He says, 'I used to drive past a lovely chalk slope on the way to our old offices at Caversham and always thought it would make a great sparkling wine vineyard.' The sparklers on Laithwaite's list include wines from: Wyfold Vineyard, part-owned by Barbara Laithwaite; from Harrow & Hope (see p. 162), owned by son Henry and his wife Kaye; the last of the wines from Laithwaite's minute Theale[33] Vineyard; wine from their Windsor Great Park vineyards (when it is available); and wines under the South Ridge label, their own English sparkling wine brand, which Mike Roberts told me accounted for one-third of Ridgeview's sales in the early years of the winery. The South Ridge brand was originally created for them by Kit Lindlar when he started his winery in Kent. When Lindlar closed the winery, he sold all his equipment to Mike Roberts, who was then setting up Ridgeview, along with the making of the South Ridge blends for Laithwaite's, where it has stayed ever since. There are several non-vintage South Ridge wines: a Cuvée Merret Brut, a Rosé, a Blanc de Blancs and sometimes a Blanc de Noirs. The first order for South Ridge was only 50 cases, but it has since grown to become 'several thousand cases' and is by far the biggest selling English sparkling wine on their list. Before Hugh Johnson moved from his country house at Saling Hall near Braintree in Essex, where he had a substantial cellar, Tony and Barbara tasted a bottle of the 1993 South Ridge, the inaugural vintage, which had lain undisturbed for over twenty years. What was it like? 'Stunning, brilliant, like Krug,' said Tony, 'it would have lasted another twenty years'.

Laithwaite's also stock two sparkling wines apiece from Gusbourne and Hambledon. Prices for sparkling wines range from £19.99 to £45.00 (less 10 per cent for mixed cases). On the still wine front, they only list two, a rosé and a white, both from Denbies under the Ashcombe Hill label, exclusive to Laithwaite's and both priced at £13.99. Both Tony and Barbara emphasize that price is an issue with English wines. It has

33 Theale Vineyard was on a sloping bank formed from the brick and rubble waste that resulted when Laithwait's built their last but one office. This was planted with 703 Chardonnay vines in 1998 at 2 by 1 metres and was partly looked after by the employees who worked in the offices nearby. As I recall it they 'adopted' vines, pruned them, ate their lunches beneath them, kept them neat and tidy and had an informal competition to see whose vine had the most grapes. The Theale Blanc de Blancs wines were made at Ridgeview and were of remarkably good quality, winning several medals and awards. The 2003 Founder's Reserve came seventh in the 2007 Effervescents du Monde competition. I served a bottle to a group of MW students and they all had it down as a top-quality Champagne retailing in the £40–£60 category. When Laithwaite's sold the offices in 2016, they offered the vines to anyone who wanted them and they ended up in Tiverton in Devon. Nobody thought that 18-year-old vines would survive the journey, but miraculously only 20 died and the others are back and cropping.

taken a good few years to get people to buy English sparkling wines at £20 and over and they are very aware that still English wines over £10 are hard to shift. 'Maybe with the large 2018 harvest we will see some still wines at under £10,' muses Tony. 'Maybe,' I say.

Taken together, Laithwaite's (and the Sunday Times Wine Club's) offering of English wines (no Welsh) is pretty impressive and whilst they do not release sales figures, we are talking about case numbers in the several thousands per year. They have a unique position in wine sales in Britain, perhaps only challenged by the Wine Society, which also has a very loyal clientele (helped by the fact that you can only buy if you become a single-share shareholder), and sell into what might be termed 'middle Britain', people who care about their wines. Their customers like the Laithwaite's philosophy, are probably more pro-British than, say, your average supermarket shopper and are probably prepared to pay a bit more for something different – all attributes which suit English and Welsh wines. Laithwaite's also has several overseas sales operations – Australia, New Zealand, Singapore, Southern China and the USA – all of whom take small amounts of English wines. In the future I suspect that as volumes rise, their exports will also increase.

When it comes to vineyard ownership in Great Britain, the Laithwaite family can claim involvement in three: Wyfold, the 2.23 hectares (5.51 acre) vineyard part-owned by Barbara Laithwaite, wines from which are now made by Henry Laithwaite at his Harrow & Hope winery; Harrow & Hope itself (see p. 162); and the Windsor Great Park vineyard. Tony Laithwaite grew up and went to school in Windsor and started the company under some railway arches there, so when English sparkling wine started to take off, he often had thoughts about having a vineyard somewhere locally. One of Windsor Castle's grace-and-favour residents thought that there were good sites for a vineyard within the Great Park, so Tony Laithwaite started discussing the idea with Crown Estates, the park's owners, and managed to secure a lease on a south-facing plot of land, known as Mezel Hill. This is between 53 and 60 metres above sea level, and overlooks the 'Great Meadow Pond', one of the large lakes that dot the southern end of the park and drain into Virginia Water. This is not the first time that Windsor has had a vineyard. According to multiple records, Henry II (1154–89) had a small vineyard in 'the Little Park' and it was apparently still there two hundred years later when Edward IV (1461–83) entertained the Governor of Holland. There was also a most productive Black Hamburg vine in a large greenhouse at Cumberland Lodge, a former Royal residence which can be seen (and vice versa) from Mezel Hill. It is recorded that in 1879, 1,134 kilograms of grapes were harvested from this one vine.

In early 2011 I was asked to take a look at the site and draw up a planting plan. The land is quite mixed, with some very sandy parts and clay in places. The drainage was not ideal and parts should have been drained before planting, but time was not on our side. Some of the very lower end of the site, most of which luckily would become headland and was not planted with vines, was covered with a thick layer of black silt that had been dredged out of the lake the site borders onto. Not ideal, but there was no alternative but to plant. The 18,500 vines were planted in early May 2011, 55 per cent Chardonnay at 1.8 metres row width by 1 metre intervine distance, 35 per cent Pinot Noir and 10 per cent Meunier, both at 1.8 metres by 0.8 metres. The total area planted was 3 hectares (7.41 acres). The narrow row width and tight spacing between vines was chosen by Henry Laithwaite, who had experience of narrow rows having worked in French vineyards and had planted his Harrow & Hope vineyard at the same density the year before. The whole Laithwaite's team felt that the wines would be better for it. The density of the Pinot Noir and Meunier, at 6,944 vines per hectare (2,810 vines per acre), is probably the highest density of any vineyard in Great Britain, beating even Nyetimber's original plantings which were at 1.6 metres by 1 metre.

The first harvest was in 2013, when enough grapes for around 2,000 bottles were picked and sent to Ridgeview for processing. The blend in 2013 was slightly tilted towards the Pinots as the Chardonnay had not established (in the wetter parts) quite so well. Yields since 2014 have been pretty regular, averaging around 14,000 bottles a year, including the frost-hit 2017 (when a -6°C frost on the night of 25 and 26 April did considerable damage) and the bountiful 2018 when the yield was almost double the average. The Windsor Great Park wine, as it is called, was launched to a considerable fanfare in February 2017 and sold out (at £34.99 a bottle in a smart box) pretty quickly. It was rationed by selling some in a three-pack containing one bottle each of sparkling wine from Windsor Great Park, Wyfold and Harrow & Hope. A second vintage, the 2014, was also launched and sold out, although a small amount was held back and released in time for the wedding of

Prince Harry and Meghan Markle in May 2018. The next vintage to be released is the 2015, in two tranches, half to pre-release customers at the end of 2018 and the other half during 2019. Commercially the vineyard has been a great success and well up to projections. If they are selling it all at £35 per bottle, and taking VAT, excise duty and production costs into account and don't have to pay a wholesaler or retailer a margin, then it must be more than paying its way.

Windsor Great Park wines will become better and better as a 'solera' of older wines is being built up to blend into more recent vintages and give them a bit more age and character. The site is fully fenced against rabbits and deer, and pheasants (of which there are plenty as the Great Park hosts a large commercial shoot) do not appear to do much damage. Anne Linder, a long-standing Laithwaite's employee, who began working for Tony as a wine buyer in 1988, says that parakeets are the most unexpected challenge and just love the ripening grapes (nobody is entirely sure how these non-native birds ended up in London but there are now thousands in the city). The Windsor vineyard has been very much her project and she takes great pride in it and its wines. Crown Estates are very pleased to have the vineyard on their land and there are ongoing discussions with the Laithwaites about planting more vines. On the sales side the Laithwaites say, 'we can already sell everything we produce and want to be able to sell it overseas.' On this basis, an expansion of the Great Park vineyard would seem assured.

Laithwaite's, both as wine retailers at home and abroad and as vineyard owners and winemakers, are a great asset to English and Welsh wine. They understand the business and appreciate the problems of vintage variation and cost of production and how that can be managed. It is good to see the second generation (Henry) involved with his own vineyard and with the making of wines from Wyfold and this bodes well for the next 50 years. Who knows what the industry will look like by then.

Llanerch Vineyard

Hensol, Pendoylan, Vale of Glamorgan, CF72 8GG.
www.llanerch-vineyard.co.uk
2.83 hectares (7 acres)

Wales' oldest vineyard with very good visitor facilities including hotel, holiday cottages, wedding venue, restaurant and café.

Llanerch was established between 1986 and 1989. In those days, like many others, the vineyard was planted with Germanic varieties, plus the (almost) obligatory hybrids: Bacchus, Huxelrebe, Kernling, Reichensteiner, Seyval Blanc and Triomphe. More Triomphe and Seyval Blanc were added in 1992 and 1995, together totalling 2.3 hectares (5.68 acres). Surprisingly, given the decline of most of these varieties and the ever-upward surge of Champagne varieties and other, more 'fancy' varieties, nothing much has changed here – at least in the vineyard. A mixture of GDC and the less well-known Lyre system (a divided canopy trellis) remain the main forms of training. In recent years, a test patch of Pinot Noir has been planted together with some Phoenix and Solaris so that the cropping area is today 2.83 hectares (7 acres). Only a very small parcel of Kernling from the 1986 plantings remains. Wines are sold under the 'Cariad' label – Welsh for 'darling'.

As situations go, Llanerch Vineyard is well placed both from a viticultural and a business standpoint. South-facing and between 46 and 51 metres above sea level, it is in the warmest part of Wales, as protected as you can get from the south-westerly winds and around 15 km (8.75 miles) from the coast, close enough to be frost-free, far enough to escape sea breezes. The soil is a sandy loam over clay. Drainage is poor in places and probably the cause of some of the problems in parts of the vineyard. From a business and tourist point of view, the vineyard is ideally placed: halfway between Cardiff and Swansea and only a few minutes from the M4 motorway, yet still surrounded by beautiful visitor-friendly countryside.

The first vines were planted by Peter and Diana Andrews, who bought what was then a dilapidated farmhouse and farm buildings in 1978 and set about restoring them, making the house habitable and converting some of the farm buildings into two holiday cottages. They also wondered what to do with the land. Eventually they came up with the idea of planting vines; given that they were only a few miles from the vineyards planted by Lord Bute at Castel Coch and Swanbridge, maybe this provided the germ of the idea. Diana was one of the first students to attend lectures at Plumpton College to learn about viticulture and winemaking. Initially a winery was built on-site, but as the growing area expanded and the tourism side became more important, the winery was converted into holiday cottages and winemaking farmed out to Three Choirs, where it remains today.

Since those early days, even if the vineyard hasn't changed much, the ownership and the enterprise certainly have. Peter and Diana Andrews sold the business in 2007 for £2.5 million to two business partners (Carol Growcott and Scott Williams) but they couldn't make it prosper and it eventually went into receivership, so it was put up for sale in May 2009 for £1.95 million. For a while it lingered on the estate agent's books and the vineyards were effectively abandoned. However, in October 2010, just as the harvest was approaching, it was bought (for £1.6 million) by the Davies family. Ryan Davies, who trained as a geologist, was persuaded to take on Llanerch by his parents who funded the acquisition and still take a keen interest in the business. Ryan's father, Gwyn, had sold his transport business in 2005 and was looking for opportunities to invest. In October 2010, with contract exchange and completion approaching, the Davies family 'jumped over the hedge' and picked all the grapes they could find, taking them to Three Choirs to be made into their first vintage, all 4,000 bottles of it. Whilst it wasn't their finest wine, it did give them something to sell when they first opened their doors to visitors.

On taking over Llanerch, several things were obvious. The vineyards were neglected and needed 'straightening up' and in many places, replanting; the buildings needed some TLC and investment; and the site had obvious potential to be expanded and to cope with many more visitors and customers, as a venue for dining, events and weddings and in the form of accommodation. Since buying the property, an 80-cover restaurant has been installed; they host around 80 weddings a year, and run at least two tours a day through the popular months (charging £12 a head for a still wine tasting, and an extra £6 if you want a 125 ml glass of sparkling). Almost all their home-grown wine is sold through the restaurant at £20 a bottle for the still and £35 for the sparkling, and they sell it at the same prices in the retail shop. 'We have so little wine and so many visitors,' says Davies, 'that we are able to charge these prices'. Annually they sell 70,000 bottles of wine from the site, more than ten times what they produce from their own vineyards, with the profit margin on house-wine better than on their own Welsh wine. 'I can buy house-wine at less than it costs me to produce our own wines,' says Davies. The site also houses a cookery school as well as two luxury holiday suites and seven courtyard studios.

The latest development at Llanerch is a twenty-six-bedroom hotel block that was being built as I visited the vineyard and which will be ready for occupation in spring 2019. Davies has also bought an adjoining 1.6 hectares (4 acres), paying £37,000 per hectare (£15,000 per acre), which will enable them to both expand their vineyards and surround themselves with vines, creating an ideal venue for weddings. At the moment, many of the weddings take place in a marquee, but this will eventually be replaced with a permanent wedding venue, together with a new farm shop selling a range of Welsh products, including other Welsh wines, plus a café and tours centre. In the vineyard, the latest investment is in a £12,000 Boisselet under-vine weeder which Davies hopes will reduce the reliance on herbicides to keep control of the weeds. The 2018 harvest, their best to date, produced 18.5 tonnes.

Taken as a whole, Llanerch offers an example of how many a vineyard in Britain fares. It is established with the enthusiasm of its founders who run it until they retire; it is then taken on by someone who finds the going tough, too tough in this case, who gives up; it is then rescued by entrepreneurs who, knowing very little about the wine business, see an opportunity to use the vineyard and wine production as a base – almost an excuse – for creating a more viable business based upon catering in all its varied forms, tourism, weddings, events and functions and yes, even vineyards and wines. Making money from growing grapes and selling the wine that comes from those grapes on its own is hard, especially if merchants and wholesalers want their share of the proceeds. Basing a business around those vineyards and those wines, adding on what might be termed peripheral activities (although in truth they are actually the mainstream activities) makes good commercial sense. Llanerch looks to be in good hands for the foreseeable future.

Lyme Bay Winery

Shute, Axminster, Devon, EX13 7PW.
www.lymebaywinery.co.uk

Devon winery (no vineyards) making award-winning wines from fruit sourced from Essex, Devon, Dorset and Kent.

Lyme Bay Winery was started in 1993 by Nigel Howard to make cider from apples grown in the South West, including from Julian Temperley's orchards at Burrow Hill in Somerset (from whom they still source fruit). Realizing that cider-making was a very seasonal affair and wanting to extend the productivity of the winery, Howard started bringing in fruit wines made at Broadlands Wineries in Cawston, north Norfolk, fortifying them and bottling them under the Lyme Bay label. Production expanded over the years and James Lambert, now managing director, was brought in from Broadland Wineries to oversee production. The winery expanded, moving from its original base to its current home near Shute, about 10 kilometres (6.25 miles) north-east of Lyme Regis. Today, the sprawling site houses a fairly large production facility and storage warehouses which produce around 850,000 litres of different products a year. Lambert says with both pride and trepidation that they make '219 SKUs (stock keeping units)' which comprise different products, different sizes, different formats and different labels. Included in that total is a significant amount of wine from English-grown grapes. Their range is enormous and includes almost every alcoholic product that one can think of: fruit wines and country wines still and sparkling; meads of all types and styles; apple ciders and fruit ciders; a wide range of liqueurs; gins and rums; and of course, English wines, still and sparkling, red white and rosé. The only product they don't make is beer, but they do sell it.

Lyme Bay's involvement with English wines started in 2009, when they planted their first vineyard. After a three-year search, some land was found at nearby Watchcombe and 1 hectare (2.47 acres) of Seyval Blanc was planted. A second, larger site at Southcote, near Honiton was found and planted in 2009 and 2010 with 7 hectares (17.3 acres) of Bacchus, Seyval Blanc and Pinot Noir. The vines established well and crops, small at first, started to be produced and made into wine by Lambert. He says, 'we were quite excited by the concept of going after the still wine market,' feeling that there was perhaps too much sparkling wine being produced in Britain, and that with the right grape varieties and good winemaking, still wines could form the basis of their English wine business. In the near-perfect conditions of 2014 their 8 hectares of vines managed to produce a grand total of 67 tonnes, but since then yields have been 'less rewarding'.

In 2015, Howard decided to sell the business (the vineyards he owned were sold separately) and it was bought by Geoff Ball, whose family firm is dominant in the floor adhesives business in Britain. Ball had stuck a toe in the wine world by buying a company called Wine Innovations (a *Dragons' Den* business which failed to secure an investor) which packaged wine in individual plastic glasses – the 'Tulip' – using a foil lid:

ideal for picnics, festivals, concerts and general out-of-doors drinking. Whilst on the face of it a great idea, it is logistically challenging, with the wine coming from France, Spain and Chile, the plastic glasses from Scotland, the foils from somewhere else and the only machine in the world that could put all the elements together sited in Malaga in southern Spain. The finished product is shipped to Britain, where Marks & Spencer is the main customer. Ball thought that Lyme Bay would make a good home for this business and decided to invest in it and marry the two together. Whether the wine-in-a-glass concept has a future is debatable. Single-serve wines are very competitively priced but concern by the public about plastics and recyclability and the relatively short shelf life of this method of packaging versus wine in cans, which has a longer shelf life and is 100 per cent recyclable, makes it doubtful.

Until early 2019, when he left to go to a new start-up winery in Essex, Lyme Bay's winemaker was Liam Idzikowski, who joined the company in 2015 having worked his way around the English wine world, taking in a degree at Plumpton, *stages* at Camel Valley, Kingscote and Hush Heath and then joining Langham Vineyard, where he was winemaker for three years and produced many award-winning wines. He also has experience in wineries around the world. Since Idzikowski joined the team, and given that the winery no longer owned any vineyards, the source of many of Lyme Bay's grapes has moved several hundred kilometres east and today it has grape supply contracts with five different producers in Essex and Kent. The company makes no bones about this and is not shy of – in fact is quite proud of – stating on the back labels and on the website where the raw materials come from. Idzikowski feels that the regularity of crops is better in the drier, less wind-swept parts of Britain and that the fruit quality is better. The fruit is picked into 300–350 kilogram covered bulk bins with SO_2 added, trucked down overnight in eight- to twelve-tonne loads, and processed first thing in the morning. Lyme pays £1,800–2,100 per tonne, depending on variety and various other quality-based parameters, which are very typical prices at the moment. They also take fruit from Dorset and Devon and find that the spread of varieties and geographical spread of vineyards enables them to space the pressing out over several weeks. The Watchcombe and Southcote vineyards were not included in the sale of the business and were subsequently sold by Howard, but Lyme Bay still take the fruit from both sites. Southcote sits at between 108 and 145 metres above sea level, and although south-facing, is very exposed and 'in a very wet part of the county' and yields, except in an exceptional year, are going to be irregular and on average, quite low.

Idzikowski is very keen on winemaking and loves to experiment with both still and sparkling wines. The winery is very well equipped with both Willmes and Europress presses (the latter new in 2018) and of course, with the very large volume of other products being produced on-site, such things as refrigeration, handling equipment, bottling and storage are all well catered for. All sparkling wine operations including riddling and disgorging take place on-site. The volume of grapes pressed has risen over the last few years, with 75 tonnes processed in 2017 – 'I would have taken 100 tonnes' says Lambert – and 260 tonnes in 2018. The main varieties processed are Bacchus, Chardonnay, Pinot Noir, Reichensteiner and Seyval Blanc, with smaller amounts of Pinot Gris. One of their growers has planted Pinot Blanc vines and these will start to produce fruit in 2019. Production is split around two-thirds still wine and one-third sparkling, although it is anticipated that the sparkling proportion will increase over the next few years. Since 2015, when they first started entering wines into the national WineGB competition, their medal tally has been impressive: three golds, eleven silvers and fourteen bronzes across three vintages and in every category. Of their three golds, all for still wines, two were for Bacchus wines, one with grapes from Essex and the other with grapes from Kent and Devon, and the third for a Pinot Noir rosé. Six of their silvers were for sparkling wines and given that these were for wines from the 2013 vintage (before Idzikowski took over as winemaker) I would expect to see their sparkling wines from later vintages clocking up the golds before too long. Their tally of awards and medals from other competitions is just as impressive.

Since the new owners took over in 2015, more investment has gone into the business. Lambert says they 'have concentrated on improving the quality of everything we do, that's equipment, systems and people.' They have gained BRC (British Retail Consortium) Global Standard Grade A – 'like two ISO 9000s,' chips in Idzikowski – which enables them to deal with all the major multiples in Britain on a national basis. Sales of Lyme Bay's English wines have been rising over the last few years and in 2016 they represented 7 per cent of turnover, rising to nearly 12 per cent in 2017. They have a lively cellar door trade which accounts for 5 per cent of overall turnover, although they sell 20 per cent of all the English wine they make in this way and this percentage is rising. And what of the future? Lambert and Idzikowski are both cautious and bullish. Cautious about the impact of Brexit – 'nobody knows what's going to happen,' says Lambert – but bullish about their business and especially about their English wines. 'The weakening of the currency has made imported wines more expensive, especially pricier ones such as Champagne, and this has started to normalize the price of English wines. The provenance of wines has become more important to people and anything produced in Britain is getting more prominence,' he continues. 'As guys [and presumably girls] are getting better at both growing grapes and making wine, the cost base is coming down which gives us better margins.' He adds that, 'everyone in the trade wants to premiumize their ranges and overall, we are seeing consumers veering away from the cheapest products, all of which helps English wines.' Lambert and Idzikowski see a positive future for their wines. 'In the last two years we have seen the interest in our English wines growing, especially since we started winning some major awards, and they have become more and more important to us. Over the next ten years I expect to see the English wine market grow significantly,' concludes Lambert. (In January 2019, Idzikowski left Lyme Bay to become winemaker at a start-up winery at Danbury Vineyards in Essex.)

With a different business model to many producers – buying grapes at fixed prices, a winery that handles what will be over 1 million litres of product quite soon, excellent production and packing facilities with the capacity to handle different formats and sizes and a sales operation that is used to dealing with a wide and changing range of products – I see Lyme Bay as having one of the most sustainable English wine businesses in the country.

New Hall Vineyards

Chelmsford Road, Purleigh, Chelmsford, Essex, CM3 6PN.
www.newhallwines.co.uk
44.61 hectares (110.23 acres)

One of Britain's oldest and largest vineyards and still in family hands. Produces a wide range of award-winning wines; twice Winemaker of the Year; major supplier of grapes to other wineries.

New Hall Vineyards was established by Bill and Sheila Greenwood in 1969, when they planted 0.47 hectares (1.16 acres) of Reichensteiner vines (purchased at auction for 23p per vine) on their arable farm. They had their first commercial crop in 1972, a modest 3 tonnes, which was sent to Merrydown Winery in East Sussex (in those days one of the few wineries in the country) for processing. By 2018 it had become one of the biggest vineyards in Britain, with 44.61 hectares (110.23 acres) of vines, including over 12 hectares of Bacchus, significant plantings of Pinot Noir, Huxelrebe, Müller-Thurgau, Schönburger and Acolon, plus a wide range of other varieties. The farm remains firmly in family hands. Sheila Greenwood is still a partner, but her son Piers, who took over the vineyard and winery in 1983, retired in 2016 and Sheila's son-in-law, Chris Trembath, took over Piers' share of the partnership. Trembath's daughter Becki subsequently joined the company. Following Piers' decision to retire, a new vineyard manager, Andy Hares, and operations manager, Lucy Winward, were brought in but during the two-year transition period which saw Piers retire and the Trembaths take over, the business continued without too many changes. Chris Trembath has known the vineyards for almost all his adult life and as a farmer of around 600 hectares (1,500 acres) on the other side of Great Dunmow, is well used to the vicissitudes of agriculture and well aware of what he has taken on as part owner of this enterprise. He says that he wanted to preserve the New Hall name, which he felt would be lost were the vineyards to be sold to another wine producer (there would have undoubtedly been a fairly long queue of buyers) and to keep the family tradition alive. With his daughter Becki helping run things, this makes New Hall one of a small handful of British vineyards where a third generation is involved and set to carry on the family business. Chris admits to being 'very naive about the detail' of the vineyard before he took over but he has learnt a lot over the last few years and now feels in a much better place to take things forward and make improvements in the business.

New Hall is situated in the village of Purleigh which lies between the estuaries of the River Blackwater to the north and the Crouch to the south. This part of Essex, which locals call the Dengie Peninsula, but which New Hall and the ten other vineyards in the area quite understandably call the Crouch Valley, is slowly becoming known for the reliability of its crops and the quality of its grapes, one of the reasons why in 2017 there were in total over 100 hectares (250 acres) of vines, and expanding. With most of the land less than 25 metres above sea level, an annual rainfall of around 500 millimetres and almost guaranteed to be frost free, one can see the attractions of this area. This should in fact be no surprise. Vineyards were planted in Purleigh between the twelfth and fifteenth centuries – one was next to the parish church, only 500 metres from the current vineyards – and Purleigh wine is said to have been drunk at the signing of the Magna Carta in 1215.

As an Essex boy, born and brought up only a few miles away from New Hall, when I first expressed an interest in viticulture as a profession in 1974, my father said, 'We must visit our local vineyard,' which we duly did. I well remember seeing the old railway sleepers used as end-posts (which are still there lining the driveway) and meeting Bill, who was one of the few men I can recall who wore both a stout leather belt and braces. Quite why that sticks in my mind I have no idea.

Piers Greenwood, who is still retained as a consultant, had what I can only call a unique perspective on how to plant, trellis, train and manage a vineyard in Britain. In 1988, working with Karl-Heinz Johner, the German winemaker who was then running Lamberhurst Vineyards, by far the biggest and highest profile vineyard and winery in Britain at that time, Piers planted 18.86 hectares (49.07 acres) of vines, using a Wagner laser-guided planting machine. At that time the only other vineyard to have been machine planted was Denbies, in 1986–7. In order to gain some income from the vineyard in its first three years, the vines were planted at 3.96-metre (13-foot) row width, enabling a forage harvester to cut the lucerne (alfalfa) which had been sown in the vineyard alleyways. This novel aspect to the planting, together with the very relaxed pruning and training regime, and the choice of varieties planted (over a quarter of the 1988 plantings were Pinot Noir and Pinot Blanc) made New Hall unique. Today, vines are still planted in rows far wider than almost any other British vineyard and still trained and managed in what one might call an 'extensive' way. At 3-metre row width, with 1.3 metres between the vines, the vine density is 2,564 hectares (1,038 acres), which is as low as any in the country. However, keeping costs down, always important where there is no upside from selling the crop in bottles, is the secret to making money from growing grapes and the wide spacing and easy pruning and training regime, whilst not one I would advocate to anyone as a way to plant and establish a successful vineyard, obviously works for the New Hall team as they have been doing it like this for 50 years. As mentioned earlier, Piers Greenwood also had a role to play in the production of bottle-fermented sparkling wine in Britain (see p. 71).

For most of the life of the vineyards, the main income has been from selling grapes and wine has played a relatively minor part. Piers was, as he often pointed out, a farmer and grapes were his crop. For many years I would meet him at harvest time, either at Lamberhurst (which I ran from 1988–91) or at Chapel Down (where I also made wine until 2000), when he would deliver grapes, usually well past 11 o'clock at night and sometimes even later, and we would share a chat and a cigarette and discuss things viticultural. Today, whilst things have changed and will change even more in the future, grape sales are still an important part of the income mix. New Hall's grapes, especially (but not only) their Bacchus, attract a premium price for their consistency of supply and quality and Chapel Down as well as some other quite well-known producers as far afield as Cornwall use them in their best wines. Even in disastrous years such as 2012, when many vineyards to the west of the meridian line struggled to produce any grapes (and many had none at all) New Hall still delivered. In 2017, when frost knocked many good vineyards hard and lowered crops by 30 to 50 per cent, New Hall had very respectable yields.

New Hall currently makes around 20–25,000 bottles of sparkling wine a year, including a new sparkling Bacchus which will be a limited edition made to celebrate the vineyard's fiftieth anniversary. They intend to raise volumes of sparkling wines in future vintages, with the rest of their crop being made into still wines for sale to their leaseholder customers (see p. 71), their other retail customers and, in limited amounts, the trade. Their two wholesalers, Hallgarten Wines and Berkmann Wines, mainly sell into the on-trade (restaurants, hotels, pubs) and to private clients. They don't export – they don't have enough wine to need to – and as Chris Trembath says, 'it's a juggling act between selling grapes and making wine'. He is taking a slightly longer-term view about the business and is prepared to invest in bottled wines, still and sparkling, putting more effort into wine sales in order to make better returns and only sell the minimum amount of grapes. He sees the transition to a point where they sell grapes only when crops are larger than their own need for wine as a 'five-year campaign'. They also make wines under contract for an increasing number of vineyards, both locally and from further afield. Most wineries do this and it is of course a good way of creating income from what are in effect fixed assets and fixed labour costs.

On the wine sales side, New Hall is again an outlier when compared to most other English and Welsh wine producers. The New Hall Annual Wine Festival, held since 1972 on the first weekend of September and now in its forty-seventh year, remains a major sales event for them and continues to attract wine lovers from far and wide. New Hall also pioneered what is commonly known as the 'rent-a-vine' scheme, but which they call Own Your Own Vineyard, referring to their customers for this as 'leaseholders'. This scheme was set up following changes to the agricultural tenancy laws in 1996, which allowed people to take short tenancies on land without creating the full three-generation agricultural tenancy which up until then had been the norm. After lengthy negotiations with HM Customs and Excise (now HMRC) it was agreed that, subject to certain conditions, customers could lease a number of vines, in New Hall's case a whole row of 80–90 vines, and contract with the landlord (New Hall) to tend them, harvest the grapes and make the wine which the leaseholder could then have back without payment of excise duty or VAT. They say that this accounts for around 'one-third of all their wine sales,' and their 250 'wine ambassadors' visit quite often, spread the word about their wines and generally contribute to making the place buzz. Other vineyards in Great Britain operate similar vine lease schemes, most notably the largest English Wine producer, Chapel Down, whose scheme on the face of it appears far less generous to their leaseholders than New Hall's. The Trembaths are also set on using the farm and its buildings for income-generating occasions such as weddings, meetings and corporate events, all of which contribute to the bottom line and help sell the wine.

Compared to many of the shiny new vineyards and wineries now scattered across much of southern England and Wales, New Hall is very definitely 'old school'. Its winery buildings, whilst serviceable and able to produce good wines (Piers Greenwood was UKVA 'Winemaker of the Year' in 2013 and 2015 and shared the award in 2016 with another winemaker), are hardly state-of-the art and certainly look like they could do with some updating. The Trembaths have plans to do just that over the years as cash flow allows and have recently invested in 60,000 litres' worth of new stainless steel tanks, bringing their production capacity up to 350,000 bottles, and a third *gyropalette* for riddling their sparkling wines. Better labelling facilities and winery equipment are next on the shopping list with a new press not far behind. On the vineyard front, they are planting another 15 hectares (37 acres) between 2018 and 2020. Varieties being planted include Meunier, which will go into the increasing amounts of sparkling wine they are producing, plus more Bacchus, for which they receive a very good price as grapes, and some Blauer Frühburgunder (Pinot Noir Précoce) for reds and rosés. They firmly believe, with some justification, that the Crouch Valley is becoming recognized as one of the best places in Britain to grow vines and the crop reliability and good grape quality can only help when it comes to selling grapes to less favoured areas. The growers in the area are cooperating with each other and there is talk of a regional association, a vineyard and winery trail and even its own PDO scheme, equivalent to a French *appellation contrôlée* (AC) system.

New Hall is most definitely unusual in the way it grows its grapes and makes and sells its wines. From today's standpoint, where Britain boasts some exceptionally modern vineyards and wineries, some of them very well-funded and financed, New Hall looks somewhat old-fashioned and out-of-date. However, one has to admire the tenacity of its owners, past and present, to stick to what they do well and make money out of viticulture. The very fact that they have survived where others failed and have made wines which, in the last ten years, have more than held their own in the face of strong competition, is a testament to their way of doing things.

Nyetimber Vineyard

Gay Street, West Chiltington, Pulborough, West Sussex, RH20 2HH.
www.nyetimber.com
258 hectares (638 acres)

Britain's largest vineyard owner and producer of a wide range of top-quality premium wines. The first British bottle-fermented sparkling wine producer to gain national and international recognition.

In 1988 the rumours started. There were some crazy people, Americans, who were planting swathes of Chardonnay in the hills above Pulborough. Not only Chardonnay, but Pinot Noir and Meunier as well. And not only those varieties but at a very high density. Where did they think they were? Epernay? Slowly but surely the facts slipped out. They were indeed Americans, from Chicago, heirs to a fortune made in dental equipment – dental chairs, it was said. They had engaged the services of Kit Lindlar, then one of the best-known winemakers in the country, who, out of the public gaze, was making bottle-fermented sparkling wines at his winery near Maidstone. He was being helped by a Champagne producer, Jean-Manuel Jacquinot, who was supplying the know-how to take the grapes from vineyard to the bottle. Vintages came and vintages went. The first harvest was in 1992, but four years later it was still maturing. By now, a winery had been built and equipped, some said lavishly equipped, behind the handsome fifteenth-century manor house that was Nyetimber. Eventually we heard that a wine had been entered into the 1997 International Wine and Spirit Competition (IWSC) and we all waited with apprehension.

That first wine, the 1992 Nyetimber Première Cuvée Blanc de Blancs (100 per cent Chardonnay) surprised us all. It won not only a gold medal, but also the English Wine Trophy.[34] Their second release, the 1993 Nyetimber Classic Cuvée (a Chardonnay, Pinot Noir, Meunier blend) went one better: a gold medal, the English Wine Trophy *and* the Bottle Fermented Sparkling Wine Trophy for the best (non-Champagne) sparkling wine in the 1998 IWSC. Their third wine, the 1993 Nyetimber Première Cuvée, was again awarded a gold medal, the English Wine Trophy and – just to ring the changes – the IWSC Most Impressive Wine Presentation Trophy in the 1999 IWSC. After these major awards most of us realized that things would never be quite the same again and that the days of German-variety-based still wines were over.

Since then, Nyetimber has become the English sparkling wine known for its exceptionally high quality and is (currently) second only to Chapel Down in terms of volume of production and distribution. To me it is Britain's Krug or Bollinger to Chapel Down's Moët et Chandon. After the original owners, Sandy and Stuart Moss, retired in 2001, the estate was bought by Andy and Nichola Hill (he best known for writing the Eurovision winner 'Making your mind up' for the appropriately named group 'Bucks Fizz') who kept it for five years until a divorce meant they had to sell. Prior to selling, they had a 69-page

34 To put this in perspective, the IWSC had awarded their English Wine Trophy to sparkling wines before: the 1991 trophy went to the 1989 Rock Lodge Impresario Sparkling, the 1992 trophy to the 1989 Throwley Chardonnay Sparkling and the 1993 trophy to the 1987 Carr Taylor Vintage Sparkling.

financial report produced which made pretty grim reading. Yields were low – the average from 1997 to 2005 was 19.5 hectolitres per hectare – and stocks were high and getting bigger. Sales were rising – 45,356 bottles in the year ending 31 March 2005 – but production was 'inefficient', stock control 'poor', the 'assumed cost of a bottle of wine of £5 a bottle was incorrect' (it was actually £8.84), there was 'no cohesive sales or marketing plan', 'the staff decided what needed doing and when' and 'leadership was required'. At this point Eric Heerema enters the picture.

Heerema, who was variously reported as being an ex-lawyer, ex-venture capitalist and businessman, had been living in Britain with his family for over a decade and had made his home there. He had already dipped his toes into English wine and had planted an 8.3-hectare vineyard at Coldharbour, his nearby country home. In 2004 he decided that he wanted to create 'a commercially viable project of quite considerable scale' and do for English sparkling wines 'what McAlpine did for still wines in the 1980s at Lamberhurst.' To this end, in April 2005, he had meetings with Hill to see whether he would sell Nyetimber, but negotiations foundered as their ideas of value were too far apart. In August 2005, the Hills having announced their separation and with lawyers involved, their need to sell became more acute and they got back in touch with Heerema. After several months of negotiations, not helped by the divorce proceedings, a price was agreed, and on 3 March 2006, for £7.4 million, Heerema, then aged 46, became the proud owner of Nyetimber.

Prior to the purchase, Heerema had already researched land in the area to expand the vineyards and between February and April 2006 was able to buy several suitable blocks. Within weeks of taking over he expanded the vineyards and in 2006, 2007 and 2008 an additional 81.4 hectares of vines – over 300,000 vines – were planted: 51.7 hectares at nearby Upperton, Tillington and Nutbourne Lane; 21.2 hectares at Bignor alongside the Roman Villa (since sold); and 8.5 hectares at Nyetimber itself. These plantings brought the total under vine by the end of 2008, including the 8.3 hectares at Heerema's house (also since sold), to 105.25 hectares. Since those early days of Heerema's ownership, Nyetimber's vineyards have grown, and continue to expand. In 2009–10, 58.31 hectares of chalk pasture land on two sites near Stockbridge in Hampshire were bought and planted; the West Chiltington

Golf Club, which adjoined the home vineyards, was bought in 2016 and planted with 47.2 hectares of vines; 19 hectares on the Chartham Downs near Canterbury, Kent were purchased in 2017 and planted in 2017–18; and a further 28 hectares at Lacton Manor, Westwell, Kent, adjoining the existing Westwell Vineyard (owned by others), between Charing and Ashford, were leased and planted in 2018 and 2019. Together these vineyards amount to 258 hectares (638 acres) with an *encépagement* of 45 per cent Chardonnay, 35 per cent Pinot Noir and 20 per cent Meunier. Heerema hasn't stopped expanding what is already the biggest vineyard holding in the country. He would ideally like to buy more land – another 200 hectares (500 acres) is being talked about – and expand still further. Whilst 500 hectares might seem an enormous area of vineyard for a British producer, compared to, say, Taittinger, with almost 600 hectares (owned and under contract), in a world context it isn't.

Since the early days, when the first three vintages were made by Lindlar (with Jacquinot's help), the winery has been in a number of hands. After the Mosses sold (Sandy Moss had been the winemaker), Peter Morgan, an ex-Plumpton student who had worked at both Ridgeview and Davenport, took over for two vintages, 2002 and 2003, before returning to Plumpton College. He was replaced by Irishman Dermot Sugrue (now star winemaker at Wiston), who had been recruited as assistant winemaker by Morgan the previous year. Sugrue stayed there for two vintages, 2004 and 2005, but left before the first vintage under Heerema's ownership, the 2006. For that vintage, a freshly graduated Plumpton student, Belinda Kemp, was employed, and together she and Jacquinot handled the botrytis-plagued vintage. Wishing to bring some stability to what is unquestionably the most important position in any wine-producing operation, Heerema looked far and wide for a new winemaker. His searches produced Canadian Cherie Spriggs, who studied in Canada (Ontario and British Columbia) and Adelaide and whose husband, Brad Greatrix, was also part of the package and helps run the winery. Cherie and Brad's winemaking CVs include time spent at wineries in Australia, Canada, France, New Zealand and the USA (Oregon) and they came to Britain with considerable international experience. Spriggs' first harvest was the difficult 2007, followed by the even more challenging 2008 – two vintages which would test any winemaker's patience. Once Spriggs had her feet under the winery table she ended the Jacquinot-inspired policy of not letting wines go through the malolactic conversion and instigated a much stricter regime with regard to cleanliness and non-oxidative pressing, handling and storage of wines. Jacquinot and Nyetimber parted company in May 2009.

Since then, there have been great changes in the winery both in terms of location and size. Initial plans by Heerema to build a dream winery at Nyetimber were shelved (owing to access problems) in favour of a site a few miles away at Brinsbury College, handily situated on the A29 road. However, with delays in design and planning and with the new vineyards coming on-stream, for the 2010 vintage a winery was fitted out in a building on an unlovely trading estate in nearby Crawley, where it remains today. In addition to this facility, a new pressing station was built in the centre of their Manor (home) vineyards for the 2017 harvest and the juice can now be tankered to the winery. Spriggs ditched the single Magnum press that they had used since the original Nyetimber winery was built for the 1995 vintage (selling it to Hush Heath) and replaced it (over the years since 2008) with six Coquard PAI presses – five eight tonne and one four tonne – the larger ones costing around €250,000 (£220,000) each. To the uninitiated, PAI might not sound like much, but to an aficionado of grape presses, these are reckoned to be the best for whole-bunch Champagne-style wines. (Monsieur Coquard was surprised to be able to say one year that he'd sold more PAI presses to the British than to the Champenoise.) At the pressing centre there is an automated loading system for grapes, which are picked into 15-kilogram crates; juice falls by gravity into settling tanks. Of course, it's not all been plain sailing. Harvests have sometimes been plagued by disease and the decision not to pick any grapes at all from the 2012 harvest must have been a disappointment. However, the event was in one sense put to good advantage in that it was seen by the outside world as a sign of the pursuit of quality at any price. Since then, the quality of the viticulture has improved so hopefully that type of event can be avoided in future.

Nyetimber's wines, from the very first releases over 20 years ago, have always impressed. Those first few, the 1992 and 1993 wines with their chunky acidity and long-aged toasty, brioche notes on both nose and palate were outstanding and won their medals and trophies with ease and on merit. They won them because they were amazingly good and so far ahead of the opposition that even the word opposition is wrong: they were playing a totally different game. Since then, once the Spriggs–Greatrix team settled in, cleared out the wines and practices they didn't like, and got to grips with the grapes they were getting from myriad different vineyards, the wines have certainly improved and taken on a style of their own. Purity of fruit, excellent balance and a lighter touch with the dosage (as the acid levels are lower) are their hallmark. Oak is used sparingly – a small proportion (less than 5 per cent) of the *blanc de blancs* is aged for less than 6 months in new *barriques* and the red proportion of the rosé (around 10–12 per cent) will also see some time in older oak. Wines are aged longer than in most British wineries, undoubtedly not having financial pressures to get wines on the market helps with that, and typically the multi-vintage Classic Cuvée will be three years on lees, with the *blanc de blancs* having five years. The multi-vintage wine, which contains reserve wines going back to Spriggs' first vintage in 2007, is the first true non-vintage wine from any British winery. Most non-vintage wines are at best a two to three vintage blend, at worst just an easy way to get over the problem of printing new labels every vintage. The multi-vintage Classic Cuvée is now Nyetimber's most widely distributed wine, and presumably made in the greatest volume. The last vintage Classic Cuvée was in 2010; they put aside around 25 to 30 per cent of production every year for the multi-vintage Classic Cuvée. Their most impressive wine (prior to the release of the 1086 range – see below) has been the Tillington Single Vineyard range of wines which retail for around £75–£80.

In mid-2018, to much fanfare and acclaim, they launched a new line of very upmarket, newly packaged prestige cuvées under the '1086' label, referencing the village's mention in the Domesday Book. The wines are a white classic cuvée from 2009 (46 per cent Chardonnay, 43 per cent Pinot Noir and 9 per cent Meunier) priced at £150 a bottle and a 2010 rosé (75 per cent Pinot Noir and 25 per cent Chardonnay) priced at £175. Those that have tasted them have given them very good reviews and on quality grounds alone, they probably deserve to stand alongside similarly priced prestige Champagnes. Whether the prestige Champagne-buying public will cough up is another matter, but it is a bold move and one that will undoubtedly make some other English sparkling wine producers sit up, take notice and probably emulate. Since the 2009 vintage all their wines have been bottled in almost black bottles, something Tom Stevenson, the wine writer, wine taster and sparkling wine specialist, thinks 'will change sparkling wine production throughout the world'. Sparkling wines can become 'light struck' if light (either natural or artificial) gets to them which will produce a smell of 'drains and cabbages'. This is a particular problem in wines bottled in clear glass such as rosé wines.

In 2017 Nyetimber launched a brand called 'N' which is gorgeously bottled in a matt gold bottle, sports a Union Jack inspired neck collar and – somewhat intriguingly – has the words 'Mayfair London' dead-centre on the front of the label (that's where the London office is). This Champagne variety blend is the only Nyetimber wine to be made partly from bought-in grapes plus some of the *taille* (second-pressings) which up until then had not been used in their other wines. It is a non-vintage with around 15 per cent reserve wines. At the moment (2017) it is only available for export to the on-trade, which I assume means upmarket restaurants and nightclubs where wine in gold bottles is presumably a common sight.

Exports for Nyetimber are still at an embryonic stage – 'We started much later than everyone else,' says Heerema – and are mainly to the east coast of the US, with Hong Kong, Singapore and Japan showing interest, plus Denmark, Sweden and Norway. Heerema would like to build up exports to 'twenty to twenty-five per cent of sales'. As of 2017 they amounted to around 8 per cent of sales.

Heerema comes over as an intensely private man and one who would rather not be talking about himself or his finances and especially not his empire of wine. At Nyetimber there is no farm shop, no public tasting room, and no tours, although there are now a limited number of 'open days' each year and certain private events are held there. Their website must also be unique for a wine producer in that there is no facility to buy wine (or even prices for that matter). They also avoid most (but not all) wine competitions, preferring not to be judged in competitions that have separate classes for wines of British origin, but judged 'amongst their peers', in other words against Champagnes and other high-class sparkling wines from around the world. From 2001–8 they entered their wines in UKVA competitions, winning an almost unbroken number of gold medals and trophies, including the Gore-Browne for best wine four years on the trot – 2003–6. Sandra Moss won the McAlpine Trophy for British Winemaker of the Year in 2001, the first year it was awarded. In 2009 and 2010 they only entered one wine a year, each of which won a silver, since when no more Nyetimber wines have been entered into this competition. They have stuck to the IWC, IWSC and Tom Stevenson's 'Champagne and Sparkling Wine World Championships', declining to enter their wines into the biggest competition, the Decanter World Wine Awards. In these three competitions their tally of top medals has been high and consistent. Over the five years between 2014 and 2018 they were awarded twenty-two gold medals, far more than their next nearest rivals, Hattingley, with sixteen, Camel Valley with fourteen, Wiston with eleven and Chapel Down with ten. In 2018, Spriggs was awarded the IWC Sparkling Winemaker of the Year, the first time this award had gone to either a woman or someone outside Champagne. I am not sure which of those achievements is more important, but either way this is a very significant moment for Spriggs herself, Nyetimber and English sparkling wine in general. Like almost all vineyards in Britain, the 2018 vintage for Nyetimber was their largest ever and with 170 hectares (420 acres) fully cropping, Spriggs said that she 'feels confident in expecting a production volume of well over a million bottles, including setting aside reserve wines'.

What the team at Nyetimber has achieved under Heerema's ownership has been quite amazing and deserves to be praised by everyone involved with growing grapes and making wine in Britain. It truly is the flagship of the fleet in terms of wine quality, branding and marketing. Of course, having enough money to spend on both infrastructure and personnel helps and getting Nyetimber to this point has not been cheap. The source of the wealth Heerema has lavished on this project is not difficult to find out about with a quick trawl on the internet, but suffice it to say that there appear to be unlimited funds for the enterprise. I had lunch with him in around 2008 and he told me that he had earmarked £50 million for the project. Interviewing him this time around, I suggested that he must be through that first £50 million and well into the next £50 million. He declined to answer, but the accounts of the Jersey registered holding company would suggest this is correct. When I asked whether there was a profit on the horizon he said, 'Yes, but not yet within our grasp.' One can only wish Heerema and his team well and look forward to many more excellent wines to come.

Above: Breaky Bottom is one of the UK's more remote vineyards, despite being only a few kilometers from Brighton. It sits in a fold in the South Downs, sheltered from the prevailing south-westerly winds that come up the Channel.

Below: Chapel Down's home vineyard was the original one planted at their Tenterden winery site. With its south facing aspect, tall perimeter hedges and rising land providing shelter from the prevailing south-westerly winds, it was once declared the 'finest site in the south-east of England' to grow vines.

Above: Flint Vineyard, one of the UK's rising star wine producers, has a simple but effective winery converted from a former grain storage barn.

Below: Harrow & Hope, one of the UK's newer vineyards, is already winning prizes and awards. High density planting and a gravel-rich, free-draining soil are the perfect combination for high quality Chardonnay, Pinot Noir and Meunier grapes.

Above: Tucked into a high valley above Henley-on-Thames in the Chilterns, Hundred Hills' award-winning winery and its immaculate vineyards are set to produce wines of world-class quality.

Below: Llanerch, Wales' oldest vineyard, still crops some of its 1986-planted vines and trains them on the Lyre system, unusual for Great Britain.

Above: Lyme Bay takes grapes from a number of vineyards spread across Great Britain and crafts them into award-wines in their very modern winery.

Below: New Hall is in one of the driest part of Great Britain, and its vineyards, on sheltered, south-facing slopes and at around 20 metres above sea level, are kept frost-free by proximity to the sea. The cropping record here is one of the most consistent in the country.

Above: Nyetimber, the largest vineyard owner in Great Britain and inarguably the producer making the country's best sparkling wines, has vineyards spread across the south of England.

Below: Sandhurst Vineyards in Kent, supplier of grapes to many well-known wineries, has been growing vines since 1986 and has a track record of cropping that is one of the best in the country.

Above: Occupying a spit of land almost surrounded by the River Dart in Devon, Sharpham Vineyards has been producing good wines (and cheeses) since the mid-1980s.

Below: On chalky soil in Barham, near Canterbury, Simpsons Wine Estate is one of the new breed of wine producers in Britain. With experience garnered selling 400,000 bottles a year from their 40 hectares in the Languedoc, they are bringing their marketing skills to bear on a superb range of both still and sparkling English wines.

Above: Simon Day at Sixteen Ridges Vineyard, also produces own-rooted vines in commercial quantities using the latest in propagation techniques.

Below: The Leckford Estate Vineyard, part of the John Lewis Partnership, produces excellent quality sparkling wines using the Champagne trio of grape varieties. These wines are exclusive to the supermarket Waitrose, also owned by the Partnership.

Above: Winbirri, Norfolk's largest and most successful wine producer, situated just to the east of Norwich, has vineyards spread across the village of Surlingham. Winning the Decanter World Wine Awards 'Best Value White Single Varietal' trophy with their 2015 Bacchus really put them on the map.

Below: Despite being in North Yorkshire, the vineyards at Yorkshire Heart produce a range of wines that sell to visitors, tourists and local outlets keen to taste and enjoy a wine from such an unlikely location.

Oxney Organic Vineyard

Little Bellhurst Farm, Hobbs Lane, Beckley, Rye, East Sussex, TN31 6TU.
www.oxneyestate.com
13.65 hectares (33.73 acres)

Britain's largest organic vineyard producing very high quality, award-winning wines.

Sitting in meetings, dealing with clients, worrying about staff, budgeting, keeping the show on the road, such is the daily diet of a business owner. Sometimes the mind starts to wander. Wouldn't it be idyllic to sell up, buy a small farm, live in the country surrounded by (one's own) fields and really get back to nature? Maybe start a small business, a vineyard? I hear English wine is becoming very well thought of. Thus it was (well, almost) that Kristin Syltevik, her partner Paul Dobson and their twelve-year-old son Isak, found themselves farming on the Kent–East Sussex border, a few miles north-west of Rye.

Syltevik, who was born in Norway, first came to Britain as an eighteen-year-old, in 1984, to work as an au pair. After studying marketing and business she worked in the PR industry, specializing in high-tech and new media accounts, becoming managing director of Miller Shandwick (now part of Weber Shandwick) in 1996, aged thirty-one. In 2000 she and a partner founded their own media agency, Hotwire, and within a few years they had nearly 200 employees in offices around the world. In 2007 the Australian Photon Group bought the company and after running it for the new owners for five years Syltevik left in July 2012.

Syltevik's first brush with the countryside and with farming was when in 2002 she bought a house and six acres near Chiddingly in East Sussex. Here she and Dobson, at the time a professional golfer, had an organic vegetable garden and a few sheep and chickens and had started to learn about earning a living from the land. Once she sold Hotwire, Syltevik decided to invest the proceeds in 'land or gold' as the stock market at the time wasn't doing so well. Luckily, she chose land and in 2009 bought her first farm, 100 hectares (250 acres) at what was then called Little Bellhurst Farm in Beckley, East Sussex. This she and Dobson, neither with any farming experience or training, decided to farm themselves. Subsequently she bought a further 243 hectares (600 acres) of farmland, some of it on the other side of the Kent Ditch, on the Isle of Oxney (after which the vineyard and winery are now known) where she and Dobson now live and farm. All farming is done organically to Soil Association standards and Dobson is now contract farming for other organic farmers in the area, putting to good use the impressive array of cultivation equipment he has at his disposal. His latest purchase has been an £80,000 Swedish precision seed drill and inter-row hoe which uses GPS and cameras to know where it is and where the crop is.

I first met Syltevik in early 2011 when we started discussing the possibilities and practicalities of planting a vineyard on the land at Little Bellhurst. From the outset, she had fairly firm ideas about what she was trying to achieve in terms both of wine style and marketing opportunities. The need to be organic was first on the shopping list and despite my doubts about the practicalities of this method of producing grapes in Britain, nothing would move Syltevik from her ideas. The land is between 15 and 20 metres above sea level, some east facing, some west facing and some level. The soil is predominantly a mixture of clay and loam, alluvial in places and slightly acid. Drainage is an issue and all the land planted with vines was pipe-drained at 10-metre intervals before planting. This part of the world is known for its mixed farms, its grazing for sheep and cattle, its hops and top fruit, and is dominated by the River Rother, the source of which is near Rotherfield in East Sussex and whose tributaries have helped shape the undulating land it flows through. Until the mid-seventeenth century the river was navigable to ships and barges and the ports of Bodiam, Small Hythe and Appledore all had access to the sea at Rye. Since then, the land has been progressively drained and protected with sea walls and drainage systems, so today there is little evidence of its once tidal nature.

The first vines went in the ground on a wet Saturday in early May 2012. I had earlier advised Syltevik to use a GPS planting machine, but fears that planting machines made trunk diseases worse persuaded Syltevik that she wanted to plant all 8,455 vines by hand, using spades. Having done this myself many times, including in 1977 when I planted my first vineyard, I knew what this involved and attempted to dissuade her, but she was adamant. The weather during April 2012 was dreadful, some of the worst on record, and rain and cool conditions meant that the site didn't get prepared in time to dry out and once it was prepared, digging conditions were bad. However, bit by bit, vine by vine, and row by row the vines went in and after about three weeks the job was done.

The varieties planted that first year were Chardonnay 46 per cent,

Pinot Noir 36 per cent and Meunier 18 per cent, amounting to 2.03 hectares (5.01 acres). In the following two years more vines were planted (this time by GPS-guided machine) including more Chardonnay, Pinot Noir and Meunier, plus, at my insistence, 5,325 Seyval Blanc vines. This variety had been suggested originally as the track record of yields of pure *viniferas* grown organically and biodynamically in Britain is poor and I knew that Seyval, despite all the bad press it has had over the years (mainly it seems from people with little experience of either growing it or making wine from it), produced results and was not for nothing known as 'save-all' when it came to cropping in difficult years and difficult conditions. 2013 and 2014's plantings brought the planted area up to 8.08 hectares (19.97 acres). In 2016, with sales of wines gathering pace, Syltevik decided that she needed to increase the size of her vineyard in order to meet anticipated sales. In May 2018, a further 23,200 vines were planted, Chardonnay and Pinot Noir (but no Meunier as the performance of those already planted had not lived up to expectations) plus 1,500 Blauer Frühburgunder (Pinot Noir Précoce) in order to bolster the ever-popular still rosé. The planted area was now up to 13.65 hectares (33.73 acres) making it the largest organic vineyard in Britain by quite a margin. The *encepagement* is now 37 per cent Chardonnay, 43.5 per cent Pinot Noir, 9.4 per cent Seyval Blanc, 7.5 per cent Meunier and 2.6 per cent Frühburgunder.

Despite never having wielded anything much heavier than a garden spade in her pre-vineyard life, and to my great surprise, Syltevik decided that she didn't need the help of fencing and trellising contractors and together she and Dobson installed all the perimeter deer and rabbit fencing, and all the many thousands of planting stakes, intermediate stakes, end-posts and anchors that go into 68 kilometres (43 miles) of vineyard. Seven years later Syltevik says 'we are still tired from doing it'. Their only very minor glitch came when they installed the end-posts in the first vineyard the wrong way round, but despite my misgivings, they appear to do the job just as well. The first vineyard was also installed using planting stakes cut from the farm's own oak, but these quickly bent and twisted in the weather and for all future vineyards, galvanized steel planting stakes were used.

Even before the first vines were planted, Syltevik had decided that she wanted to have her own winery. She also knew that she wanted to create a destination where visitors, hopefully all wine buyers, could come and taste the wines. In a previous life the farm had grown hops, the only remaining evidence of this being the classic square oast house, complete with wooden cowl, which today houses part of the winery and the farm shop. For the 2018 harvest a much larger barn for additional tank space and wine storage was built. The winery is fully equipped for both still and sparkling wines, including for riddling and disgorging. Winemaking is a joint operation between Syltevik and winemaker Ben Smith, who 'does the hard work'. Winemaking consultant David Cowderoy was used for the initial vintages.

To date Syltevik puts the bill for the vineyard and winery enterprise (not including the land) at 'around £2 million'. She says that it's difficult to be exact about the total investment as the wine side is just part of the partnership's farming and leisure enterprise. Apart from the farms, the flock of sheep and the vineyards, there are also some very tasteful holiday cottages, two bijou shepherd's huts, and two biomass boilers to heat not only all the accommodation on both farms, but also a huge barn which can hold 'hundreds of tonnes' of their prize organic wheat, barley and oats, all of which can be dried using woodchips from their own woods.

The first harvest at Oxney Organic was in 2014 and produced around 1,650 bottles (75 cl) of a delicate, delicious Pinot Noir and Meunier still rosé, released in May 2015 and sold out – at £14 a bottle – straight away, plus 2,000 bottles of classic cuvée sparkling. Harvest 2015 produced 5,000 still rosé and 4,500 sparkling; harvest 2016 was relatively small as the flowering was poor, but despite the frost, 2017 produced just under 20 tonnes – 9 tonnes of which came from the 1.28 hectares (3.16 acres) of Seyval – and 2018 produced their best yield to date, 57 tonnes, with some grapes left on the vines as they ran out of tank space. Now that the 2012–14 plantings are getting more mature and Syltevik and her crew are getting better at both disease- and weed-control – the two tasks which are most difficult in organic vineyards – yields are settling down and improving, subject to vintage variation. Yields in organic and biodynamic vineyards in Britain are never going to be as large as those in conventional vineyards (in themselves not large by world standards) and it seems that if Oxney can average 4–5 tonnes per hectare (1.6–2 tonnes per acre) then they will be as good as any in the country. They have also started to produce organic bottle-fermented cider using fruit from local orchards.

On the wine quality side, the tally of medals and awards, mainly golds and silvers, is impressive and better than that of a lot of non-organic vineyards. Their first sparkling wine, the 2014, was released in December 2016 and gained a silver in the IWC and a score of 17/20 from the notoriously tough-marking Jancis Robinson MW, while their 2015 Rosé was awarded the Waitrose Rosé Trophy in the WineGB awards. From such a young vineyard, especially an organic one, this is an impressive start. Growing vines organically and producing economically viable yields in Britain was never going to be easy, and Syltevik and her team have to be admired for the way they have taken on the challenge and made an impressive start. As the new vineyards start cropping and volumes rise, Oxney Organic wines are bound to become much better known.

Sandhurst Vineyards

Hoads Farm, Crouch Lane, Sandhurst, Kent, TN18 5NT.
29.95 hectares (74 acres)

One of the largest (and oldest) vineyard owners in Britain, supplying top-quality grapes to several important wineries.

Chris Nicholas has been growing grapes since he planted around 550 vines in his garden in 1986, aged 25. The varieties he planted – Bacchus, Cascade, Reichensteiner, Siegerrebe and Seyval Blanc – were pretty standard for the day. He was so encouraged by the way they established and the high yield they achieved in their second year, that he started to think about vines as a commercial crop for the family farm, which had been bought by his maternal grandparents in 1939 and taken over by his father and mother in 1956. It was principally a hop farm, with some arable, fruit and sheep – a very typical Wealden farm for its day – and Chris has been working on it since 1981, a year after he left agricultural college. He came to see me at Tenterden Vineyard, to talk about growing vines commercially. He wanted to know if I was interested in helping, to both supply vines and set up the vineyard, but more importantly, in persuading his fairly sceptical father that vines could be a profitable enterprise. As I recall, with some hesitation, his father agreed that Chris could plant 0.61 hectares (1.5 acres) of Seyval Blanc on a field above their oast house which had just come out of hops. This for me was the first of many plantings, on both this farm and others, that I undertook as I started my career as a viticultural consultant. In order to gain experience, Chris also took on the running and management of nearby Castle Vineyards (today called Bodiam Vineyards) which had been planted in a fit of enthusiasm by a very large local farming estate, but with which they had become disenchanted. Chris ran this 1.82-hectare (4.5-acre) mixed variety vineyard – there were nine varieties planted including (rarely for the time) some Pinot Noir and Auxerrois – and brought the grapes to me for contract winemaking, which was the other half of my fledgling business. He also planted, managed, and took the grapes from another little local vineyard called Challenden, owned by a family friend. Sandhurst wines always did quite well in competitions, winning gold medals with Bacchus wines on three occasions and the Bernard Theobald Trophy for Best Red with a Pinot Noir.

Since those early days, almost three decades ago, Chris has planted more and more vineyards. He started in 1989–90 with Bacchus, Reichensteiner, Schönburger and Seyval Blanc under contract to Lamberhurst Vineyards (where I took over as winemaker and general manager from 1988 until 1991) followed by a block of reds – Dornfelder, Pinot Noir Précoce, Regent and Rondo (then still called Gm 6494-5) – in 2001. As his experience as a grower developed and as grapes as a financially rewarding crop started to prove themselves, more and more plantings followed. By now Lamberhurst had gone its own way, but its contracts had been taken over by Chapel Down, which recognized both Chris' qualities as a grower and the quality of his grapes, especially of his Bacchus, which has often been the mainstay of their Bacchus Reserve. As the quality of his grapes became better known and as the sparkling boom got under way, other wineries approached him to grow for them, and fairly large blocks of Chardonnay, Meunier, Pinot Noir and Pinot Blanc were planted. He also continued to have relatively small volumes of wine made from some of his grapes and planted a 0.4-hectare (1-acre) block of Albariño for his own wine, and as an experiment to see how it would do. Having grubbed-up the last Seyval Blanc vineyard in 2004, when Lamberhurst stopped using it and Chapel Down didn't want it, he has since replanted new vineyards with it, plus Reichensteiner for wineries that want to make entry-level wines and for which larger quantities of cheaper grapes are required. Latest plantings have been of Bacchus, Chardonnay, Reichensteiner and Pinot Gris for a winery in the south-west of Britain which cannot grow anything like the necessary quality and the quantity of grapes in their region. All vines today are planted at 2-metre row width, with most varieties since 2012 planted at 1-metre intervine distance instead of 1.2 metres and 1.3 metres. Chris finds that the higher density gives earlier yields, often taken in year two, better quality and better quantity – all things that make a huge difference to someone who lives by growing grapes alone and who cannot rely on any further income from selling wine by the bottle. All grapes are supplied on long-term grape supply contracts.

Over the years, land has been bought and sold, some rented and then given up, but today the farm is 142 hectares (350 acres), split into two major blocks either side of the village of Sandhurst. There are 29.95 hectares (74 acres) of vines, 52.61 hectares (130 acres) of hops and a small area of cherries. The remainder is arable and woodland; the sheep and the apples have gone. In addition, the Nicholases also look after 14.97 hectares (37 acres) of Bacchus and Meunier on land next door to their farm for Chapel Down. Chris gave up having wine made on his own account in around 2000, preferring to stick to what he and the family do best – growing good quality grapes. Since his father retired in 1996, Chris has run the whole farm with a minimum of staff. His wife Nicola works full-time on it, plus in recent years their two sons have joined the team: Alex looks after the vines and Sebastien is the hop specialist. In 2018 Chris nominally retired, although he can still be found during the growing season sitting on the back of a tractor more often than not.

One way in which the Nicholases differ from other growers is in the cost structure of both planting and establishing their vineyards and the way they manage and run them. Having supplied every vine they have ever planted, I know that they always use good quality plants which, since 2000, have been GPS machine planted. They do almost all the site preparation themselves, and in most cases use the minimum of bought-in (new) materials, putting up the trellising using second-hand hop wire, with second-hand end-posts and anchors, although of course, some new inputs are inevitable. Having erected (and sometimes taken down or repaired) hop gardens since 1939, working with posts and wire, putting in anchors and erecting trellising comes as second nature and the team they use knows what they are doing and understands how to do it efficiently and economically. Typical establishment costs (without the land, but including all vines, trellising materials and labour) would be around £15,000 per hectare (£6,000 per acre) – about half what many growers would spend using contractors and high-end galvanized metal posts, anchors and wire. They also try to ensure that their new vines establish well so that they can take a crop in year two – a crop that in many instances is enough to pay for 50 per cent of the establishment costs.

On the running costs side, the Nicholases score by keeping it in the family, employing only one full-timer plus, when needed, casual labourers (who can also help with the hand-work in the hops) and doing as much of the work as possible themselves – pretty much all of the pruning, all of the tractor work and spraying (thus keeping the casual labour costs down as much as possible). One example is spring lower shoot removal, which almost all other growers do by hand at considerable expense, but which Sandhurst do by spraying twice with an approved material, something which hop growers have always done as a matter of routine. Three men, one tractor and 5 litres of herbicide (cost £315) does the job in one 10-hour day on 30 hectares (75 acres) of vines – something which would take a team doing it by hand many days. One area where costs are not spared, and if anything might even be higher than those of other growers, is in two essentials: the cost of protecting the vines against pests and diseases; and the costs of vine nutrition. Their experience in hops over the decades has shown them that money spent on good sprayers and good spraying is an effective insurance policy against losses, and that when you grow good yields you need to replace the nutrients the crop removes. Their annual costs for spraying will seldom be less than £1,200 per hectare (£486 per acre) and often nearer £1,400 per hectare (£567 per acre), excluding application costs. To keep the application costs as low as possible, 2018 saw the purchase of a new £24,000, 1,500 litre twin-axle Berthoud sprayer which sprays three rows at a time and is capable of getting around all 30 hectares in two and a half days. This replaces single-row Victair sprayers, better suited to hops, where over-the-row spraying is not possible.

Overall, the annual cost of farming their vineyards (excluding picking costs) is not much more than £5,000 per hectare (£2,000 per acre) which is probably 70 per cent of that in many other vineyards. The vines are walked by an agronomist every two weeks who advises what to spray and they keep on top of the nutrient status of their vines with regular petiole analysis. Light brown apple moth and spotted wing drosophila (SWD) are monitored and sprayed against when necessary. Windbreaks and shelter belts are trimmed back as the ripening period starts in order to reduce the numbers of wild blackberries, a favourite breeding ground for SWD. They would prefer to use a predator against both of these insect pests (much as they do in hops against red spider mites and aphids) and Chris feels sure that eventually one will be developed for vines. Having grown a good crop, they are more than anxious not to lose it. Of course, there are unknowns on the horizon, Brexit and the casual labour issue for one. 'Picking could be a nightmare,' says Chris, 'unless we can get overseas pickers'. He is hopeful that he has an advantage with both hops and grapes to harvest, giving pickers a longer period of work than just grapes.

Financially, grapes have been a good crop for the Nicholases. Average yields over thirty years and across all varieties have been around 8.65 tonnes per hectare (3.5 tonnes per acre) with varieties such as Reichensteiner achieving 10.62 tonnes per hectare (4.3 tonnes per acre) and Seyval Blanc 11.12 tonnes per hectare (4.5 tonnes per acre). In 2017, a year when late April and early May frosts took much of their early growth, they still picked 177 tonnes off 25.9 hectares (64 acres) – a rate of 6.83 tonnes per hectare (2.77 tonnes per acre). In 2018 they picked their largest crop to date, a shade under 400 tonnes off 25.9 hectares (64 acres), which averages out at 15.44 tonnes per hectare (6.25 tonnes per acre). Prices of grapes have fluctuated over the years with varieties such as Seyval Blanc in the 1980s and 1990s going for £650 per tonne (picked and delivered) and Schönburger better at between £1,400 and £1,600 a tonne depending on sugar level. At the time, Schönburger was Lamberhurst's most expensive wine and won them the Gore-Browne Trophy for English Wine of the Year in both 1985 and 1990. Today, prices achieved, especially for lower yielding varieties such as the reds and the Champagne varieties, are higher than average, in some cases considerably higher, although nowhere near the ultra-high prices that some grapes have gone for in recent years – sometimes as high as £3,500 per tonne (and even higher, it is rumoured). These high prices have been occasioned by several factors: the very low (or even non-existent) crop in some vineyards in 2012; the realization by some large, established growers that their sites are incapable of producing yields much above 5 tonnes per hectare (2 tonnes per acre); the realization by some growers that their growing costs are very high and that even at seemingly quite high prices, buying grapes is cheaper than growing grapes themselves;

and finally the entry into the grape-buying market of several producers who don't grow any grapes at all, don't have (or have run out of money to buy) any more land or who just want extra grapes because their sales are getting ahead of their stocks. 'Everyone has tried to buy grapes off us,' Chris says. 'Everybody asks us for grapes. We just have to say no, we don't have any.' Whilst for commercial reasons it would not be right to discuss actual prices, and in any event, contracts differ with regard to quality levels (sugars and acids) and delivery arrangements (some prices are delivered, some collected), their average prices across all varieties, and selling grapes to six different wineries, would be getting towards £1,800 a tonne, less picking costs of say £200 per tonne. Translate this into income and at 8.65 tonnes per hectare (3.5 tonnes per acre) it comes to around £13,840 per hectare (£5,601 per acre), leaving a margin after growing costs of around £8,840 per hectare (£3,577 per acre), which is quite healthy when compared to some other crops. And all grown, it has to be noted, on fairly heavy Wealden land, with clay in places and not an ounce of chalk in site. Well sheltered, well established and well managed beats open, exposed, chalk downland every time.

Having first met Chris' mother, Anne, in around 1977, when she taught my children at primary school, and known Chris and his family since 1986, when he first visited me at the winery, I have huge respect for the family's skills as farmers and, more specifically, grape growers. Sure, there have been ups and downs, good years and bad years, high sugar years and high acid years, but taken over three decades, they have managed to create one of the best, most productive and most sustainable vineyard enterprises in Britain. I doubt if there are many other grape growers in the country who do as well. They stand or fall on what they produce. To see the fourth generation of the family take the farm over (with the fifth coming along), with the huge optimism that there is in grape growing and winemaking in Britain today, must be very gratifying.

Sharpham Vineyard

Sharpham Estate, Ashprington, Totnes, Devon, TQ9 7UT.
www.sharpham.com
3.4 hectares (8.4 acres)

One of the oldest vineyards in Britain, on the banks of the River Dart in South Devon. Produces high-quality wines and cheeses, and runs good visitor facilities and an excellent café.

A few miles from Totnes, overlooking the River Dart, Sharpham Vineyard is situated in one of the most beautiful parts of the country. The 226-hectare (550-acre) Sharpham Estate is owned by the Sharpham Trust, a charitable trust set up by Maurice and Ruth Ash, the estate's original owners, in the early 1980s. The Sharpham Trust is, as the website explains, 'an education and conservation charity connecting people with nature and fostering mindfulness and well-being through our programme of retreats, mindfulness courses, outdoor learning and the arts.' The Ashes' interests included the arts, Buddhism, conservation and rural regeneration and these are very much still at the heart of what the Trust does. The estate comprises several farms and enterprises, including Sharpham Meadow, a green burial site, and the Sharpham Partnership, founded in 1981, which produces both wines and cheese. The cheese is produced from a herd of Jersey milking cows which traces its lineage back to the herd that the Ashes brought with them (by train) when they moved from Essex to Sharpham in the 1960s.

The Sharpham Partnership, which was once a partnership of various members of the Ash family, plus Mark Sharman, has been a limited company since 1997. As members of the family left the partnership for different reasons, Sharman acquired 100 per cent of the company. Sharman was brought up on a farm in south Devon, although his parents gave up farming when he was eleven, persuading him that farming 'wasn't a way of life to follow'. After university in Newcastle upon Tyne, where Sharman studied mining engineering – and gained a first, specializing in rock mechanics – and three years in northern Ontario working in gold mining, he returned to south Devon in 1985 to work at Beenleigh Manor, a fruit and cider farm which his cousin, Marian Ash, daughter of the Sharpham founders, and her then husband, owned. Sharman had often helped Marian on her farm, tractor driving during the apple harvest and getting involved with the cider making, even at quite a young age. The job at Beenleigh enabled him to return to Devon and settle down with his partner Debbie Mumford (now head cheesemaker at Sharpham). After Marian and her husband parted company in 1988, leaving Mark and Debbie without a home or a job, Maurice suggested that Sharman come and work for him to run the vineyard which he had planted on the Sharpham Estate between 1981 and 1985. Sharman was sent off to Plumpton College in 1989 in the very first intake of eight or nine students and over six months did a six-week viticulture and winemaking course (with David Cowderoy as the winemaking instructor) on a one-week-per-month basis. Sharman's first job on the vineyard was to finish the trellising of the most recently planted vines and get to grips with running both the vineyard and the apple orchards at Beenleigh.

The first harvest to make it into bottle was in 1986, the 1985 having been too small for commercial production. Having then no winery of their own, the grapes were taken 400 kilometres (250 miles) to Kit Lindlar's High Weald Winery near Maidstone, then one of the very few wineries in Britain offering contract winemaking services. When the wine was returned in bottle, all involved were less than impressed. 'Too Germanic,' said Maurice (a fully-signed up Francophile who had a house in Cap d'Antibes where he spent a lot of the time) and after the 1987 harvest turned out much the same way, they moved the winemaking for the 1988 vintage to Three Choirs. This was not only nearer (half the distance) but also the winemaking team, headed up by another Kit, Kit Morris, was more amenable to suggestion about wine style than Lindlar had been. Sharman gained some winemaking experience during the 1988 and 1989 vintages by helping Morris out in the winery, but for the 1990 vintage, a straw barn at Sharpham was converted and equipped as a winery.

The vineyards since those early days have undergone considerable changes. The first sites, steep and quite small, were planted with a selection of varieties commonly found in British vineyards in the 1980s and 1990s and once totalled 6.47 hectares (16 acres). Auxerrois, Huxelrebe, Kerner, Kernling, Pinot Gris and Reichensteiner have all gone, and today there are 3.4 hectares (8.4 acres) of vineyards with the major variety being Madeleine x Angevine 7672, plus Blauer Frühburgunder, Dornfelder, Phoenix and Pinot Noir. Some of the MA 7672 was supplied by me in 1993 with vines grafted from scion wood taken from Robin Don's Elmham Park vineyard – now grubbed-up – which were known to have come from Ray Brock's Oxted vineyard. They differ slightly in bunch shape from Sharpham's older vines of this variety, which were supplied by Gillian Pearkes (who got her vines from Brock's originals), but the leaves appear the same and the wine quality is just as good. In principle, the vineyards are all trellised on the Scott Henry divided curtain system, although some of the vineyards have reverted to standard VSP training.

Today, the Sharpham Partnership operation comprises three distinct businesses: the vineyard and winery, the cheesemaking and the dairy herd. All the land and buildings they occupy are owned by the Sharpham

Trust, but the Sharpham trademark for both wines and cheeses is owned by the Partnership. The winery uses the grapes from their own vineyards, around thirty tonnes in an average year, plus grapes from Sandridge Barton Vineyard, an 8.51-hectare (21.03-acre) estate on the other side of the River Dart. They have in the past taken grapes from other vineyards as well. From Sandridge Barton they now take Bacchus, Chardonnay, Frühburgunder, MA 7672, Pinot Gris and Pinot Noir and expect around sixty to seventy tonnes a year. The 2018 crush, at 105 tonnes, was their largest ever: 40 from Sharpham, 60 from Sandridge Barton and 5 from Manstree Vineyard near Exeter. They make both still and sparkling wines and sell around 35 per cent of their wines (by volume) from their retail shop and to the café which is rented by an unrelated caterer, and 65 per cent to various trade customers, St Austell Brewery and Waitrose being the most important. By value the split is nearer fifty–fifty. Sharman says they were late into the sparkling wine business, making their first sparkling wines in only 2003 but are now winning prizes and medals for it.

One of Sharpham's most unusual wines is the Beenleigh Manor red which sells at £32 a bottle. The history of this wine goes back to 1979, when Marian Ash planted a very small area of Cabernet Sauvignon and Merlot vines under plastic tunnels and tried to produce a full-bodied red wine from them. Sharman says the vines were planted 'to steal a march' on her father's intentions to plant a vineyard of his own at Sharpam. This venture became a casualty of her divorce and the vines were abandoned for a year or two. Sharman eventually took pity on the 'vineyard', buying it together with a sleeping partner in January 1989 and resurrecting it. He still owns it, replacing the plastic every six or seven years and taking the grapes to the Sharpham winery, where he makes the wine. Around three to five hundred bottles are produced most years and in the 1990s and early 2000s the wine consistently won the 'best red' trophy and 'best small volume wine' award. Given that the vineyard occupies only 1,300 square metres (0.32 acres), to get a gross return of between £6,000 and £10,000 a year isn't bad going. Sharman says, 'it pays for a week's holiday somewhere nice for the two of us'.

The cheesemaking is run by Sharman's partner, Debbie Mumford, and accounts for 50 per cent of the Partnership's turnover. Over the years since they started making cheese in 1981, the same year as the first vines were planted, it has established itself as one of the best cheese dairies in the country. They now not only make cheese from their herd of

Jerseys, but have also expanded into cheese from both goats and sheep, buying their milk in from local flock owners. The dairy herd has been relocated to a farm on the Dartington Estate and although the animals are still owned by the Sharpham Partnership, they are cared for and milked by another farmer. They use an Angus bull on some of the Jerseys, providing them with calves that can be reared for beef production on the land released by moving the herd away.

The cheesemaking is housed in a completely separate building from the winemaking and is bursting at the seams as production rises. Long term, Sharman would like a 'fairy godfather/godmother' to fund a co-operative winery for all the South Devon growers (similar to the Sonoma Valley cooperative winery Grand Cru Custom Crush) so that they could move their winemaking operations and expand the dairy, wine shop and tourism-related activities into the winery buildings. The team that runs the whole operation is a mixture of old hands and new. Sharman and his partner Debbie have been there since 1985 and Duncan Schwab, now head winemaker (with Sharman as executive winemaker) has been there since 1992, as has Abby, their office manager.

The Sharpham farming enterprise shows what can be achieved through a combination of good land use, specialization, the production of a range of high-quality agricultural products and making the best of a location through visitor friendliness and tourism. Over the last thirty-five or so years they have created a strong, viable business that is a credit to the vision that Maurice and Ruth Ash had and to the hard work and perseverance of Sharman and his team.

Simpsons Wine Estate

The Barns, Church Lane, Barham, Canterbury, Kent, CT4 6PB.
www.simpsonswine.com
16.59 hectares (41 acres)

Up-and-coming producer with innovative marketing ideas, making very good still and sparkling wines. Have been owners of a 40-hectare wine estate in the Languedoc since 2002.

Charles and Ruth Simpson make a formidable pair. With degrees in international marketing and international relations and backgrounds in the world of pharmaceuticals and in the humanitarian sector, their decision to give up the glamorous world of international business and buy a slightly down-at-heel wine estate in the Languedoc must have surprised their nearest and dearest. Charles went to Michigan State University to do his degree and was hired by the global pharmaceuticals company Merck, Sharp & Dohme on their sales side, where he was taught about marketing, joining Glaxo Wellcome (now GlaxoSmithKline or GSK) and moving to Britain four years later. In 1999 and just married, he was asked to relocate to Baku in order to open up a sales office looking after Azerbaijan and Georgia.

Living in an ex-KGB building on the banks of the Caspian Sea and dreaming about life together, newly-weds Charles and Ruth contemplated their future together. What did they want to do? What did they *really* want to do? Not this, for sure. Over the next few cold Soviet nights (with nothing else to keep them warm) they did some brainstorming and discussed 'areas where our skillsets could intercept, and thought about a business to which we could add value.' With Ruth coming from a family whose fortune had been made in alcohol – in this case whisky – wine popped up into their field of vision fairly quickly. Through her mother, Ruth is a fifth-generation member of the Grants whisky company (famous amongst many other products for Glenfiddich), which, despite being the third largest Scotch whisky company, is still family owned and managed. Having decided that wine production might be an area to investigate, their travels took them to Australia, where the Grants' tie-up with the Mildara wine company gained them access to several wineries, and then to New Zealand. It was whilst they were there in 2001 that the 11 September attacks on the World Trade Center took place, bringing home to them just how far away from their families they were. As a result, they decided that Europe, specifically the Languedoc region of France, ought to be the area to investigate.

They chose the Languedoc for several reasons. They had decided that 'it was the only part of France where you could do a "new world" project'. Here wine producers had the freedom, outside of the AOC system, to plant the grape varieties and make the wines they wanted without someone saying they didn't conform to rules and regulations. Domaine Sainte Rose lies 12 kilometres north-east of Beziers in the heart of the Pays d'Oc wine region. The property was owned by an incomer from north-east France who had managed to unsettle the locals by being unfriendly and charmless, and so was on the market. In 2002, cashing in their flat in London at a time with the pound was strong against the euro, and with their first child due three weeks later, they bought the 40-hectare (99-acre) Domaine Sainte Rose. 'As 29- and 30-year olds, we thought we could change the industry in an afternoon,' says Charles. However, they soon found that things were not quite as flexible as they had hoped. 'Sixteen years later, knowing that however hard we push, whatever we do, whatever quality improvements we make, we cannot sell Languedoc wines for more than £18 a bottle [British retail price] makes life difficult.' Wine prices are so heavily tied into the AOC system, which in turn governs the price of the land, that it's almost impossible to break the connection. When all is said and done, apart from the land, the cost of producing wine – the vineyards, the labour, the machinery, the winery and the winemaking – does not vary much wherever you are, but only being able to sell your wine at €3–5 per bottle ex-cellars puts a limit on the amount of income that can be produced off any given area of land.

It was in 2010 that the Simpsons first started thinking about English wine. They had tried Nyetimber and Ridgeview and knew that the wines had quality. After further research they decided that 'England was the most exciting, dynamic [wine] area that we could think of. It was the sort of place that had attracted us to the Languedoc sixteen years earlier.' The moment of truth came on New Year's Eve 2011. They were staying at the Cameron House Hotel on the shores of Loch Lomond with Ruth's mother and brother, Neil Gordon, and after a few glasses of Champagne, Charles and Ruth suggested to the family that they ought to 'buy some land [in England] and sit on it.' They had read an article in *Decanter* about 'vineyard land' on Kent's chalk-rich North Downs that Strutt & Parker was selling (and for which I had been commissioned to survey, take soil samples and write a report about its suitability for vines). The asking price was £25,000 per hectare (£10,000 per acre). After getting in touch with Strutt & Parker (and demanding that I be there when they viewed the land) they made an offer for 35.2 hectares (87 acres) of land (which included 2.83 hectares of woodland) at £21,000 per hectare (£8,500 per acre), which was accepted. It was spring 2012. They also looked at 4 hectares (10 acres) of established vineyards at Halnaker, just outside Chichester which was on sale for the very high price of £360,000. With its trelliswork in a dreadful state and the vines not much better, they declined to make an offer.[35]

35 This land was eventually bought by Gusbourne vineyard for the asking price.

Initially the idea had been to sit on the land and see what happened. However, with President François Hollande recently elected and threatening a wealth tax, with their eldest child about to change schools and with Domaine Sainte Rose 'profitable and paying off the investment' the Simpsons started to have other ideas. Domaine Sainte Rose was running itself from the vineyard and wine production side (although not the marketing side which is still theirs). Not wanting any more exposure to France – 'we felt we had another project in us' – the Simpsons started looking into actually planting the land the family had bought.

From their perspective their decision was surprisingly easy. They knew how to plant, establish and run vineyards, they knew how to build and equip a winery and make wine. The rest is marketing – a subject that they probably know more about than any other part of the wine business. As Charles says, 'the question was do we spend our lives selling €3–5 ex-cellar Languedoc wines or £15 ex-cellar English sparkling wines? … When you sit down with the wine buyer for southern French wines, the question is: what's the price? When you sit down with the wine buyer for English wines the question is: how much can you let me have?' They moved back to Britain, renting a house in Barham, and sending the children to school in Kent.

Planting started in 2014, in the smaller of the two fields now known as the Roman Road site (so named because its eastern boundary is the site of a Roman road). Vines were sourced from VCR (Vivai Cooperativi Rauscedo), the world's largest vine nursery, with bases in both northern Italy and southern France, from where the Simpsons had obtained vines for Sainte Rose. VCR also helpfully shipped in a GPS planting machine along with an excess number of vines and planted the whole vineyard for a budget price. In 2014, 9.12 hectares (22.54 acres) of vineyard were planted: 46 per cent Chardonnay, 33 per cent Pinot Noir and 21 per cent Meunier. Rootstocks used were Fercal and 41B, with a very few on 420A. The clones chosen were all CIVC and Burgundy clones, plus Chardonnay 548. There are around ten clones of Chardonnay, six of Pinot Noir and seven of Meunier. The vines were planted at 2-metre row width by 1.2-metre intervine distance. Their second site, Railway Hill, slightly steeper, slightly higher and more east facing,was planted over two years, 2016 and 2017. The 2016 plantings were at the same 2-metre by 1.2-metre spacings as Roman Road, but the 2017 plantings were at 2.2 metres by 0.8 metres as the site slopes slightly to one side and it was felt that the wider spacing would help tractors maintain their stability. To date their plantings total 16.59 hectares (41 acres) with 2 hectares still to plant. 'Maybe we will plant something interesting and unusual' says Ruth. Yields to date have been modest. In 2016 (when only the 2014 planted vines cropped) the yield was 30 tonnes, which was made into over 20,000 bottles of sparkling and 600 bottles of still Chardonnay. Owing to the hard frosts which hit many British vineyards at the end of April and beginning of May, 2017 was a disappointing year, yielding just 25 tonnes. In 2018 the harvest was phenomenal, with the 2016 plantings coming into production and perfect growing conditions. Yields across the two vineyards were around 8–10 tonnes per hectare (3.2–4 tonnes per acre), depending on the variety and clone, and in total around 200 tonnes were pressed. Their latest 2018 picking was some 'squeaky clean' Chardonnay on 3 November.

The 2014 vines established well and it was clear that for the 2016 harvest a winery would be required. Wanting a building of some sort, if only to keep tractors and equipment in, the Simpsons applied for and obtained planning permission on the Roman Road site for an agricultural building. However, one condition of the planning permission was that when they started digging foundations, they would have to employ an archaeologist to keep an eye on proceedings in case anything of interest turned up, the area around the road having possibly been Roman and Anglo-Saxon burial grounds. In the end they didn't need to even start on the building as they put an offer in on some existing agricultural buildings and were able to persuade the owner – the same person they had bought the land from – that their offer was the best he was likely to get, and if he didn't accept it now, they would go ahead with the new building and he'd lose out.

The development of their winery site, which now includes office space and a tasting room, has proceeded in stages and has been partially grant-aided. In 2016 they received a grant of £143,154 from the RDPE (Rural Development Programme for Europe), which is managed by the Rural Payments Agency. This represented 37.5 per cent of the total cost of the project. The winery was officially opened by Oz Clarke in October 2016. The original two barns have been completely renovated with added insulation, external cladding and new floors. A third building has been erected and both additional winery space and bottle storage are in the planning stages. A retail facility is not open yet, but will go ahead when they have enough stock to sell. One item which they declined to spend their money on was a £250,000 'bio-bubble' plant to treat any processing water coming from the winery. Asking around they heard that most wineries, at least those bothering to treat their wastewater, used a contractor to cart it away. After installing a large underground storage tank, they found a local cesspit emptying contractor who for around £300 a year will take three to four 16,000 litre loads of wastewater away and dispose of it in a licensed soakaway.

If there's one thing that most British vineyard owners struggle with, it is marketing. Spending money on well planned and planted vineyards and building and equipping lavish wineries is one thing and can be done by most with some help and a healthy bank balance. Creating wines that the market wants, constructing a brand that will attract your customers and finding a home for the wine that your relentless wine factory is programmed to produce is another. For most it's a question of suck it and see. Start slowly, feel your way as supplies increase, and hope that production, stock levels and sales reach a happy equilibrium. For the Simpsons, who have spent sixteen years selling 400,000 bottles a year of Domaine Sainte Rose wines into export markets – none is sold in France – the task takes on a different form. Currently 20 per cent of their French wines are sold in the US and they see this market as ideal for their English wines too. The US 'three-tier system' of importers, distributors and retailers is notoriously difficult to understand, let alone break into and it took the Simpsons ten years to work out how to do it. They have their own import company and using worldwide wine logistics company J. F. Hillebrand to manage all the paperwork and shipping, they send their wine direct to the US, using the warehousing and distribution services of USA Wines West. The product remains theirs and at their risk until sold, but it does mean that they can issue price lists in US dollars, rather than FOB (free on board) prices in euros, which US distributors and retailers find less easy to deal with. The cost of getting their wine into the US and into a New Jersey warehouse ready for onward sale is around US$20 per nine-litre case of 12 bottles. Their US agent, with whom they have worked for ten years, has got them into around twenty states and is 'doing a great job'. The Simpsons don't go for the obvious east- and west-coast cities, where most adventurous wine drinkers are located and to where most importers head, but have deliberately chosen to target less obvious states – Texas and North

Carolina are cited as examples. Export markets need to be serviced and they feel that an annual visit is the bare minimum. Visits typically last two weeks and follow a similar pattern: breakfast sales meetings for the distributors, lunchtime events for the trade, with sales representatives, and dinners for consumers – day after day after day. But persistence pays, and sales of their French wines are good. In all their presentations in the US they now add a few slides at the end about their English wines, expecting a few chuckles, but are amazed to find that their audiences are 'already well aware of the product and only waiting for it to become available.' They know a few names, Nyetimber and Ridgeview being the most quoted. To illustrate this enthusiasm, the Simpsons recount how, when attending the Colorado Springs Wine Festival in 2018, a bottle of their Roman Road 2016 Chardonnay (still wine) sold for US$750 at the Gala Charity Auction.

One innovative idea of the Simpsons has been to work with Naked Wines (now owned by Majestic) and pre-sell 1,200 six-bottle packs of their 2016 sparkling wines, both French and English, at £94 a unit. The deal was that customers received four bottles of their 2016 English fizz, with the balance made up of a new sparkler from their Languedoc vineyards. They offered Naked Wines' 'wine angels' the chance to select the blend they preferred – Blend B, the Expressive Blend came out on top – and got them to also suggest a name. Fizzy McFizz Face was rejected in favour of 'Beora', the name of the Saxon chief after whom the village of Barham is named. They also asked a local art college to come up with some label designs which again went through the Naked Wines selection process. For their pains, the Simpsons have pre-sold £112,800 worth of wine, banked the money and used it for equipping the winery. Nice marketing with plenty of free publicity for both their English and French wines.

I ended my interview with my standard last question: 'so what's the total bill to date?' Without much hesitation Charles offered some figures: 'Around £800,000 on the land, £600,000 on the vineyards, £400,000 on the barns plus agricultural and winery equipment – maybe £2.5 million in total.' By my reckoning that's not bad for a fully functioning, fully equipped vineyard and winery enterprise with a productive capacity of around 115,000–125,000 bottles of what should be very high-quality sparkling (and occasionally still) wine. You can find plenty of vineyards in Britain who have spent far more and achieved far less bang for their buck. Of course, the Simpsons still have more to finance. Between three and five years' stock at cost of production could come to another £2.5 million, but by then they will have started to pull in some income from both sparkling and still wines and the payback will have begun.

The Simpsons are an interesting couple with an interesting approach to making a sustainable business out of growing grapes in Britain, making wine and selling that wine. 'We not only want to make a profit, we need to make a profit,' says Charles, and from what I have seen they have set off down the right path. It will be interesting to see how their wines turn out, what price points they achieve and where they sell, but it's my guess that when it comes to profitability and repaying their investment, Simpsons Wine Estate will be viewed as a text-book example.

Sixteen Ridges Vineyard

Haygrove Evolution, Dragon Orchard, Ledbury, Herefordshire, HR8 2RG.
www.haygrove-evolution.com

Winemaking, viticultural advice, own-rooted vines – all under one roof.

Simon Day, born in 1970, is a second-generation viticulturalist, his father Tom having been farm (and then vineyard) manager at what became Three Choirs Vineyard, when it was planted in 1972. Day's brother-in-law, Martin Fowke, has been the winemaker at Three Choirs for over thirty years. Growing up at Three Choirs, Day had always been interested in the wine business and at weekends, evenings and during the school holidays had helped out on the vineyard and in the winery. On a trip to Trier on the Mosel in 1982 and aged only 12, it dawned upon him that maybe vines and wine could be a career. Despite parental opposition, after a biochemistry degree at Sussex University he worked in wineries in Australia, New Zealand and Oregon to gain experience. He then returned to Britain to work at Denbies, Lamberhurst and at La Mare in Jersey. In 2001 his father died and Day took over the vine importing and consultancy business which his father had built up over the years, calling it Vine and Wine. He also started his own cider-making business, Once Upon A Tree, making craft ciders from locally sourced apples.

In 2007, Worcestershire farmer John Ballard, who at the time owned a wedding venue called Carradine Barns, decided he would like to plant a vineyard and called on Day's expertise. During 2008 and 2009, 3.6

hectares (8.9 acres) of vines – Pinot Noir, Pinot Noir Précoce and Seyval Blanc – were planted between 35 and 60 metres above sea level on a sheltered south-east facing slope that faces down towards the Severn and is contained in a natural amphitheatre. The soil is a fertile, sandy loam over old Devonian sandstone and the vines are trained to the less commonly found (in Britain at least) Scott Henry training system. The first vintage of Sixteen Ridges, as the vineyard became known, was in 2011 and made at Three Choirs. In 2013, Day started to buy grapes from this vineyard to establish his own English wine brand, an arrangement that continues to this day. It is planned to expand plantings here with an additional 2.4 hectares (6 acres) being planted over the next 2–3 years.

In 2012, Cilla Clive, mother of soft fruit grower Angus Davison, asked Day to plant a vineyard at Redbank at Little Marcle, just outside Ledbury. In 2013 1.45 hectares (3.58 acres) of mainly Bacchus, with smaller plantings of Chardonnay, Muscaris, Ortega, Pinot Noir and Solaris were established at Redbank. In 2016 an additional 1.58 hectares (3.93 acres) of Pinot Noir was planted, the variety having proved itself over the previous three years, together with Pinot Noir Précoce. Further vineyards totalling 2.43 hectares (6 acres) of Madeleine x Angevine 7672, Muscaris, Chardonnay, Pinot Noir and Pinot Noir Précoce were planted in 2018, some of which are with Day's own-rooted vines (see p. 222). The vineyards at Redbank will be expanded as the existing orchards get to the end of their productive lives and it is anticipated that an additional 14 hectares (35 acres) will be planted over the next five years. There are also other suitable south-facing farms available nearby with potential permission for polytunnels should this method of growing prove successful (see p. 221).

The south-east facing site at Redbank lies between 60 and 95 metres above sea level on the Ledbury Wall Hills and is sandy loam and Devonian red sandstone, a soil capable of retaining heat. The Bishop's Vineyard, as one of the plots is called, is named after St Thomas Cantilupe, the thirteenth-century Bishop of Hereford (and Lord Chancellor in 1264) who in 1276 caused the Ledbury vineyard on the south-facing slopes of Wall Hills to be replanted. He reputedly sent some wine to the Pope, together with some *verjuice*, then (as now) a condiment used in place of vinegar.

Of all the vineyards I have seen in Britain, the Redbank site is undoubtedly one of the best. With its vineyards all facing south, all below 60 metres above sea level, with rising ground to the north and falling ground below for frost drainage, this is a text book location. Yields are, by average British standards, high, with Bacchus and Pinot Noir cropping at between 11.12 and 14.83 tonnes per hectare (4.5–6 tonnes per acre), the shy-cropping Pinot Noir Précoce at 7.41 to 8.65 tonnes per hectare (3–3.5 tonnes per acre) and the reliable Seyval Blanc at around 14.83 tonnes per hectare (6 tonnes per acre). Planted at 2.5-metre row widths with 1.4 metres between vines, the combination of the excellent site and the Scott Henry trellising system definitely brings results. I know of almost no other sites in Britain with these levels of production.

In 2014, a new company, Haygrove Evolution, was formed which incorporated Day's cider, vineyard consultancy, contract winemaking, vine propagation and vine sales businesses. A new winery was built and equipped on the Haygrove Redbank site, which can handle the winemaking from both the Sixteen Ridges and the Redbank vineyards. There is an ever-increasing number of contract customers – currently it is seventeen – and Day sees this as a major part of the enterprise. The business has two full-time winery staff, plus Day during harvest and at other critical times, as well as two full-time staff looking after sales and business development.

Sixteen Ridges wines are sold via merchants and wholesalers as well as regionally with supermarket Waitrose, with very little going from the cellar door or to visitors. Vineyard tours are very low-key and remain 'a business opportunity yet to be developed'. The 'runaway success' has been the red wine. Made initially from Pinot Noir Précoce but now with an addition of Pinot Noir, this wine is fermented with a small addition of oak chips and some in barrels and retails for £18. Its quality is due to the very high level of ripeness the grapes achieve even in what might be termed poor vintages. Day says that this wine is 'all on allocation' and is looking forward to when the new plantings come on stream so he can expand the production beyond the current 3,000–3,500 bottles a year. Day finds that Seyval Blanc is a very good partner to Pinot Noir in the Signature Cuvée sparkling where (for the 2013) it accounts for around twenty-five per cent of the blend. This wine was taken by supermarket Sainsbury's and can be found in 200 stores. Day is also a Bacchus fan and notes that for this variety, vine age really does bring benefits to wine quality. From 35-year-old Bacchus vines he makes superbly flavoured wine.

Day is also experimenting with growing vines in polytunnels to see how this affects them in relation to both yield and quality. Growing under plastic means you have a much greater flexibility on which varieties you plant and Day currently has Cabernet Franc, Cabernet Sauvignon, Chardonnay, Chasselas, Gewürztraminer, Merlot, Riesling and Sauvignon Blanc, all for winemaking. Dessert varieties (table grapes) were considered, but with little enthusiasm from the multiple retailers, this idea was shelved.

As well as importing vines from French and German nurseries, Day is pioneering the production of own-rooted vines (i.e. not grafted onto rootstocks) in Britain. This was a business that his father started in a small way, mainly to supply the demand for varieties not usually produced by overseas nurseries, principally MA 7672. Own-rooted vines are slightly controversial as phylloxera is present in some British vineyards. However, Day feels that the benefits of own-rooted vines – lack of a graft, no rootstock (which can carry what are known as 'trunk diseases') and ability to plant potted vines in the autumn (as opposed to the spring, the normal time for British vineyards to plant vines) – outweigh the disadvantages of what he feels is the 'remote possibility' of a phylloxera infestation. 'As long as one is careful about biosecurity, not using equipment, machinery or picking boxes that have been in other vineyards, then the risk is minimal, ' he states. Another benefit, which I find intriguing, is Day's claim that own-rooted vines hang on to their leaves much longer than grafted vines, giving them an ability, post-harvest, to restock with carbohydrates prior to the winter. If this is true (and I have no reason to doubt Day on this) it is a significant factor and one that ought to be trialled on a scientific basis. Watch this space.

Day started producing own-rooted vines on a commercial scale in 2013, initially in beds covered in black plastic, but found that losses were high and too many vines had poor roots, making them unsaleable. Since then he and the Haygrove propagation team have developed a system of growing them in individual pots, six pots joined together in one tray, with each pot having its own irrigation and fertigation supply. Growing them in pots means that the rooted vines can easily be lifted (or more precisely picked up), knocked out of their pots and planted directly into the vineyard without disturbing the roots. It also enables growers to receive their vines in the autumn, still in leaf in September or October through to dormant vines in November or December, so that the vines have a chance to bed in over the winter and make an early start on growth in the spring. The current level of production should see Day selling around 50,000 own-rooted vines in 2018–19. Having no graft, the vines can be sold with trunks if the grower wishes, acting in effect like 'high graft' vines which offer the promise of cropping in year two. Taken together, these own-rooted vines potentially have some significant advantages over traditional grafted vines (except that is for that vine louse). Day is also offering a massal selection[36] service to growers who wish to expand (or replant) their vineyards with wood taken from an existing vineyard. So far, this service has only been taken up by a couple of growers, but it is a start.

Taken together, the vineyards, the wine sales, the contract winemaking, the vine propagation and the vine sales, Day has developed what appears to be a very viable, sustainable business, all based around British viticulture. As a second-generation viticulturalist, he has seen the transformation from grape growing based upon Müller-Thurgau, Seyval Blanc and Reichensteiner to an industry based upon Chardonnay, Pinot Noir and Bacchus, and has the experience to take good vintages with the bad and come out the other side. The next twenty-five years should be both interesting and rewarding for him.

Tinwood Estate

Tinwood Lane, Halnaker, Chichester, West Sussex, PO18 0NE.
www.tinwoodestate.com
36 hectares (89 acres)

One of Britain's larger growers, starting to make an impression with high-quality bottle-fermented sparkling wines.

Born in 1985 into a farming family, agriculture was probably in Art Tukker's blood from an early age, certainly earlier than many of today's British winegrowers. His Dutch grandfather had owned glasshouses in the Netherlands and made a living growing tomatoes and other salad crops. His father, Arie, being the youngest son, was not going to inherit the farm, so became a consultant and travelled the world overseeing tomato and lettuce production for Marks & Spencer. In 1983 Arie settled in England near Chichester, buying (and renting) land in the South East in order to grow lettuces for British supermarkets; at one time he was growing over 600 hectares (1,500 acres) of lettuces, making him

36 Massal selection is where scion wood for grafting is taken from an existing, cropping vineyard, rather than a single-clone mother-block.

one of the largest suppliers in Britain. Art decided to study agricultural business management, specializing in farm diversification, at London University's Department of Agriculture, then based on their country campus at Wye College in Kent. For his degree dissertation in 2005, the topic Art chose was 'The Profitability of Planting Vines in Britain'. While writing this, and after tasting some wines, he and his father were encouraged enough to investigate the possibility of planting a vineyard of sufficient size to make grape growing a commercial (i.e. profitable) enterprise.

Various wineries were approached to see if they wanted to team up with a professional supplier of grapes. Nyetimber, their nearest large wine producer, was approached on the basis that Eric Heerema, its new owner, and the Tukkers were both Dutch, but their suggestions fell on stony ground. Next on the list was Mike Roberts at Ridgeview, who proved more amenable to the idea. As the deal to supply grapes was being discussed, Arie decided to investigate the possibility of buying a stake in Ridgeview. His experience of 'being hammered on price' by the buyers of his lettuces, mainly the major British supermarkets, wasn't great. They were tough to deal with and you were always at risk of being undercut by other producers. (Sainsbury's had recently introduced a 'how low can you go' on-line timed auction system for suppliers of non-branded products where the lowest, often uncommercial, price won the contract.) In discussions with Mike Roberts, it transpired that Ridgeview needed more winery capacity if they were to take on a new grape supplier of the size being proposed and they needed funds to expand their winery. Where was the money to come from? Arie Tukker proposed that he provide it and in late 2006 he and his wife ended up buying 24.4 per cent of Ridgeview. (Following the death of Mike Roberts, Arie Tukker became Chairman of Ridgeview.)

With the knowledge and confidence of their abilities as growers and the security of having a stake in their buyer, and with the help of Mike Roberts who specified the varieties and clones, the Tukkers planted a total of 19.64 hectares (48.53 acres) over two years, 2007 and 2008, on the home farm at Tinwood, just to the east of Chichester. This farm is around 9.5 kilometres (6 miles) north of the coast at Bognor Regis, and far enough away to escape the worst of any cooling sea breezes. The 100-hectare (250-acre) farm sits on alluvial chalk with a high flint content, so is naturally well-drained, and is very gently south facing at between 25 and 33 metres above sea level. Its only drawback, as was seen in 2017, is that in times of frost, the air drainage is minimal. The whole farm is laid with a network of irrigation mains, needed for the lettuces and latterly strawberries that were grown there, but to date, no vines are irrigated, although anti-frost irrigation has been discussed. Since those initial plantings, more vines have been planted and by 2018 the total was 36 hectares (89 acres). There is an additional 40 hectares (100 acres) of land suitable for vines that could be planted, and the plan is to plant these additional acres over the next ten years.

The vines at Tinwood established well, and in 2009 a total of 45 tonnes of grapes were produced from the 2007 plantings at a rate of 3.87 tonnes per hectare (1.57 tonnes per acre) – not bad for vines under three years in the ground. Crops since then have been good, averaging around 8 tonnes per hectare (3.24 tonnes per acre). The vineyard is managed by five full-time employees (with a further three on the retail and tourist side), plus contract labour when required. All vineyard tasks are mechanized wherever possible; they are probably the only British vineyard using an automatic tucking-in machine. Weed control is currently with herbicides and looking at the high flint content, the soil might not lend itself to mechanical hoeing.

The quality of the Tinwood Estate site can partly be gauged by the earliness of their harvests. In all but the latest years they are finished by the end of September (where most other vineyards are often picking Chardonnay in the third and fourth weeks of October) and by their excellent sugar levels. Initially a relatively small amount of wine for sale under the Tinwood Estate label was made at Ridgeview, around 15 per cent of the weight of grapes delivered, but the contract has been renegotiated and since 2016, they receive 10,000 bottles of sparkling wine made for every 50 tonnes of grapes delivered. With current production of around 200 tonnes, this equates to 40,000 bottles a year, an amount that the Tukkers reckon they will be able to build up to selling from the on-site retail shop, to local on-trade outlets, and to the Goodwood Estate (their largest customer). All the wine for sale comes back to the estate to be matured in their new temperature-controlled wine store but they have no plans to build their own winery.

In 2012, as the wine they had available for sale increased in volume, a smart tasting room with both inside and outside tasting areas was created, and tours and tastings, both daily during the summer and by appointment, now form part of the tourist and visitor offering. The nearby Goodwood Estate, with its Glorious Goodwood horse racing, the Goodwood Festival of Speed and Goodwood Revival car-themed events and open days, hotel and other offerings, is a great draw to the area and must help with wine sales. Two years ago, the Tukkers, Art and his wife Jody, got planning permission for three luxurious 'vineyard lodges' which are available for rent and proving very popular.

To date the Tinwood Estate enterprise has had around £1.6 million invested in it (including the new lodges and wine store but excluding the land, which was already owned by the family). Art reckons that with the record-breaking 2018 crop of 275 tonnes 'they might make a profit' but he accepts that owning a vineyard, creating a brand, and getting to the point where the investment starts getting repaid is a long haul. Still, with youth on his side, with the benefit of a proven site and a guaranteed buyer for their grapes and with all the upside that having an on-site outlet brings, he is not too worried about the massive increase in plantings which is taking place and which seems to be picking up speed. If only they could get planning permission for the house they would like to build on-site, things would be even better.

Waitrose

Waite House, Doncastle Road, Bracknell, Berkshire, RG12 8YA.
Leckford Estate Vineyard, Winchester Street, Leckford, Stockbridge, Hampshire, SO20 6JG.
www.waitrose.com; www.leckfordestate.com
6.75 hectares (16.68 acres)

Major British retailer selling large volume and very wide range of English and Welsh wines. Unique in having its own sparkling wine vineyard on a Hampshire farm.

It is a very lucky thing for English and Welsh winegrowers and wine producers, in this day of cut-throat, take-no-prisoners retailing, that Waitrose exists. It, or I should say its parent company, the John Lewis Partnership, is a remarkable organization. The John Lewis Partnership has been owned by its employees since 1929, when the son of the founder (John Lewis) gave it to them. Today there are 85,000 'partners', all of whom have a stake in the business both as employees and part-owners. The partnership owns around 50 department and 'At Home' stores under John Lewis, Peter Jones and other brand names, around

350 Waitrose and Little Waitrose stores, getting on for 30 Waitrose outlets at motorway service stations, plus a fair-sized export market in branded goods which go to more than 50 countries. Its market share of Britain's grocery trade is just over 5 per cent. The partnership also owns the Odney Club, home to a residential conference centre (which the Masters of Wine and WSET use regularly), and the Leckford Estate, known now as the 'Waitrose Farm', a 1,620-hectare (4,000-acre) estate in Hampshire. The farm, not only home to a large arable enterprise, plus dairy, chicken, mushroom and fruit farms, also has the 6.75-hectare (16.68-acre) Leckford Vineyard. This was established in 2009 and expanded with an additional 2.05 hectares (5.07 acres) in 2017. This puts Waitrose in a unique position as both a producer and a retailer of English and Welsh wines and makes it doubly aware of the problems and issues facing wine producers both at home and abroad.

Waitrose was one of the first British supermarkets to see the business sense of having a specialist wine department, staffed by dedicated and knowledgeable people, and in the early 1970s employed Julian Brind, who had just become a Master of Wine, to set up and run the wine side of the company. Brind was given relative freedom to source wines that he felt the decidedly middle-class Waitrose customers, who never bought solely on price, would find interesting and enjoyable. In 1973 New Zealand Sauvignon Blanc made an early appearance on a British supermarket shelf courtesy of Brind and it was he who started Waitrose's interest in Britain's home-grown wines. Brind also made sure that the buying team had a good sprinkling of Masters of Wine on it (at one stage there were five) and today, the department is headed up by Pierpaolo Petrassi MW, with another two MWs on the team: Rebecca Hull MW and Xenia Irwin MW.

Petrassi, thoroughly British despite his very Italian name, looks after not only wine buying, but also buys beers, ciders and perrys (made from pears), spirits and tobacco and has been doing so since 2010. Hull has worked for Waitrose in one capacity or another since 2006 and was buyer for English and Welsh wines between 2008 and 2018. Together, Petrassi and Hull have an acutely focused view of where English and Welsh wines, both still and sparkling, are in terms of price and quality and where they fit into the generality of wines available to the supermarket shopper in Britain today. Petrassi is very keyed in to the whole Waitrose ethos. 'In the way that we first looked at New Zealand before anyone else, we felt that English and Welsh wine offered something of real value and this hasn't changed across the two to three decades that we have been doing it,' he says. 'We have an obstinacy, a desire to do something different and English and Welsh wine fitted in to that philosophy.'

Part of my reason for interviewing Petrassi and Hull is that they have a unique insight into English and Welsh wines, both still and sparkling, and where they fit into the overall firmament of wine sales in Britain. Waitrose is undoubtedly the largest retailer of wines produced in Britain, with the market research company Nielsen, which tracks sales of wines (amongst many other products) through British retailers, putting their sales share of English and Welsh wines at 60–70 per cent (compared to sales of 7.7 per cent of all wines sold).[37] Petrassi feels that English and Welsh wine has a great story to tell and that this is part of its attraction to him as a retailer. But from a producer standpoint he also sees the diversity of distribution as 'one of the jewels in the crown of English and Welsh wine, and the fact that you can inspire customers to buy at the cellar door as one of the real points of difference.' He also says that their customers 'like to be involved with the whole local, regional hand-made kind of romance of the [wine] industry and are prepared to trade up a bit more to English and Welsh wines if they feel they are getting the whole back story that goes with it.'

Their English and Welsh wine offering, taking both physical stores and on-line together, comprises 110 wines: 46 sparkling, ranging from £17 to £42 a bottle, and 64 still wines priced from £8.99 for their own-label 'Dry White' (made by Denbies), their best-selling still wine, to £19.99 (a 37.5 cl dessert wine). Chapel Down's 'Flint Dry' at £12, Denbies' Flint Valley at £9.49 and Chapel Down's Bacchus at £13.99 are the next most sold still wines. Taking still and sparkling wines together they sell around 86.5 per cent from stores and 13.5 per cent via Waitrose Cellar, their on-line wine shop, with sparkling wine selling slightly better online. Four still wines and four sparkling are available in more than 300 stores, with the other 100 or more wines having local or regional distribution. In the last six weeks of 2016, a period that included two weeks when there was a 25 per cent off promotion running on all wines, and of course included Christmas and New Year, by far the busiest period for

37 Nielsen's statistics are skewed with regard to English and Welsh wine as they only track major retailers and multiples and do not track retail or trade sales made at the cellar door. They also do not track on-trade sales or sales made via independent and small chain wine merchants.

sales of sparkling wines, English and Welsh sparkling wines sold at the rate of one bottle of English and Welsh to ten bottles of Champagne. Whilst this may sound quite a small comparison to make, it is almost double the amount that Waitrose estimated they would sell and when you put it into the context of overall sales of Champagne, which are running at about 28 million bottles a year in Great Britain, this equates to sales of English and Welsh sparkling wine of 3.5 million bottles, which is more than double the amount currently available for sale.

On still wines Petrassi and Hull are surprisingly upbeat. Hull says that she 'would definitely stock more English still white wine if it was available at the right price,' and that, 'availability is very much part of the equation'. She feels that volumes are a limiting factor. I ask about Bacchus: 'Do customers recognize it as a grape variety or a brand?' Hull says that 'Bacchus does resonate with a lot of customers,' as being a quality term, but that 'customers are quite happy with wines made from Reichensteiner and Seyval Blanc blends [such as Denbies' Flint Valley] if the price is right.' Hull says that it's 'better for the [English and Welsh wine] industry if you can get younger people in on a cheaper purchase buying still wine,' and that 'we ought to be doing more to promote still wines.' We discuss English and Welsh rosé wines – they offer 14 sparkling and 9 still on their website – and how they are very popular. I suggest that from a producer's standpoint, a still rosé selling at between £12.99 and £14.99 is both profitable and creates ready cash compared to a sparkling version which requires much more work, more packaging materials and 3–5 years of ageing. They agree. As I am about to wrap the interview up, Petrassi asks me what I think about English and Welsh red wines. Now I am not so sure who is interviewing whom. I discuss the very few decent English and Welsh Pinot Noir based red wines that I have tasted (principally those from certain vintages from Chapel Down and Gusbourne) and he tells me that Bolney Estate's 'Dark Harvest' at £10.99 is 'usually reliable' although I see later on Waitrose's website that it gets three one-star, one four-star and two five-star ratings. Mixed opinions. Bolney's Pinot Noir at £15.99 gets much better ratings, with seven out of eight reviewers giving it four or five stars.

Waitrose's own Leckford Brut sparkling wine has been on sale since the first vintage, the 2011, was available and today (when it is available) it sells for £24.99. I suggest that this is under-priced, that the quality is good, and that there are over 20 English sparkling wines they sell at higher prices and that they are in the enviable position where they could charge more. Petrassi and Hull demur. I get a feeling that they don't want to be seen overcharging for their own wine, although they do accept that the price will probably rise in the not too distant future. Leckford Brut is available in around 200 outlets, with small amounts being exported to the Middle East (they have nine stores in the UAE) and South East Asia. Both Petrassi and Hull are very keen on their own wines and have seen them improve vintage upon vintage. Leckford Brut is also used for any Waitrose and John Lewis events where sparkling wine is served (and where previously Champagne would have been used). Production varies from vintage to vintage with 35,000 bottles in 2014, a meagre 10,000 in frost-ridden 2017, but a massive 80 tonnes, which will produce around 65,000 bottles, in 2018. Such are the vicissitudes of vineyard ownership in Britain. The estate operates as an independent commercial unit, so Hull has to buy it at a normal commercial price, and they make the same margin as with any other English and Welsh sparkling wine. It is made at Ridgeview Estate.

On pricing Petrassi thinks that their customers recognize quality and 'are prepared to pay a bit more for a wine with a good story.' He says that despite the average price of Champagne across all British retailers being under £20 – 'not ours, I hasten to add, ours is a lot higher than that' – he thinks that English and Welsh sparkling wine at between £24 and £40 a bottle 'represents good value for money'. He does however think that 'it would be naive to assume that people don't draw a comparison between English and Welsh sparkling wine and Champagne,' and that they try to make sure everything they sell is value for money. At the end of my interview Petrassi also touches on competitors to English and Welsh sparkling wines and mentions high-end ciders and perrys. He says that plantings of perry pears, which had been declining since the heady days when Babycham (a perry) was the tipple of choice for some members of the drinking classes, are now rising and that he sees 'more and more interesting stuff come across the desk of my beer and cider buyer, in a format which looks like high-end sparkling wine'. Selling at £10–15 these ciders and perrys advertise the fact that they have been made using the traditional method for sparkling wines, many of them using Champagne yeasts for the secondary fermentation. Petrassi feels that these drinks are 'something to keep an eye on, as their sales will grow on the coat-tails of English and Welsh sparkling wines.'

Petrassi also considers Nyetimber's rejection of the whole of its 2012 crop as being of too low a quality to be a masterly PR stroke. 'It's part of the richness of the Nyetimber story and is something they can use from time to time, again and again,' to persuade people that quality comes first. It certainly seems to have worked with Waitrose customers as Nyetimber's wines are among their best-sellers, despite being at the top end of their price range for English and Welsh wines. Hull says that Nyetimber's multi-vintage Classic Cuvée 'is of consistently high quality and customers have grown to love it and trust it.'

On the future for English and Welsh wines, both Petrassi and Hull are optimistic, but realistic. They are 'proud of our range of Champagnes and of English and Welsh sparkling wines, but one [English and Welsh wine] is on more of a journey than the other.' They both think that producers will start producing more non-vintage wines than they currently do and that from their favourite producers, 'the aspect of reserve wines is becoming more and more significant.' They feel that non-vintage is important to help iron out quality differences between vintages and to help balance out supplies as quantities vary between vintages. They also feel that 'the customer is really not bothered about vintage or non-vintage.' It's interesting to note that of the many English and Welsh sparkling wines available on the Waitrose Cellar website, none of the 37 wines listed on the front page have their vintages showing and it's only when you open up an individual wine that you can see the vintage (if they have one). I guess with the variability in supply of different vintages and with the small amounts available of some wines, dealing with vintages is a logistical nightmare and going non-vintage (whether it's a true non-vintage made from wines from at least two vintages, plus a fair dollop of reserve wines, or just a vintage wine labelled as non-vintage for ease of labelling and distribution) makes life slightly easier from a multiple retailer's point of view. They also see 'a gradual shift in quality [upwards] as people build up reserve stocks.' However, they do accept that 'in a market where you are trying to tell a story, vintage wines gives you a unique opportunity to do that.' They also say that whilst 'quality has come on in leaps and bounds, Becky [at the time of the interview, still English and Welsh wine buyer] still has to kiss a few frogs.'

With the hectares of sparkling wine vineyards having doubled from 2009, when it was 1,215 hectares (3,002 acres) to 2018, when it is officially 2,329 hectares (5,755 acres) and very little sparkling wine from the last six year's plantings yet on the market, the amount of English and Welsh sparkling wine about to hit the shelves, or at least be available for sale, is set to increase dramatically. 'Will there be shelf space for it?' I inquire. 'Yes, it will win more shelf space'. 'What will go? Champagnes?' 'No – other sparkling wines,' comes the reply. 'Definitely not Prosecco'. My guess is that its Cava and maybe some New World sparklers will lose out.

Finally I ask about packaging: 'Does a smart box help sell high-end sparkling wine?' Hull says, 'Only at Christmas, when customers are present hunting. People like to read the back label and that's not possible with a box. It gets in the way.' Often the same information is printed on the back of the box, but apparently people like to touch the bottle. There must be a lesson there for any producer looking to spend £2 or more on a box for their wine. The first vintage of Leckford Brut, the 2011, was initially packed in a box, but when they ran out of boxes, it was dropped. 'Better to spend the money on promoting the wine,' says Petrassi. Hull says that 'people spend a lot longer looking at Champagnes and sparkling wines and are much more likely to pick up a bottle and look at the back label.' She says, 'labelling has got much better in the last couple of years,' and they always encourage producers with labels they consider less than perfect to go into a branch and see what others are doing.

The Waitrose team is most definitely the single most influential conduit between producers of English and Welsh wines and the wine-buying public. Their comments and observations therefore need to be taken seriously. Compared to many other retailers and multiple off-licences, Waitrose offers a consistency of personnel which I know producers admire and find helpful and allows them to build up relationships so that there is mutual understanding of the trials and tribulations of being a wine producer in a fickle climate such as Britain's. Long may it continue.

Winbirri Vineyard

Bramerton Road, Surlingham, Norwich, Norfolk, NR14 7DE.
www.winbirri.com
13.5 hectares (33 acres)

Relatively new Norfolk vineyard producing exciting wines, especially from Bacchus. Winner of major Decanter World Wine Awards Trophy.

Steve and Lee Dyer (father and son) are the driving forces behind Winbirri, Norfolk's largest wine producer and inarguably its most successful. With around 13.5 hectares (33 acres) planted (of which 10.5 hectares are cropping) and more planting in the pipeline, they are getting very close to the top twenty of British producers. This part of Norfolk – which is generally 'very flat' as Noël Coward would say – actually has a few humps and bumps in it, despite being very close to the river Yare, which wends its way from Norwich (7.5 kilometres away) to Great Yarmouth (22.5 kilometres away). Their highest vineyard is actually 29 metres above sea level. The soil, being near the sea and the Broads, is mainly sandy with a liberal sprinkling of flints, and is great potato country (once you have buried the flints).

The Dyers have built their business from scratch, have 'never borrowed and don't owe anybody a penny,' and through trial and not too much error, got themselves a great enterprise, one that I see going from strength to strength. Steve started out his working life 'with a cart and a handbell,' selling fruit and vegetables through the streets of nearby Norwich. His grandfather had been a small-scale market gardener, growing tomatoes and mushrooms, and Steve had helped him out as a boy. From these small beginnings he built up a sizeable business – Mr Fruity – delivering fruit and vegetables, both fresh and pre-prepared, to greengrocers and catering outlets. With 47 employees and a £5m turnover, this company has, after 40 years of Steve's ownership, been sold in a management buyout, giving Steve (aged 67) plenty of time to spend on running the vineyards and keeping the deer – red, roe, fallow, Chinese water and muntjac – away from their young vines.

Unusually for British vineyards, the Dyers own very little of the land upon which they have planted vineyards. Apart from what one might call the home farm – a hectare of land adjacent to their winery, wine store and tractor shed which was once used for growing 'fancy lettuce' – all the land they farm is leased from a local farming estate. 'You can't buy land around here,' they say and even if they could, I am not sure they see buying land (at £22,500 per hectare) as a sensible use of their capital. They noted the bits of land that were 'rubbish and stony' or too small or irregular in shape for the potato harvester and took 25-year leases on them. They pay a reasonable rental – a little bit over the £300–400 per hectare their landlord might get for grazing or arable, but nothing excessive – 'just enough to keep them interested'. At the end of the tenancy, what will they do? Renegotiate, or if that proves a problem, grub the vines, reinstate the land and lease some more somewhere else. After all, their brand, the most valuable part of their business, is not tied to the land. The Dyers take the view that it's what you do with the grapes that counts, what value you add to them via processing and how and where you sell the wine made from them. This very much chimes with their experience in the fruit and veg business, where a carrot may be worth one price as a carrot, but sliced and diced, grated and packed and sold to a busy chef in ready-to-go portions, 'you can make a lot of money,' as Steve puts it.

The first plantings, in 2005, in what was then a fairly vine-barren region, were 200 Madeleine x Angevine 7672 and Siegerrebe 'just to see what they would do'. Steve made their first wine 'just for the family' using an 80-litre Idropress. This wine he cautiously gave to Lee on his return from Thailand, where he had been on what appears to have been an extended gap-year. What did Lee think of it? 'Not much,' says Lee. 'Can you do any better?' Steve asked him. 'I can and I will,' was Lee's reply, and very soon he took himself off to Plumpton College to learn the ins and outs of winegrowing and winemaking. Since those first 200 vines, land has been leased and vines planted. Bacchus, Chardonnay, Dornfelder, Madeleine x Angevine 7672, Pinot Noir, Regent, Rondo, Seyval Blanc, Siegerrebe and Solaris all have their place. The first vines were planted at 1.8 metres between the rows. 'A big mistake and they are too close together,' so later plantings are at 2.25 metres row width. From today's standpoint, where many vineyards (especially more recent ones) only grow the three Champagne varieties, or if they do grow still wine varieties, tend to major on Bacchus or just one or two more mainstream still wine varieties, the Winbirri list looks a bit random, even old-fashioned (I am quite surprised that Müller-Thurgau doesn't show up). However, when it comes to producing a crop year in, year out, a spread of varieties which includes the tried and tested hybrid Seyval Blanc and a selection of the best of the newer interspecific crosses (Rondo, Regent and Solaris) isn't such a foolish decision. Vineyards in Norfolk have always struggled. After all, Norwich is on about the same latitude as Hanover and there are not many vineyards there. In addition, Norfolk, especially near the east coast, lacks shelter from anything approaching a hill and is prone to cooling winds, which are not conducive to good flowering or fruit-set. Elmham Park, Harling, Heywood, Lexham Hall and Pulham were all there in the '70s and '80s, but are gone now. Some even made some good wine. Pulham's 1979 Magdalen Rivaner was a Gore-Browne Trophy winner and one of the first English wines I liked (and actually bought). Of course, with climate change, even Norfolk's climate has been improved and judging by Winbirri's performance, they are just as able to grow Chardonnay and Pinot Noir (albeit only for sparkling) as vineyards on the south coast, some 200 kilometres (125 miles) further south. It's as far from Norwich to Plumpton as it is from Plumpton to Épernay.

The Dyers manage their vineyards and the winery between them. Steve, with the help of a couple of part-timers and some students during the busy summer months, looks after all their vineyards and Lee does all the winery work, except of course for bottling and disgorging, when extra hands are required. Their 1.5 tonne Scharfenberger Europress is most definitely too small for their current planted area, let alone what's in the pipeline, and a new four or five tonne capacity one is being considered for the next harvest. Yields are not massive, they say that they aim for 5 tonnes per hectare (2 tonnes per acre), which would not be viable if you were only selling grapes. But when selling pretty well 100 per cent in the bottle (they have in the past sold some grapes, but not recently) their returns are reasonable. To date, in buildings, vineyards and winery and farming equipment, they have invested around £600,000–700,000. Always on the lookout for new income streams, they are buying a machine which will turn their prunings (which a different machine already chips and bags up directly in the vineyard) into briquettes which they can take round shops and garages and sell as an alternative to barbecue charcoal.

Sometimes in any business it's a random piece of luck that takes you forward to the next level, although as Gary Player (maybe) said, 'the harder I practise the luckier I get.' In the 2017 Decanter World Wine Awards (DWWA), where I chair the panel for English and Welsh wines, we gave a gold medal to an exceptionally vibrant and pure 2015 Bacchus still wine. It – along with the other eleven wines, still and sparkling that we awarded golds to – later went before the panel of super jurors, whose job is to award trophies and platinum medals to those wines that are 'best in class'. Our gold medal Bacchus was shown in the Best Value White Single Varietal class alongside a number of similar wines i.e. single varietal, white, under £15 retail wines from around the world.

And it came top. It was of course the 2015 Winbirri Bacchus, which had already won the 2016 Gore-Browne Trophy for the English Wine of the Year. Within days, the press went mad: the *Guardian*, *Daily Mail*, *Daily Telegraph*, *The Times* and countless other publications and news disseminating websites pushed it further into the stratosphere. My comment that 'the Winbirri 2015 Bacchus is one of the best wines made from Bacchus that I have ever tasted. Its nose is fresh and fruity and although the colour is very pale, the wine packs a powerful, fruit-filled palate,' was quoted all over the place. Bacchus now accounts for 19,000 of Winbirri's 52,000 vines, with more going in in 2019 and 2020.

Lee's telephone never stopped ringing. He told me that he had 4,000 unanswered emails in his inbox and they could have sold every bottle in a week. It was lucky that they hadn't sold any Bacchus grapes from the 2015 harvest as there was plenty of demand for them and Lee thought that they had quite a bit of the 2014 still to sell. Luckily they had decided to make the entire crop into wine and hadn't even started selling it when the award was announced. The price of the 2014 had been £13 a bottle and they decided to generate some goodwill with their existing customers, trade and private, and keep the 2015 at the same price. They restricted private customers to a maximum of two bottles of the Bacchus so long as they took a mixed case with some of their other wines, and kept supplying their trade customers as they had before. Waitrose, who would have taken every bottle and could have pushed the price up for the bottles they had, kept to the agreed pricing and of course, sold out in seconds.

Winbirri Vineyard is representative of many British vineyards but unlike a lot (probably the majority) has managed through sound business sense, not overspending, not wasting money on non-paying assets and taking the decision, one that suits them, of leasing land rather than owning it, to create a viable business that I am sure pays them a decent living. Had it not been for the excellence of their Bacchus, I might have said that their wines are good, but not great. Many of the varieties they grow might be considered second-class by some of the posher producers down south, but they work in Norfolk. Over time I am sure they will rationalize what they grow, perhaps taking out some of the poorer performers and majoring in Bacchus. They are certainly a good example of what can be achieved in Britain with a wine-producing business and all in less than 15 years.

Yorkshire Heart Vineyard

Pool Lane, Nin Monkton, York, North Yorkshire, YO26 8EL.
www.yorkshireheart.com
6 hectares (14.83 acres)

One of Britain's most northerly vineyards which, despite its location, is successfully making wines and selling them to appreciative customers.

I guess that when you have spent your life dealing in one sort of liquid in a bottle – milk – dealing in another type – wine – is almost second nature. Chris and Gillian Spakouskas (the surname comes from Chris' Lithuanian grandparents who, escaping a pogrom in 1911, stopped off in Britain on their way to America and stayed) spent almost thirty years running milk rounds in and around York. Both are from farming stock with Gillian's family being local dairy farmers. Wanting to maximize returns from their dairy, it seemed like a sensible extension to the family's business to bottle the product their cows were producing and to get Chris and Gillian to distribute it, so they started buying milk rounds. However, with the home-delivery of milk going through difficult times as supermarkets undercut the traditional milk rounds, Chris and Gillian started to think of alternative ways of using their family land and making a living from it.

Gillian had always made wine at home 'from anything that would ferment' says Chris, but one night, sitting up in bed with his cocoa and reading a wine book – Hugh Johnson's *World Atlas of Wine* seems the most likely culprit – he suddenly realized that 'proper' wine was *only* made from grapes. A visit to George Bowden at Leventhorpe Vineyard in 1998, then Yorkshire's only even faintly commercial vineyard, followed. A request to buy some grapes from Bowden was swiftly rejected, leaving them with the only other option: grow your own. The following year they bought 35 vines from Stuart Smith at the Vine House – Madeleine Angevine, Phoenix, Solaris, Rondo and two Regent – and got planting. Planted in their garden on a gentle south-west facing slope and trained to a single pole system (later changed to conventional posts and wires), it wasn't long before grapes were produced and Gillian could practise 'proper' winemaking. 'The whole point of planting grapes,' said Chris, 'was to make wine. That's what interested us.' They had caught the bug.

As they reduced their reliance on milk, selling off the rounds one by one, planting vineyards took over. With the help and encouragement of people like David Bates at Welland Vineyard in Leicestershire with his 'training days' and support from other enthusiastic members of the Mercian Vineyards Association, they started planting Yorkshire's second commercial vineyard in earnest in 2006. By 2018, their total planted area amounted to 4.47 hectares (11.05 acres) with a further 4,000 vines, around 1.5 hectares (3.71 acres), to be planted in 2019. Main varieties (in order of area planted) are Solaris, Seyval Blanc, Rondo and Ortega, with smaller plantings of Regent and Pinot Noir, plus a wide range of other varieties such as Acolon, Madeleine x Angevine 7672, Siegerrebe and one of the very few British plantings of Cabernet Franc. Apart from some of their initial plantings which are at 2 metres by 1 metre, all vines are now planted at either 2.5 metres by 1 metre (for Seyval Blanc) or 2.5 metres by 1.5 metres for Solaris and Rondo. Although the first blocks of vines were planted in a more or less north–south direction, the Spakouskases find their vines perform better when planted east–west, as the prevailing winds run down the rows rather than across them.

Yields, as one would expect at this latitude, are never huge, with average yields being around the 5 tonnes per hectare (2 tonnes per acre) mark, with heavier yielding varieties such as Rondo, Seyval Blanc and Solaris achieving nearer 7.5 tonnes per hectare (3 tonnes per acre) in good years such as 2014. In 2018, an exceptional year, some of the hybrids hit 12.5 tonnes per hectare (5 tonnes per acre) and even the Cabernet Franc produced its 'first fermentable crop'. They run the vineyards with a minimum of extra labour, doing as much of the work as they can themselves and with the help of family members. Their daughter-in-law is now trained to use the sprayer and takes over when Chris is giving tours. Vines are still hand-trimmed and hand deleafed, a task that ideally should be mechanized, but that equipment is 'still on the shopping list'.

Their biggest disaster to date was in early May 2010 when a -7°C spring frost wiped out all their growth in one night. They had expected some degree of frost and had sprayed an anti-frost spray the day before, leaving that evening to drive to Sussex to pick up some sparkling wine equipment. Returning the next day, their jaws dropped (and their hearts sank) as they saw their once green-shooted vineyards turned to blackened wisps. Of course, the damage was done and nothing could bring that year's crop back; yields were badly affected. However, even as they saw their damaged vines, thinking that perhaps they might have been killed by such a severe frost, Gillian says that she knew how addicted they had become as they started discussing what varieties they would replant.

Their winery has been simply equipped, using a lot of second-hand equipment and budget stainless steel tanks. 'Fine if you're careful with them,' says Chris, 'but they don't take too much mishandling'. For their first small crop in 2009 they bought a small second-hand Vaslin screw press but have since upgraded to a bigger Slovakian airbag press as their volumes increased. Altogether they have spent no more than £60,000 on the winery equipment (not including the building) which seems like something of a bargain. They make both still and sparkling wines, selling them mainly (80 per cent) from the farm gate. Prices for still wines are £12–£13 a bottle, with sparklers at £25. Visitors, tours, coach parties and wedding parties are the mainstay of their clientele, all of whom appear to want something to take home. 'If they can't afford a bottle of wine, then they will take a bottle of beer or a card. They have to take something,' says Gillian. They fully admit that their customers are not 'educated wine people,' but nevertheless they know what they like and appreciate the time and trouble taken on tours to explain the processes and how different varieties and the changing vintages affect the style and taste of the wines.

In order to supplement the vineyard and wine production business, they decided in 2010–11 to start a small brewery. 'We knew that the vineyard would keep us out of the poorhouse,' said Chris, 'but we needed something to make us some money.' Some seven years on, they admit that brewing is a hard road to riches, although profitability is definitely on the horizon. 'There's a craft brewery around every corner and we are all selling to the same customers,' says Chris, adding 'this makes life difficult, especially as pubs are notoriously bad payers.' 'We gave too much credit to start with,' says Gillian, 'and learnt the hard way,' but they now feel they have a better balance of pubs, restaurants and farm shops, who take their beers and the minority of the wine they don't sell direct. They don't need – and indeed do not have the volume – to sell wine through multiples or merchants.

Chris and Gillian Spakouskas would be the first to admit that establishing a vineyard north of York might seem like a brave (some may say foolhardy) venture. Yields are not as good as in the southern counties of Britain and with the need to grow hardier varieties than those found in the more favourable parts of the islands, wine quality is always going to be compromised. However, unless you try, how do you know what's possible? Chris and Gillian have shown that by doing the job well, looking after the vines with a high degree of professionalism (better than many high-profile vineyards in Kent and Sussex) and adapting to the climatic conditions they have to deal with, a business based upon growing vines can be created in unlikely locations. Whether it's a blueprint for others to follow, whether the business has the legs to be sustainable in the long term, only time will tell. One thing is certain though: it will not be for a lack of hard work and dedication.

7

MAFF & DEFRA: WINEMAKING AND LABELLING REGULATIONS

EARLY DAYS

In the early days of the viticultural revival, Britain's Ministry of Agriculture, Fisheries and Food (MAFF) took an active interest in the subject and for 20 years there was an official National Vines Adviser who could be called upon to advise growers through MAFF's own consultancy arm, the Agricultural Development and Advisory Service (ADAS). The first person to occupy this position was Tony Heath, a soft-fruit adviser based at the Efford Experimental Husbandry Station (EHS) at Lymington near Southampton. Although principally a strawberry specialist, he took a great personal interest in vines and was responsible for writing two MAFF publications on the subject: *Outdoor Grape Production* (1978) and *Grapes for Wine* (1980). After Heath retired, his position was taken in turn by Joanna Wood, Sheila Baxter and Jerry Garner, all of whom gave advice to growers on matters viticultural. Efford EHS had its own vineyard, planted in 1975, which undertook variety and trellising trials, as well as trials on vine nutrition, fungicides and weed control. It published several useful reports, hosted open days and while it lasted, provided some useful information to Britain's small but growing band of winegrowers. In 1986 MAFF decided that running the vineyard was an expense it could do without and it was grubbed-up. In recent years, with the privatization of ADAS, the position of National

Vines Adviser has lain dormant, and advice, certainly free advice, on viticulture is no longer available.

Relations with MAFF, as the authority governing the production of wine both before Great Britain joined the European Union (EU) and, since 1973, after it joined, have always been important for British grape growers and winemakers. To begin with, the English Vineyards Association (EVA) was invited by MAFF to meetings on an irregular basis to discuss matters that affected the industry, such as vine varieties, winery practices, labelling legislation, pesticide registrations and a wide range of other topics. This committee, which became known as the English and Welsh Wine Liaison Committee, was purely advisory and its deliberations and decisions carried no official weight. Once the area of vines in Britain was known to exceed 500 hectares (which happened in 1987) relations between the industry and MAFF were put on a more formal basis, with meetings held regularly. In addition, a Vine Varieties Classification Committee (VVCC) was formed, the task of which was to oversee changes to the lists of vine varieties permitted to be grown in Britain. In 2001, a new government department, the Department for Environment, Food, and Rural Affairs (DEFRA) came into being and took over MAFF's portfolio including vines and wine production.

QUALITY AND REGIONAL WINE SCHEMES

The reaching of the 500-hectare limit in 1987 caused Wine Standards (WS) to start the process of drawing up a vineyard register – a national list of all vineyards containing exact plot (parcel) locations and sizes, together with the number of vines and the variety, clone and rootstock types. The following year MAFF conducted a statutory survey of all vineyards over one-tenth of a hectare (100 ares) then known to exist. Given that it was not then obligatory to register the ownership of a vineyard unless it was producing a 'wine sector product' (grapes, grape juice or wine), this survey was bound to be a little bit hit and miss.[38] However, comprehensive or not, the survey showed a remarkable increase in the

38 Today, a vineyard of 0.1 hectares or more is meant to register with the WS within six months of planting. This legal requirement has never been enforced, hence many vineyards fail to register and their presence is only officially picked up when they produce their first grapes and process them into wine or take them to a winery.

area under vines. From 546 hectares with 382 hectares in production in 1988, the total jumped in one year by over 60 per cent to 876 hectares with 652 hectares in production. More interesting were the yield figures. Declared production in 1988 was 4,110 hectolitres – equivalent to 548,000 75 centilitre bottles – but in 1989 the figure shot to 21,447 hectolitres – 2,859,600 75 centilitre bottles. That's a 520 per cent increase! Although this was partly due to better weather in 1989 and therefore a larger yield, it was obvious that the pre-1989 surveys were only picking up the smaller, less productive vineyards and those with larger yields had, for whatever reason, declined to send in returns.

The reason for concern over the high yield figure, both within the industry and with British officialdom, was the existence of an EU-wide vine-planting ban which applied in all member states whose annual production was in excess of 25,000 hectolitres of wine. (This limit had originally been set at 5,000 hectolitres and a planting ban had been mooted in 1979 to take effect in 1980–1981, but the EVA had successfully petitioned MAFF at the time and the limit was raised by the EU to 25,000 hectolitres.) In 1993, when a 26,428-hectolitre yield was announced for the 1992 harvest, MAFF successfully appealed to the Commission to take a five-year average yield figure rather than one single year. The limit was then raised to 50,000 hectolitres, taking Britain well out of the danger zone. This was the situation until 2007 when, as part of the general EU wine regime reforms, it was announced that a planting ban in those member states that did not already have one, would never (or at least would be highly unlikely to) take place.

The only official way around the planting ban was either to buy planting rights from a grower who was permanently giving up growing vines (the usual way for growers in the remainder of the EU to expand their vineyard holdings) or to apply to the authorities for permission to plant vines. In this latter case, growers who wished to plant new vineyards could only do so for 'the production of certain [still] Quality Wines which could be shown to be in demand by the market.' Back in the 1990s, the discovery that Britain had what was probably nearer 1,000 hectares of vines rather than 500 hectares and that in good years was capable of producing well over 25 hectolitres per hectare, meant that the country's wine industry was in serious danger of breaching the 25,000-hectolitre barrier which would, according to the strict interpretation of the regulations, have precipitated a planting ban in Britain.

Given that the country had no Quality Wine Scheme (QWS), a crop in excess of this figure would have ended all new vine planting in Britain.

In early 1990, as soon as the results of the 1989 vineyard survey were known, MAFF decided that the solution to this potential problem was to set up a Quality Wine Scheme Committee (QWSC) whose task would be to draw up a full 'Quality Wine Produced in a Specified Region' (QWpsr) scheme to give still (i.e. not sparkling) English and Welsh wines full *appellation d'origine contrôlée* status. To satisfy the EU regulations was in one sense the easiest, and in another the hardest of the committee's problems. The regulations had been drawn up with a fairly broad brush so that they could cope with the myriad different production conditions across the climatic and cultural spread of Europe. They had also been drawn up with one eye on the preservation of each region's 'traditional practices'. The fact that Britain had played no part in drawing up the original regulations and in any event was a relative newcomer to winegrowing and winemaking, meant that its tally of 'traditional practices' was fairly small. The one big impediment to getting a scheme that satisfied both the regulations and the majority of growers was the thorny problem of hybrids (vines with some non-*Vitis vinifera* genetic material in them). Under a clause in the EU regulations these were denied the right – in whatever proportions – to be made into Quality Wine.

For many growers in Britain the exclusion of hybrids was a difficult pill to swallow. As well as Seyval Blanc, which at the time was the third most widely planted variety in terms of area and the most widely planted in terms of the number of vineyards having the variety, there were a number of older hybrid varieties (Cascade, Léon Millot, Maréchal Foch and Triomphe) together with some newer ones (Orion, Phoenix, Regent and Rondo[39]) which growers found useful. Hybrids covered over 15 per cent of the total British vine area and produced approximately 25 per cent of Britain's wine – a higher percentage than their area because of two factors: their higher than average yield and the fact that they were often blended with wines from *vinifera* varieties. Their exclusion from Quality Wine production was a hangover from history. Apart from the fact that they existed in many British growers' vineyards and, in most cases, were useful, disease-resistant varieties, the grapes from them made perfectly good wine.

39 These four varieties have since been declared 'true' *viniferas* and can now be made into PDO wines.

The arguments over whether hybrids could or could not, should or should not, be included in the QWS went on for many meetings. Representations were made to the Commission and their ruling was that they could not, and furthermore the basic regulations could only be altered by a qualified majority of the Council of Ministers. Officials from MAFF pointed out quite forcefully to the EVA committee members that this was a highly unlikely occurrence. Knowing that a 25,000-hectolitre yield could be just around the corner and knowing that a Brussels-imposed vine-planting ban would not reflect well upon them or help relations with the general farming community ('MAFF introduces vine planting ban' was not the headline anyone wanted to see), MAFF decided that a scheme should go ahead without the inclusion of hybrids.

In many other respects, the QWS was fairly straightforward to design. Apart from the issue of varieties, there was less contention over such subjects as minimum natural alcohols, the geographical areas covered, whether wines could be made in one area from grapes grown in another, whether irrigation should be allowed (it was not) and what the yield restrictions should be. As to what should actually constitute a Quality Wine, the committee relied heavily on the existing EVA Seal of Quality regulations. With only a few amendments and adjustments to the analytical requirements, it was able to lift the Seal regulations in their entirety and place them into the QWS. Wines would be subject to a fairly stringent analysis which looked at not only the simple physical aspects such as the alcohol, acid, sulphur dioxide, iron and copper contents, but also the wine's sterility status (bacteria and yeasts) and its stability with regard to both proteins and tartrates. It had been found with the operation of the Seal that the sterility and stability requirements had been valuable in weeding out those winemakers whose winemaking and bottling practices were not really up to standard and while they might have been able to produce wines of fine quality on the day of the tasting, they did not keep once in the hands of the wine merchant or final customer. The wines would be tasted by a panel of between five and seven members, at least two of whom would be Masters of Wine,[40] and would follow the twenty-point tasting scheme that had proved simple

40 This last requirement was changed as it proved difficult to get MWs to turn out (unpaid) for what were often tastings of only five to ten wines. Today, there is no requirement for any MWs to be present, although there is usually at least one on the tasting panel.

and workable for the Seal. The minimum natural alcoholic strength of wines eligible for Quality Wine status, i.e. their potential alcohol level at harvest and before enrichment (chaptalization) was set at 6.5 per cent (1.5 per cent more than the level for Table Wine). A derogation existed that allowed member states to reduce this to 6 per cent and this was applied for but was not granted until December 1991, too late for it to apply to wines from the 1991 vintage.

By the early summer of 1991, a basic scheme had been drawn up and was almost ready to be submitted to the Commission for its comments. The issue of hybrids remained unsettled, with a majority on the committee unwilling to see a scheme introduced which discriminated against these varieties. This majority suggested that the scheme be held in abeyance until such time as a planting ban was threatened. However, MAFF thought otherwise. Fearing the arrival of a crop higher than 25,000 hectolitres, it was determined to press ahead with the scheme's introduction for the 1991 harvest. In an attempt to placate the pro-hybrid lobby, the then Junior Agriculture Minister, David Curry, went to Brussels and on 30 May 1991 returned waving a piece of paper (in what some of us thought was a rather Neville Chamberlainesque 'Peace for our Time' sort of way) which promised that 'the Commission will study the possibility of including inter-specific [hybrid] varieties in the list of varieties deemed suitable for the production of Quality Wine produced in a specified region.'[41]

The last hurdle to be overcome before the scheme could be submitted to the Commission was that of the geographical delineation and naming of the 'specified regions' of production. An obvious solution was to create regions based upon the existing regional vineyards associations' areas – East Anglia, South East, Wessex, South West, etc. – but this was quickly found to be unacceptable once the rules on the naming of Quality Wine regions had been fully digested. Under the rules contained in Council Regulations 823/87 (as amended by Regulation 2043/89)

41 The pro-hybrid lobby took the view that they would believe this 'study' when they saw it. Annual requests for it to be undertaken were partially satisfied with a financial provision for it making an appearance in the EU's budget. There was then more delay as the Commission couldn't find anyone impartial enough to undertake it. Eventually, more than 12 years after the promise was first made, a wholly unsatisfactory paper exercise took place, in which the wine industry took no part. The result was even less satisfactory than the method of its undertaking. The study concluded that, under certain circumstances – surprise, surprise – hybrids could be made into perfectly satisfactory wine. This result of course did nothing to sway the Commission and non-*viniferas* are still excluded from all PDO wines.

grapes grown in one region could only be made into a Quality Wine in the same region or in an administrative region (taken to mean a county) that was in immediate proximity (taken to mean having a common border) to the one where the grapes were grown. This meant that grapes from Essex, for example, could not be made into Quality Wine in East Sussex as these two counties would not have been in adjacent Quality Wine regions. The only derogation to these rules was if the practice was both traditional and had taken place continuously since before 1973 besides meeting other specified conditions. Since the first two restrictions could not be met by any winery in Britain, no one bothered to enquire what the other specified conditions were. As a trade in grapes between vineyards and wineries across Britain existed, it was felt that the 'multiple region' approach was too inflexible for most British growers and winemakers and that a 'two regions' approach (where one region was entirely contiguous with another) would be best. Another problem which a multiple region system would have exacerbated was that juice used for sweetening Quality Wines (*süssreserve*) had to originate from the same region in which the grapes were grown and two large regions would make for more flexibility than several small ones. The option favoured by the industry members of the committee was to split Britain into two adjacent regions – England and Wales – which would have resulted in two descriptors: English Quality Wine psr and Welsh Quality Wine psr. Given these two regions, Welsh grapes could be taken to wineries in English counties bordering Wales (and of course vice versa), which was an important consideration given the location of the Three Choirs winery in Gloucestershire which made wines under contract for several smaller Welsh growers. Everyone agreed that this was a practical, pragmatic solution and it was incorporated into the draft regulations.

The question of what to call Table Wines also had to be addressed, given that the WS – responsible for policing labelling in Britain – felt that English Quality Wine psr and English Table Wine (and the Welsh equivalents) would not have been acceptable to the Commission. One solution, which had the approval of the industry members of the QWSC, was to call them all United Kingdom (or UK) Table Wines. This solution was accepted by the committee and a final draft of the 'Pilot Quality Wine Scheme' (as it was initially known) was sent out to all growers in August 1991 so that wines from the 1991 vintage would be able to be considered for Quality Wine status. The WS stated that they felt that the scheme was being hurriedly introduced and that they were really not ready to handle the additional work as the Vineyard Register was not fully completed.

Feedback from the industry soon showed that producers were less than keen on renaming their Table Wines by the proposed descriptor United Kingdom Table Wines, especially those with wines which, because they were made wholly or partly from hybrids, were not eligible for inclusion in the QWS. Once the WS also pointed out that certain information on labels, such as the name of the vine variety and the vintage, could only appear on wines where the Geographical Indication (GI) covered an area smaller than the member state, this solution was effectively dead. The industry members of the committee urged MAFF to reconsider the idea to have both English Quality Wine and English Table Wine or some other variant which incorporated the words England or English (and likewise Wales/Welsh), but it was felt that the Commission would not accept this, despite there being examples in, for instance, French wine labelling (*Vin de Pays du Jardin de la France*). After considerable discussion and several additional committee meetings, and with the 1991 harvest already completed, a typical bureaucratic solution was arrived at. Two regions would be created, one called Northern Counties (Durham, Humberside, South Yorkshire and West Yorkshire) which contained almost no vineyards and one called Southern Counties (i.e. the rest of the south of the country, including Wales), which contained almost all existing vineyards. In addition, vines for Quality Wine production had to be situated below 220 metres above sea level, a height chosen with some care, as it was known that no vineyards were planted above this height, yet it further defined the geographical limits of the region.

However bizarre it seemed, this solution did allow grapes and juice to be shipped around the wine-producing counties, got around the problem of renaming Table Wines and satisfied MAFF and the Commission. Despite general industry opposition, letters to the Minister of Agriculture and a leader in *Decanter*, in January 1992 this solution was steamrollered through the committee. With the 1991 wines already made and eligible for Quality Wine status, a decision had to be made quickly and the committee was advised that this was the best stop-gap solution. Industry members of the committee felt that MAFF should have been more forceful in interpreting the regulations to suit Britain's geographical and climatic circumstances, especially as MAFF was prepared to base regions on nothing other than what was, in reality, administrative convenience. The regulations stated that a Quality Wine region had to 'describe a wine-growing area ... which produces wines with particular quality characteristics', but this did not seem to bother anyone from MAFF or the Commission too much. With the best will in the world, wines from the Southern Counties (i.e. the whole of Britain's vineyard area) could hardly be said to show any particular quality characteristics that would distinguish them from those of the Northern Counties especially as no wines from this area existed.

At the same January meeting, the use of two alternative wine descriptors was accepted and it was agreed that wines could be labelled Quality Wine or Designated Origin. Originally it had been hoped, at least by most industry committee members, that a single descriptor – that of Designated Origin (similar to that used in *all* other EU member states apart from Germany) would have been acceptable to MAFF. The thinking behind this was that growers whose wines were ineligible to be entered for the scheme – mainly because they were made in whole or in part from non-*vinifera* grapes – would be at a disadvantage by the appearance of the word Quality on some wines, but not on theirs, even though they might be of equal – or even better – quality. However, MAFF officials announced that the Minister could not ban the term Quality Wine produced in a specified region and risked prosecution if he did so. Again, the fact that most wine-producing member states *had* interpreted the regulations to suit their own purposes and had effectively banned the use of this alternative term counted for nothing – another example of British officials playing by the rules to the disadvantage of their own citizens.

The completed scheme was quickly agreed by the Commission, the necessary Statutory Instruments were drawn up and issued, and the pilot Quality Wine Scheme was incorporated into British legislation. The English Vineyards Association had been appointed to be the recognized industry body (RIB) responsible for handling applications to the scheme and sending wines to be analysed and tasted. The first tasting was held on 18 May 1992 at which ten wines, which had already been analysed and had cleared the analytical requirements, were tasted. All passed and after the producers' winemaking records were inspected, were given Quality Wine status.

Over the years since the original pilot scheme was incorporated into British legislation, several changes have been made. Some sort of sense prevailed in the naming of the regions and after considerable argument in committee about what other member states were allowed to do (i.e. get away with) MAFF accepted that the terms English Vineyards and Welsh Vineyards could be used as the names of the 'Specified Regions'. These regions covered all English and Welsh counties that contained vineyards, so long as those vineyards were no more than 220 metres above sea level. These terms were felt to be sufficiently different from English Table Wine and Welsh Table Wine not to incur the displeasure of the Commission. In 1996, when a Regional Wine Scheme (RWS, equivalent to the French *Vin de Pays* category) was introduced to give some sort of status to wines made from non-*vinifera* varieties, the terms English Counties and Welsh Counties were adopted, covering exactly the same geographical areas as the Quality Wine regions, but being sufficiently different as vines growing over 220 metres above sea level were accepted (despite the fact that no vines were being grown – or indeed would be likely to ripen grapes – at this altitude), but below 250 metres above sea level.

Thus, in the naming of the three categories of wine allowed to be produced in Britain –Table Wine, Regional Wine and Quality Wine – the three descriptors and the regions they cover are, while in fact the same, on paper sufficiently different to satisfy the *amour-propre* of both ministers and officials, as well as offering lip service to the regulations, thus keeping Brussels happy. What a strange world we inhabit.

It has now been almost thirty years since the Quality Wine regulations were 'imposed' upon winegrowers in Britain and despite initial misgivings from some that it would lead to alarm and panic among vine growers and winemakers, the net effect has been – surprise, surprise – a gradual improvement in the quality of the wines being produced in Britain. At the time of its introduction, I was, because of the hybrid problem, one of the most vociferous against it. While I have not changed my mind that the exclusion of the old hybrids (principally Seyval Blanc, the fifth most widely grown variety, often used for blending with other varieties for both still and sparkling wines) is divisive and has *nothing* to do with wine quality, I knew that the imposition on growers of a set of rules and regulations which related directly to the quality of the wines they were producing would, in the long-run, be a good thing.

In 2004 DEFRA (as MAFF had then become) was informed by the EU that the terms English Table Wine and Welsh Table Wine were illegal as a Table Wine may not bear a GI smaller than the area covered by the member state, unless that Table Wine has some redeeming features and has been adjudged to be a Regional Wine. This in itself was no surprise to me at all and was something that had already been pointed out in committee several times. In all probability, EU officials thought that England was an alternative name for Great Britain, an understandable mistake since most mainland Europeans refer to anyone from across the Channel as 'English'. The upshot of this was that the categories of wine able to be produced were, once again, changed: basic Table Wine, untested and untasted, was to be called 'UK Table Wine', with the categories Regional and Quality Wine remaining much as before, although Regional Wine now has to be grown at less than 250 metres above sea level (Quality Wine remains at below 220 metres, while UK Table Wine can be grown at any height above (or, I suppose, even below) sea level.

The good thing about these changes was that a UK Table Wine would be unable to bear a vintage or the name of any vine variety used in its production. Thus most growers, used to having both a vintage and a vine variety on their labels, would be more likely to put their wines up for Regional or Quality Wine status and therefore their wines would be tested and tasted before being offered to the public. While at the time I kept my own counsel about this benefit (not wishing to make myself any more unpopular with some growers than I already was), the result of this change is exactly as I surmised. Very few wines, and certainly very few wines of interest, were labelled as UK Table Wines and the overall quality of the still wines produced in Britain has gradually risen over the years.

Other changes to the rules for the production of Quality and Regional Wine were small and mainly aimed at making the schemes more user-friendly. Wines entered for Regional Wine status could be accompanied by an analysis certificate drawn up by the producer, rather than requiring (an expensive) one from a laboratory and tastings for Regional Wine status could now take place as part of a properly organized tasting competition. Thus wines entered for the national competition or one of the Regional Association's competitions, if they achieved the correct score and were accompanied by the correct paperwork, gained Regional Wine status automatically. Regional Wines were also permitted to bear the name of a county (or unitary authority), meaning there are 18 English GIs and 11 Welsh GIs, and bottles can be labelled Cornish Regional Wine or Pembrokeshire Regional Wine.

The one big hole in the whole apparatus of Quality and Regional Wine status was the exclusion of sparkling wines. Under current EU legislation, there are three basic types of sparkling wine: Aerated Sparkling Wine, a wine produced by the addition of carbon dioxide (which must be stated on the label); Sparkling Wine, a sparkling wine produced by tank fermentation (Charmat method), transfer method or bottle fermentation, but which has not spent a minimum time on the lees; and Quality Sparkling Wine, a wine which has spent a minimum of nine months on lees.[42] (This is a very broad summary of the categories; there are myriad additional requirements which define each of these three types.) This means that most producers of sparkling wine in Britain, virtually all of whom produce wine by bottle fermentation and who leave it on the lees to mature, are able to call their wines 'Traditional Method Quality Sparkling Wine', thus immediately gaining (in the eyes of all but anyone extremely familiar with both winemaking and wine labelling regulations) instant recognition for their wines, irrespective of their intrinsic quality. The added (if wholly illogical) bonus is that the word 'Quality' in 'Quality Sparkling Wine' refers to the method of production, *not* the base materials from which it has been made, thus allowing Seyval Blanc and other hybrids to be made into 'quality' sparkling wine.

CHANGES IN WINE REGULATIONS – 2009 TO 2011

In 2009, after much discussion between the major wine-producing countries – in which Britain played little part – major changes to the terminology used on labels and some slightly less major changes to wine production processes were agreed by the EU. Quality Wines became known as Protected Designation of Origin (PDO) wines, Regional Wines as Protected Geographical Indication (PGI) wines and 'wines with no PDO or PGI' that had been through a simple 'Certification Process' (in reality just a tick-box exercise) as Varietal Wines. Anything

42 There are also semi-sparkling wines and aerated semi-sparkling wines, but no producer currently makes either of these.

other than that would be known as UK Table Wine. The most important change was that wines, still and sparkling, without a GI (Geographical Indication), i.e. those wines which had not been through the QWS, RWS, or any subsequently agreed schemes, were allowed to be labelled as Wine of England, Product of England or Produced in England (and the Welsh equivalents) rather undermining the exclusivity of the word 'England' or 'Wales'.

In 2011, Britain proposed a quality scheme for sparkling wines. Up until then, most producers of sparkling wines were quite happy with the labelling situation as under the slightly bizarre EU regulations, the word 'quality' on a bottle of sparkling wine refers to the method of production, not the grape varieties. Thus growers of hybrids, in Britain principally Seyval Blanc, could happily label their sparkling wines, so long as they were bottle fermented, 'English Quality Sparkling Wine' without having to put the wine through any sort of testing or tasting procedures. However, the rise to prominence (and dominance) of 'proper' sparkling wines meant that the larger growers wanted a proper EU-approved PDO scheme. Thus was one born. Its basic requirements were the use of one or more of six 'classic' grape varieties – Chardonnay, Pinot Noir, Meunier, Pinot Blanc, Pinot Gris and Pinot Noir Précoce (the last also known as Blauer Frühburgunder) – plus a minimum of nine months on lees in the bottle. Whether the 'classic' Pinot Noir Précoce should have been included in the varietal line-up is debateable, but it was felt that as quite a few growers had it and treated it as if it were Pinot Noir, it didn't really make a lot of difference. Producers using Seyval Blanc weren't too upset by the new sparkling PDO as they were able to call their wines English Regional Quality Sparkling Wine (if PGI wines) or just Quality Sparkling Wine if neither PDO nor PGI.

NEW PDO SCHEMES

In 2012, Camel Valley Vineyard lodged an application for Britain's first 'single-site' PDO. This covered the 7-hectare 'Darnibole' land, only for Bacchus, plus a few other qualitative parameters (8 tonnes per hectare maximum yield, hand-picked, low-pressure pressing). This application was granted in time for the 2014 vintage. In 2015, plans for a 'Sussex' PDO scheme for both still and sparkling wines were drawn up and an application was lodged with the EU by Sussex Wine Producers, an organization whose prime mover and shaker is Mark Driver from Rathfinny Vineyards, who at that stage was yet to release any wines made from his own grapes. Apart from confining it to grapes grown in and wines made in the counties of East and West Sussex, the scheme for sparkling wines allowed for wines made 'principally' from Chardonnay, Pinot Noir and Meunier (without defining what 'principally' means) plus 'in addition Arbanne, Pinot Gris, Pinot Blanc, Petit Meslier and Pinot Noir Précoce may be used'. Quite why Arbanne and Petit Meslier may be used is a question I asked (and did not get an answer to) since they are only planted in extremely small numbers in Britain, although of course accepting that they are two of the six varieties permitted to be used in Champagne. Various other minor quality tweaks over and above the English Sparkling PDO were included. For still wines, the Sussex scheme was much the same as the English still wine PDO, although with a slightly bizarre list of permitted varieties (Acolon, Gamay, Riesling, Roter Veltliner?) and a few minor qualitative tweaks. At the time of writing, the application is still making its way through Brussels and will probably not be finally determined until the UK leaves the EU, although growers are apparently allowed to use the new PDO terms in the meantime.

WINEMAKING RULES AND REGULATIONS

The regulations governing the production of wine from home-grown grapes have only altered a little since Britain joined the Common Market in 1973. The minimum natural (i.e. potential) alcohol level which grapes have to reach before they can be harvested and made into wine, both still and sparkling, is at the fairly low level of 6 per cent (it used to be 5 per cent for Table and Regional wines). For all categories of wine, enrichment (i.e. chaptalization) levels used to be plus 3.5 per cent in normal years, with an additional 1 per cent allowed in years when climatic conditions are 'exceptionally unfavourable', but in 2009 these were lowered to plus 3 per cent, with an additional 0.5 per cent permitted in poor years. This extra 0.5 per cent allowance may be restricted to certain parts of the country or certain grape varieties. Some growers have experimented with 'cryo-extraction' or 'freeze concentration' where grape juice is concentrated by cooling to freezing point and removing the resultant ice. This technique is allowed up to a point where the natural alcohol level is increased by no more than 2 per cent.

For enriched PDO and PGI wines, there is a maximum total alcohol level (total alcohol is the sum of the actual plus the potential alcohol) of 11.5 per cent for white and 12 per cent for red and rosé wines and a maximum of 15 per cent *total* alcohol for non-enriched wines of whatever colour. Wines with more than 15 per cent *total* alcohol cannot be PGI or Varietal wines and have to qualify for PDO status before they can be sold in the EU. It is important therefore to exclude non-*vinifera* grapes from these wines as only 100 per cent pure *vinifera* wines qualify for PDO status.

Still PDO and PGI wines must have at least 8.5 per cent *actual* alcohol when bottled and PDO wines must have a minimum total alcohol of 9 per cent, although unenriched white wines may, subject to EU approval, be bottled with 8.5 per cent *actual* alcohol. Acid levels of all bottled still wines must be at least 4 g/l (total acidity expressed as tartaric acid). Deacidification of juice and wines still in fermentation[43] is allowed without limit, but finished wines may only be deacidified by a maximum of 1 g/l. For both PDO and PGI sparkling wines, many of the same rules apply, with minimum *actual* alcohol levels of 9 per cent in the cuvée and 10 per cent after secondary fermentation. Deacidification of a cuvée is permitted without limit (something most winemakers would not need to do) and a cuvée may be acidified by up to 1.5 g/l, but not a deacidified cuvée. Lees ageing times for both PDO and PGI sparkling wines are 9 months from the start of fermentation until release for sale. These are only the very basic rules governing the production of wine in Britain and the full regulations can be downloaded from the 'Food and Drink' section of the DEFRA website. The 'Darnibole' and 'Sussex' PDOs have slightly different rules.

The restrictions on total alcohol levels of enriched non-PDO wines to 11.5 per cent for whites and 12 per cent for reds and rosé wines can lead to problems. A medium-dry wine with say 9 g/l of residual sugar, which equates to a potential alcohol of just over 0.5 per cent, may only have an actual alcohol of, at the very maximum, 11 per cent in order to keep under the 11.5 per cent total figure. In reality winemakers have to aim slightly lower than the 11.5 per cent total alcohol figure as there are always inaccuracies in the initial measurement of sugar levels and

43 'Still in fermentation' is defined as before the wine is racked off its gross lees.

sugar to alcohol conversion rates are never that predictable. This means that many wines are bottled with between 10 per cent and 10.5 per cent actual alcohol which, by today's standards, is quite low. Wines from warmer parts of the winegrowing world are much more likely to be bottled with at least 12.5 per cent and typically for many regions 13.5 to 14 per cent actual alcohol. This relative lack of alcohol in the wines of Great Britain is noticeable to wine drinkers more used to other contemporary wines, and whilst it might appeal to the health conscious, there are still plenty of consumers for whom the alcohol level is a key decider – within reason, the higher the better. One solution to this problem is to make more PDO wines, where the upper limit on total alcohol is 15 per cent. However, this does not help those wines made in whole or in part from hybrids, which cannot, under present EU legislation, be Quality Wines. This means that producers of red wines, which are the wines that really might benefit from having actual alcohols in the 12.5–13.5 per cent range, have to make sure that they don't use any hybrids in their blends. Luckily, the 2002 ruling by DEFRA (following, I have to say, five years of lobbying by myself) that four modern interspecific-crosses – Orion, Phoenix, Regent and Rondo – would henceforth be considered to be *viniferas* has helped red wine producers, as Rondo and Regent are both successful red varieties and both quite widely used.

The question of the use of *süssreserve* for the pre-bottling sweetening of wines seemed to exercise minds greatly in the 1980s, but no longer seems such an issue. Many winemakers, now using temperature regulated stainless steel tanks, can stop fermentations more or less at will, using strains of yeast that are easier to stop, as well as racking-off and cooling. *Süss* – as it tends to be called when it is used – is either imported (almost entirely from Germany with Müller-Thurgau and Bacchus being the most popular varieties) or is home-grown, where Müller-Thurgau and Reichensteiner (and occasionally Bacchus) are the preferred varieties. This change has come about partly because it is a requirement for PDO wines that material used for sweetening originates in the same region of production as the wine being sweetened. Stopping fermentations of course gets around the problem of finding suitable English or Welsh *süssreserve*. If sweetened, the *total* alcoholic strength may not be raised by more than 4 per cent (around 68 grams per litre residual sugar which ought to be enough for most palates) or raise it above 15 per cent *total* alcohol. For sweetening sparkling wines i.e. in the *dosage*, most producers use Rectified Concentrated Grape Must (RCGM in English or MCR in French), which being liquid, odourless and colourless is a very easy product to use.

Residual sugar levels in English and Welsh wines have come down markedly over the past 20–30 years, mainly because of the change in tastes of the wine-buying public, many of whom now prefer wines with relatively low levels of residual sugar. Geoff Taylor, whose 'Corkwise' analytical laboratory has been the principal analyst to English and Welsh winegrowers since 1988, says that most English and Welsh wines now fall into the official 'dry' and 'medium dry' categories where, with sufficient acidity, wines can have up to 9 g/l (dry) and 18 g/l (med-dry) of residual sugar. Very few English and Welsh wines are now bottled with more than 25 g/l of residual sugar, which was far from the case in the 1980s. Taylor also says that in the almost 30 years he has been analysing English and Welsh wines he has noticed that acidity levels have come down, due to riper grapes, better deacidification and the use of malolactic fermentation. He also says that alcohol levels have risen (as they have worldwide) which he feels is due to growers leaving their grapes to ripen more fully, coupled with the use of yeasts with better sugar-to-alcohol conversion rates and the wider use of refrigeration in British wineries. This leads to gentler fermentations and less alcohol loss. He also says that without a doubt, the overall quality of English and Welsh wines has risen very substantially and many of the poorer producers now appear (thankfully) to have given up the struggle. This is surely good news for the industry.

8

VINEYARD ASSOCIATIONS

THE ENGLISH VINEYARDS ASSOCIATION

By the mid-1960s there were enough vineyards in the country for a growers' association to be formed and discussions were held with MAFF to determine how this could be done. It was eventually decided to form a company registered according to the Industrial and Provident Societies Act (IPSA) and under the auspices of the Agricultural Central Cooperative Association Ltd. In October 1965 a meeting was held at Lord Montagu's Palace House at Beaulieu to elect a Steering Committee and to choose a name for the new association. It was agreed that it would be called The British Viticultural Association. This name, however, was rejected by the Board of Trade (why, history does not tell, but perhaps the absence of vineyards in Scotland had something to do with it). An alternative, The English Vineyards Association (EVA), was accepted. Wales was not included in the name as a Welsh Vine Growers Association had already been formed in September 1965. A Steering Committee was elected and held its first meeting over a year later (the naming problems had taken up the intervening 12 months) on 15 November 1966. The first Annual General Meeting was subsequently held on 18 January 1967 at which the following were elected: President, Sir Guy Salisbury-Jones; Vice President, Lady Montagu of Beaulieu; Chairman, Jack Ward; Vice Chairman, P. Tyson-Woodcock; Secretary, Irene Barrett; and Director, Robin Don. In addition to the elected officers, there were eight full members and 12 associates.

The growth of interest in winegrowing in the country over the next few years was quite remarkable. By the end of 1968, although the number of full members – those owning at least half an acre of vines – had only risen to 15, the number of associate members had shot up to over 100. This was the start of the era of much larger, more commercially orientated vineyards and over the next five years, a number of major vineyards were planted. These, together with a large number of smaller vineyards, really caused the public, especially the wine-buying and vineyard-visiting public, to take an interest in the country's vineyards and their wines. By the end of 1972, the EVA had 330 members and associates, farming 200 acres of vines, with an additional 100 acres ready to be planted in the spring of 1973.

In the early years, the EVA was run very much on a shoestring and the amount it could do to help winegrowers was necessarily limited. Members' events included annual tastings, visits to overseas shows, and symposia on winegrowing. It also published an annual newsletter which continued until 1978 when the *Grape Press*, a bi-monthly publication, replaced it. The EVA also recognized that it had a duty to members of the public who were interested in buying English and Welsh wines, and therefore did what it could to promote them as well as answering the many enquiries it received on the subject. The Association also felt it had a duty if not actually physically to help growers improve their wines, then to do what it could to recognize those wines that were good.

In 1974, the EVA established the English Wine of the Year Competition and Margaret Gore-Browne donated a magnificent silver bowl in memory of her husband Robert (who had died in 1972), which was to be presented to the best wine in the competition. Since then, as the number and styles of wines entered has increased, the Gore-Browne Trophy has been joined by a number of other trophies. The competition has, by showing growers and winemakers what their peers have been making, greatly helped to improve wine quality.

In 1978, after six years of negotiations with the authorities, the EVA received permission to introduce a Certification Trade Mark – known as the EVA Seal of Quality – which gave wines, after they had been analysed and been before a tasting panel – and approved on both counts – a recognized seal of approval that could be affixed to bottles. (This scheme ran until 1995, when the official EU approved Quality Wine Scheme, Britain's *appellation* system, was introduced.)

Another function of the EVA was the need to represent the interests of growers and winemakers and as soon as it was founded, it held regular meetings with the various authorities who had a hand in regulating and controlling the industry: the Home Office, MAFF and its successor, DEFRA, HM Customs and Excise (now HM Revenue and Customs – HMRC) and the Wine Standards Board (now the Wine Standards Team at the Food Standards Agency) being the main ones.

By 1978, for legal reasons, substantial changes to the status of the EVA were needed and in February 1979 it was incorporated as a company limited by guarantee, rather than one registered under the IPSA. The finances of the Association were always balanced fairly finely, and during the early 1970s subscription income rarely covered expenses. In 1976, in addition to an annual subscription, a levy on each acre of vines in production (vines under four years old were exempt) was introduced and this greatly helped matters. In 1980, the management of the association also required changes as Irene Barrett of Felsted Vineyards, who had been unpaid Secretary since its inception, retired. Her place was taken by Kenneth McAlpine, owner of Lamberhurst Vineyards, which at that time was by far the largest wine producer in Britain. McAlpine also became Treasurer. In April 1981, Sir Guy Salisbury-Jones decided to retire from his position as President of the EVA and his place was taken by Lord [Edward] Montagu of Beaulieu. Jack Ward also stepped down from his position as Chairman of the Board of the EVA, a post he had held since the founding of the Association in 1967, and his place was taken by Colin Gillespie of Wootton Vineyards. With these changes in place it felt very much like the 'old guard' stepping down in favour of a new, more commercially minded, management team.

As more and more vineyards were planted and production levies started to produce solid income, the finances of the EVA improved, and at the AGM in April 1985 the membership felt that the Association was sufficiently strong to consider appointing its first full-time employee. In October 1985, Commander Geoffrey Bond RN (retired) was appointed to the post of Chief Executive and for the next ten years he ran the EVA from an office in his house in Eltham in south London, dealing with a multitude of enquiries from all and sundry, handling press enquiries, talking to groups and associations and generally being 'Mr English Wine' whenever required. The EVA also appointed Anthony Steen, MP for South Hams in Devon, as its official (paid) parliamentary adviser, and for six years Steen made sure that the industry's concerns were heard in Westminster.

During the 1980s, the EVA prospered, with new vineyards being planted all over the south of England, some good harvests and a buoyant membership list. A combination of subscription income and production levies allowed the association's reserves to build to a considerable size.

As a result of this optimism in the industry the regional associations, which had been formed to cater for the local needs of vineyard owners, also became strong and started, to a certain extent, to take over some of the functions of the EVA, considered to be the central body and therefore more concerned with national issues.[44] Some members of the regional associations saw no need to belong to the EVA: they felt that they were getting all the benefits locally so why belong to both associations? From about 1990, the membership of the EVA began to fall and with it, its income, while its work continued to grow. More was spent on publicity, the duties of its staff did not contract and negotiations with the authorities grew as changes to the EU Wine Regime threatened to harm growers. By 1992–3 it had become clear that the situation could not continue indefinitely and changes to the way the EVA was both constituted and funded had to be made.

The next 18 months were taken up with the long, and at times difficult, process of changing the entire structure of the EVA. After considerable discussion and debate with both its own members and those of the six regional associations, a situation was reached where it was generally agreed that the EVA would go into voluntary liquidation and a new company, the United Kingdom Vineyards Association (UKVA), would be formed to take over its assets, its liabilities and its duties. This company would be owned, managed and financed by the six existing regional associations, its members would be those who were members of those regional associations and no others and its board of directors would be nominated by the regional associations, plus one representative from a new organization, English Wine Producers (EWP), which was set up

44 At the time, there were six regional vineyard associations: East Anglian Winegrowers' Association, South East Vineyards Association (which started out life as the Weald and Downland Vineyards Association), the Wessex Vineyards Association, the South West Vineyards Association, the Mercian Vineyards Association and the Thames and Chilterns Vineyards Association. There was also a Larger Growers and Producers Group which eventually turned into English Wine Producers (EWP)..

to represent the Larger Growers and Producers Group. UKVA would have no independent means of raising revenue from its members and all funding would come from the affiliated regional associations.

On paper this looked a workable solution and a further twelve months were taken up with the practicalities of drawing up and approving the new company's Memorandum and Articles of Association. By the midsummer of 1996, everything was in place for a handover of control and assets from the EVA to UKVA. In the event, only five out of the six eligible regional associations decided to become affiliated. The Thames and Chilterns Vineyards Association (T&CVA), which had been party to the negotiations and deliberations right up until the last moment, decided (somewhat churlishly perhaps) that they did not wish to be affiliated.[45] The first meeting of UKVA was held on 15 July 1996.

The functions of UKVA remained much the same as those of the EVA: organizing meetings for members, the AGM and the Symposium, publishing the *Grape Press*, running the annual Wine of the Year Competition and the prizegiving, operating the Quality and Regional Wine Schemes (see below), liaising with members of the public, wine trade and media seeking information about English and Welsh wine, arranging tastings of one sort or another, organizing council meetings, meetings with DEFRA, HMRC and WS, plus the hundred and one other things that a national association gets asked to do. The fact that the regional associations were now responsible for both the running and the financing of the association meant that some of the work previously carried out by the central organization could now be left to the regions. In 1998, UKVA formed a British Winegrowers Committee under the auspices of the Wine and Spirit Association of Great Britain (now the Wine and Spirit Trade Association), thus giving it a more powerful voice when looking after the interests of its members.

In cooperation with the committees of the six affiliated regional associations UKVA looked after the interests of its members and promoted, as far as its finances allowed, English and Welsh wines. It secured a grant of £30,000 from MAFF/DEFRA to create an English Wine Quality Marque, which although short-lived, was a genuine attempt to create a distinguishing mark which could be used by growers to publicize the quality of their products. It persuaded Food From Britain to support the annual English Wine Producers' St George's Day tasting which

45 The T&CVA eventually joined in 2000.

has become a showcase for wine writers and the wine trade to taste a comprehensive selection of the best of British-grown wines. It assisted DEFRA in its negotiations with the EU over the reform of the Wine Regime and by supplying valuable data about the growth of vineyards and wine production in Britain and by showing that Britain was by no means a 'faraway country' of which little was known, DEFRA was able to support the other Zone A countries (the northerly EU wine-producing member states) who wished to retain the right to enrich (in other words chaptalize) their wines with sucrose, in keeping the enrichment level at 3 per cent, plus an additional 0.5 per cent in 'difficult' years (2.5 per cent had been proposed). And last, but by no means least, it helped secure for ever the right of the small producing member states (Britain, Belgium, the Netherlands, Denmark and Ireland) to plant vines in the future without the threat of a planting ban.

For larger growers the EWP went from strength to strength under the guidance and hard work of its marketing director, Julia Trustram Eve, and her enthusiastic staff. The EWP's thirty members represented around 30 per cent of all English and Welsh wine production. The annual tasting became a firm fixture on the wine circuit with an ever-increasing number of exhibitors and wines. As the volumes of wine available for sale increased, so too did the efforts of the EWP to promote it, help market it and generally support all those engaged in its production and sale.

WINEGB

In 2015–16 it was decided that the structure of UKVA had outgrown its purpose and that a reorganization was necessary. The area under vine had almost trebled since UKVA was formed, vineyards had grown larger and more professional and needed a more professional organization to help and guide them. After much deliberation and consultation with all interested parties, an amalgamation of UKVA and the EWP was proposed and at an EGM held on 4 July 2017, a new organization, initially called British Wine Producers Ltd, but subsequently changed to Wines of Great Britain Ltd – WineGB for short – came into being. With a high-profile board of directors, a management advisory committee comprising around twelve 'working groups', each responsible for a different aspect of the industry, a full-time Secretary and Chief Executive, and a finance officer and marketing assistant in the office, WineGB looks fit for purpose and ready to take English and Welsh wines, still and sparkling, into the future.

APPENDIX: OTHER NOTABLE VINEYARDS

a'Beckett's Vineyard

www.abecketts.co.uk
3.58 hectares (8.85 acres)

Wiltshire's largest vineyard, producing still and sparkling wines, as well as apple juice and cider from their own orchards.

Adgestone Vineyard

www.adgestonevineyard.co.uk
3.51 hectares (8.67 acres)

First planted in 1968, Adgestone is one of the oldest vineyards in Britain. Now producing around 28,000 bottles a year, it is open to visitors for tours and visits and has a café and farm shop. It is also licensed for weddings.

Albourne Estate

www.albourneestate.co.uk
12.2 hectares (30.15 acres)

Albourne Estate is a boutique producer of single-estate still and bottle-fermented sparkling wines and English vermouth with their own modern on-site winery.

Albury Organic Vineyard

www.alburyvineyard.com
4.95 hectares (2.23 acres)

Albury Vineyard is a biodynamic vineyard producing award-winning still and sparkling wines in the heart of the beautiful Surrey Hills. Visitors are welcome on open days throughout the year.

Alder Ridge Vineyard

www.cobbsfarmshop.co.uk
2.9 hectares (7.17 acres)

Multiple award-winning vineyard nestled into the chalky slopes of the North Wessex Downs and producing exceptional English sparkling wines. The 2014 Blanc de Noirs was awarded 'Best in Class' at the 2017 Champagne and Sparkling Wine World Championships.

Aldwick Estate

www.aldwickestate.co.uk
4.59 hectares (11.34 acres)

Aldwick Estate is a family-run farm, well known for its hospitality and bucolic ambience. It is a popular wedding and conference venue and is supported by effervescent, zealous staff. A pre-arranged 'Tour, Taste, Toast' experience is available, plus optional professionally home-cooked catering.

Ashling Park Vineyard

www.ashlingpark.co.uk
17.23 hectares (42.58 acres)

Supremely sociable, totally delicious sparkling wine boasting DWWA and WineGB gold and Sommelier Awards silver medals. Elegant landscapes, tempting tastings and stays in luxurious accommodation designed by Will Hardy (of Channel 4's *Amazing Spaces*) are available.

Astley Vineyard

www.astleyvineyard.co.uk
2 hectares (4.94 acres)

Originally planted 1971, this small commercial vineyard is now under new ownership and produces a range of award-winning wines. There is an impressive new winery and visitor centre, and tours are available with prior booking.

Bearley Vineyard

www.bearleyvineyard.co.uk
0.44 hectares (1.09 acres)

This boutique vineyard produces award-winning wines from its small plot of Pinot Noir Précoce vines and has won British gold for its sparkling Seyval Blanc.

Biddenden Vineyards

www.biddendenvineyards.com
8 hectares (19.77 acres)

Kent's original vineyard, Biddenden was established in 1969 and is celebrating its fiftieth anniversary in 2019. It produces award-winning English wines, ciders and juices; visitors are welcome at the vineyard all year round.

Black Dog Hill Vineyard

www.blackdoghillvineyard.com
6.48 hectares (16 acres)

Black Dog Hill is a family-run, boutique vineyard planted on chalky soil below Ditchling Beacon on the South Downs. The wines are made by Dermot Sugrue at Wiston Estate. Personal tastings are available by appointment.

Bluebell Vineyard Estates

www.bluebellvineyard.co.uk
33.88 hectares (83.72 acres)

Situated on the edge of the Ashdown Forest, near the famous Bluebell Steam Railway, the vineyard is home to the award-winning range of 'Hindleap' English Quality Sparkling Wines. Established in 2005, the Estate specializes in the production of English sparkling wines using the classic Champagne varieties plus Seyval Blanc.

Bolney Wine Estate

www.bolneywineestate.com
16.8 hectares (41.51 acres)

British Winery of the Year 2017, Bolney Estate specializes in making both top-quality still wines – they are experts in Pinot Noir and Pinot Gris – and award-winning sparkling wines. They have a visitor centre with a restaurant, tour room and balcony overlooking vines.

Bride Valley Vineyard

www.bridevalleyvineyard.com
10 hectares (24.71 acres)

Owned by Bella and Steven Spurrier, Bride Valley Vineyard produces a range of both traditional method sparkling and crémant sparkling wines from the classic Champagne varieties. New visitor facilities open in 2019.

Brightwell Vineyard

www.brightwellvineyard.co.uk
5.76 hectares (14.23 acres)

Brightwell Vineyard, south of Oxford, adjoins the River Thames and has gained a reputation for producing some of Britain's best red wines, winning Harpers Winestars and *The Times* newspaper recommendations in 2018.

Carr Taylor Vineyards

www.carr-taylor.co.uk
15.65 hectares (38.67 acres)

Established in 1971, Carr Taylor Vineyards is one of the oldest vineyards in Britain, producing a wide range of award-winning still and sparkling wines. There is an on-site shop open to visitors for tours and tastings throughout the year.

Castle Brook Vineyard

www.castlebrookvineyard.co.uk
1.8 hectares (4.45 acres)

Tucked away in the meandering Wye Valley of South Herefordshire, Castle Brook Vineyard was re-established in 2004 on the site of an ancient Roman vineyard. It is committed to producing only the finest quality English sparkling wines.

Chafor Wine Estate

www.chafor.co.uk
4 hectares (9.88 acres)

Award-winning boutique wine estate set in the heart of rural Buckinghamshire. Specializes in private functions and corporate events.

Charles Palmer Vineyards

www.charlespalmer-vineyards.co.uk
12.5 hectares (30.89 acres)

Charles Palmer Vineyards is a family-run wine estate located in Winchelsea, just over one mile from the south coast. The vines are planted on a bed of Kimmeridgian clay, an ideal terroir for producing a range of traditional method sparkling wines.

Chilford Hall Vineyard

www.chilfordhall.co.uk
7.4 hectares (18.29 acres)

Chilford Hall Vineyard was planted in 1972, making it one of the oldest in Britain.

Coates and Seely – Wooldings Vineyard

www.coatesandseely.com
12 hectares (29.65 acres)

Coates and Seely use grapes from chalk-based Hampshire vineyards to produce award-winning sparkling wines. These are listed in some of the best restaurants and hotels in the world, including the George V and Hotel Bristol in Paris and the Dorchester and Savoy in London.

Court Garden Vineyard

www.courtgarden.com
6.8 hectares (16.8 acres)

Award-winning family-run estate situated near the attractive village of Ditchling. Winner of IWC 2015 English Wine of the Year.

Davenport Vineyards

www.davenportvineyards.co.uk
8.62 hectares (21.3 acres)

Davenport Vineyards, first planted in 1991, is one of the oldest and largest organic vineyards in Britain, with plantings in both Kent and East Sussex.

Dedham Vale Vineyard

www.dedhamvalevineyard.com
2.61 hectares (6.45 acres)

Set in gorgeous Suffolk countryside, Dedham Vale produces both still and sparkling wines, plus cider. Has good visitor facilities offering tours and tastings and a beautiful oak-framed barn, ideal for weddings.

Denbies Wine Estate

www.denbiesvineyard.co.uk
89.7 hectares (221.65 acres)

Denbies Wine Estate is the largest single-estate vineyard in Britain, producing a wide range of internationally award-winning still and sparkling wines. The superb visitor facilities include both vineyard and tasting experiences and they have a hotel, new in 2019, on-site.

Digby Fine English Wines

www.digby-fine-english.com

Named after the inventor of the modern glass bottle, Digby sources grapes from fine vineyards over the South East and has them crafted into award-winning wines by Dermot Sugrue at Wiston Estate winery.

Domaine Evremond

www.evremond.co.uk

27.07 hectares (66.89 acres)

Majority owned by Champagne Taittinger, Domaine Evremond, established in 2016, was the first British vineyard to be planted with the involvement of a Champagne house. With further plantings planned, wines from this producer are eagerly awaited.

Eglantine Vineyard

www.eglantinevineyard.co.uk

1.28 hectares (3.16 acres)

Small Lincolnshire vineyard which makes the only icewine in Britain and regularly wins awards with it.

English Oak Vineyard

www.englishoakvineyard.co.uk

8.06 hectares (19.92 acres)

English Oak Vineyard, located 5 miles from Poole, produces award-winning sparkling wines. Wine sales, tastings and tours are held in a purpose-built visitor centre. Electric vehicle charging also available.

Exton Park Vineyard

www.extonparkvineyard.com

21.52 hectares (53.17 acres)

Exton Park Vineyard is planted on Hampshire's famous chalk downs and focuses on producing wines that express their origin and have a consistency of style. There is a modern on-site winery and the wines have won multiple awards in top wine competitions.

Fox & Fox Vineyard

www.foxandfox.wine

11 hectares (27.18 acres)

Grower–producers of outstanding sparkling wines including the unique

Inspiration Pinot Gris, Meunier Blanc de Noirs and Essence Pure Chardonnay, which won 96 points in *Decanter* for the 2011 vintage.

Furleigh Estate

www.furleighestate.co.uk
5.5 hectares (13.59 acres)

Family-run wine estate near Dorset's Jurassic coast, making award-winning still and sparkling wines.

Giffords Hall Vineyard

www.giffordshall.co.uk
4.6 hectares (11.37 acres)

Giffords Hall is a family-owned vineyard planted on the site of an ancient glacial riverbed near Long Melford in Suffolk. Their sandy/clay soil produces quality grapes, high in natural sugars and acids, that lend themselves particularly well to both sparkling and dry, aromatic still wines.

Greyfriars Vineyard

www.greyfriarsvineyard.com
16.2 hectares (40.03 acres)

Established in 1989, Greyfriars is one of the largest vineyards in Britain. Planted on the south-facing slopes of the North Downs near Guildford, it produces mainly sparkling wines. It has its own winery, complete with cellars dug into the chalk.

Gusbourne Vineyard

www.gusbourne.com
88.8 hectares (219.42 acres)

Gusbourne strives to create wines that stand up alongside the finest offerings across the globe. Only estate-grown grapes, traditional methods and modern technology are used to produce wines that reflect the land where they are grown.

Hambledon Vineyard

www.hambledonvineyard.co.uk
90.29 hectares (223.11 acres)

Hambledon is England's oldest vineyard, having been established in 1952, and now one of its largest. It currently produces 100,000 bottles of sparkling wine a year, but with new plantings this will rise to 1 million over the next decade. A brand-new underground cellar, capable of holding 2 million bottles, is currently under construction.

Hattingley Valley Vineyard

www.hattingleyvalley.co.uk
24 hectares (59.3 acres)

Family owned and managed, Hattingley offer tours of the state-of-the-art winery throughout the year (excluding harvest) and tastings of the multi-award-winning sparkling wines. Head winemaker, Emma Rice, has twice won Winemaker of the Year.

High Clandon Vineyard

www.highclandon.co.uk
0.4 hectares (0.99 acres)

Planted on the chalky Surrey Hills, High Clandon makes long-aged, exceptionally high-quality sparkling wines. Multiple medal- and award-winning wines, the vineyard has uniquely twice won the IWC 'Cellar Door of the Year', in 2017 and 2018.

Hush Heath Estate

www.hushheath.com
22.29 hectares (55.09 acres)

Established in 2002, Hush Heath Estate has produced many award-winning wines and is one of the leading British vineyards. They have recently opened a stunning state-of-the-art visitor centre and winery extension in the heart of their beautiful 160-hectare Tudor estate. The cover photograph of this book shows the home vineyard and Hush Heath Manor and Oast House.

Jenkyn Place Vineyard

www.jenkynplace.com
5.7 hectares (14.1 acres)

Jenkyn Place is a small family-run boutique vineyard which constantly outperforms, producing top awards and medals with its wines. Tours and tastings are run throughout the year.

Kerry Vale Vineyard

www.kerryvalevineyard.co.uk
2 hectares (4.94 acres)

Family-run vineyard on the Welsh border of Shropshire. Planted in 2010 on what was the Roman Fort of Pentrheyling, it has a superb visitor centre with a café and shop selling Kerry Vale's award-winning wines.

Kingscote Estate

www.kingscoteestate.com
24.28 hectares (60 acres)

Kingscote is set in beautiful Sussex countryside and has a stunning fifteenth-century Tithe Barn surrounded by vineyards, orchards and lakes. The barn is available for weddings and corporate events throughout the year. The Bluebell Railway also runs through the estate so visitors can arrive by steam train at nearby Kingscote Station and enjoy a walk to the vineyard.

Knightor Winery

www.knightor.com
5.01 hectares (12.38 acres)

Knightor Winery is located in Cornwall, just half a mile from the Eden Project, and produces a broad range of wines, all quintessentially English. Tastings and tours are available throughout the year.

Langham Wine Estate

www.langhamwine.co.uk
11.77 hectares (29.08 acres)

Langham is the largest single-site vineyard in the South West and regularly produces gold medal winning sparkling wines. All wines are made on-site, with tastings and a café housed in an old dairy.

Lavenham Brook Vineyard

www.lavenhambrook.co.uk
3.74 hectares (9.24 acres)

Lavenham Brook, planted on a south-facing chalk slope, makes award-winning still and sparkling wines.

Leventhorpe Vineyard

www.leventhorpevineyard.co.uk
2.21 hectares (5.46 acres)

Established in 1985 and within the Leeds City boundary, Leventhorpe is Yorkshire's longest established commercial vineyard. Leventhorpe produces a range of multi-award-winning wines: dry whites, sparkling and red. Visitors are welcome and it is open for sales most days.

Lily Farm Vineyard

www.lilyfarmvineyard.com
0.59 hectares (1.46 acres)

A small family-run boutique vineyard voted Best Drinks Product by readers of *Devon Life* magazine in 2015. Has TripAdvisor 2018 Certificate of Excellence-rated vineyard tours and has cellar door wine sales outlet.

Mannings Heath Golf and Wine Estate

www.manningsheath.com
16.5 hectares (40.77 acres)

Planted in 2016 and 2017, Mannings Heath Vineyard is a wine and golf centre featuring wines from its South African property, Benguela Cove. It will eventually be producing sparkling and still wines from its British properties, which include a vineyard at nearby Leonardslee House.

Marden Organic Vineyard – Herbert Hall Wines

www.herberthall.co.uk
4.5 hectares (11.12 acres)

Boutique organic vineyard making award-winning sparkling wines.

Nutbourne Vineyards

www.nutbournevineyards.com
9.51 hectares (23.5 acres)

Nutbourne is a family-run boutique wine producer, making a range of distinctive award-winning still and sparkling English wines. The wines of handcrafted style and character are produced in the estate's winery in the heart of West Sussex.

Oatley Vineyard

www.oatleyvineyard.co.uk
1 hectares (2.47 acres)

Oatley is a small, family-run, eco-friendly vineyard in the Somerset countryside, an unspoilt, uncommercial kind of place. Old vines, red soil, and crisp, dry, white, international-award-winning wines. Visitors enjoy 'wild tasting' under ancient apple trees.

Painshill Park Vineyard

www.painshill.co.uk
0.73 hectares (1.8 acres)

The vineyard at Painshill Park, a magnificent award-winning eighteenth-century landscape garden based in Cobham, Surrey, was re-established in 1992 on a site first planted in 1738.

Parva Farm Vineyard

www.parvafarm.com
0.99 hectares (2.46 acres)

This Welsh vineyard was planted in the beautiful Wye Valley in 1979 and since then many awards have been won for its red, rosé, white and sparkling wines. Vineyard tours and free wine tastings are available.

Pinglestone Estate Vineyard

19 hectares (46.95 acres)

Pinglestone Estate is owned by Champagne producer Vranken-Pommery, the second Champagne house to own vineyards in Britain. Initially planted in 2018, the vineyards will expand over the next few years.

Plumpton College

www.plumpton.ac.uk
8.6 hectares (21.25 acres)

Plumpton College is Britain's centre of excellence in wine training, education, and research. The award-winning Plumpton Estate sparkling and still wines are produced by the wine students, who work alongside a team of vineyard and winemaking experts.

Polgoon Vineyard

www.polgoon.co.uk
3.6 hectares (8.9 acres)

Polgoon Vineyard is set on sheltered slopes overlooking Mount's Bay in Cornwall, where it's protected from prevailing winds and able to benefit from a unique microclimate that's perfect for growing grapes. The vineyard shop is open all year, with tours and events from April to October.

Quoins Organic Vineyard

www.quoinsvineyard.co.uk
1 hectares (2.47 acres)

Quoins is a small family-run organic vineyard just outside Bath. Tours and tastings are a speciality, with a chance to see and try a wide range of lesser-known fruits.

Rathfinny Estate

www.rathfinnyestate.com
70.96 hectares (175.34 acres)

Rathfinny Wine Estate is based in Alfriston on the Sussex Downs and is one of the largest vineyards in Britain. It has excellent visitor facilities, including a restaurant, cellar door and accommodation.

Redfold Vineyards – Ambriel Sparkling

www.ambrielsparkling.com
9.41 hectares (23.25 acres)

Situated on free-draining greensand overlooking the South Downs, this family-run vineyard and winery produces award-winning wines made from the classic Champagne varieties. Bespoke tours can be arranged.

Ridgeview Wine Estate

www.ridgeview.co.uk
6.48 hectares (16.01 acres)

Ridgeview is a family-owned and run producer dedicated to crafting traditional method sparkling wines. Winner of numerous international trophies, Ridgeview has been served at four state banquets and is exported around the globe. With beautiful views over the South Downs, it is open to visitors every day.

Sedlescombe Organic

www.englishorganicwine.co.uk
44.21 hectares (109.24 acres)

One of Britain's oldest biodynamic vineyards, which has recently changed hands and is now under the same ownership as Kingscote and Bodiam Vineyards.

Shawsgate Vineyard

www.shawsgate.co.uk
5.5 hectares (13.59 acres)

One of East Anglia's oldest vineyards, producing a range of still and sparkling wines.

Somborne Valley Vineyard

no website
11 hectares (27.18 acres)

Somborne Valley Vineyard has three separate parcels, each planted on a different terroir in the Test Valley. Mainly a supplier of grapes to other wineries, it also makes sparkling and red wines.

Somerby Vineyards

www.somerbyvineyards.com
5.5 hectares (13.59 acres)

Somerby is situated on the edge of the North Lincolnshire Wolds and is planted on chalk bedrock. Three varieties of grape are used: Solaris for a dry white, Rondo for a Reserve Oaked red and Pinot Noir for a traditional method sparkling.

Squerryes Estate Vineyard

www.squerryes.co.uk
20.88 hectares (51.59 acres)

Planted on the chalk of the North Downs, Squerryes Estate produces high-quality, long-aged wines. The superb new winery with wine shop is part of a 1,000-hectare estate that has been in the same family for over 300 years.

Stanlake Park Wine Estate

www.stanlakepark.com
10 hectares (24.71 acres)

Established in 1979, Stanlake Park is one of the oldest vineyards in Britain and produces a wide range of quality wines. It has its own winery and runs highly rated tours which can be booked via the website.

Stopham Vineyard

www.stophamvineyard.co.uk
5.6 hectares (13.84 acres)

Ten year old vineyard established on a sandy south-facing site and producing excellent still wines from Pinot Blanc and Pinot Gris.

Three Choirs Vineyard

www.three-choirs-vineyards.co.uk
34.9 hectares (86.24 acres)

First planted in 1973, Three Choirs Vineyard is the largest vineyard in south-west England and has consistently won awards both nationally and internationally. The vineyard has hotel rooms and a restaurant, and is open to the public throughout the year. Also has vineyards at Wickham in Hampshire.

Westwell Wine Estates

www.westwellwines.com
12.95 hectares (32 acres)

Westwell is located just beneath the Pilgrims Way on the North Downs in Kent, a route used for centuries by pilgrims travelling to Canterbury. Four different vine varieties are grown: Meunier, Pinot Noir, Chardonnay and Ortega, and all wines are made on-site from fruit grown on the estate.

Wiston Estate

www.wistonestate.com
10.16 hectares (25.11 acres)

Multi-award-winning wine producer on classic chalk downs site just north of Worthing.

Woodchester Valley Vineyard

www.woodchestervalleyvineyard.co.uk
22.21 hectares (54.88 acres)

Established in 2007 in the heart of the Cotswolds Area of Outstanding Natural Beauty, Woodchester Valley offers luxury accommodation, a cellar door and both public and private tours.

BIBLIOGRAPHY

Barty-King, Hugh, *A Tradition of English Wine*, Oxford: Oxford Illustrated Press, 1977.

Barty-King, Hugh, *A Taste of English Wine*, London: Pelham Books/Stephen Greene Press, 1989.

Bede, the Venerable, *An Ecclesiastical History of the English People*, Jarrow, 731.

Brock, Raymond Barrington, *Report No. 1 – Outdoor Grapes in Cold Climates*, Oxted, Surrey: The Viticultural Research Station, 1949.

Brock, Raymond Barrington, *Report No. 2 – More Outdoor Grapes*, Oxted, Surrey: The Viticultural Research Station, 1950.

Brock, Raymond Barrington, *Some Aspects of Viticulture in Southern England*, Oxted, Surrey: The Viticultural Research Station, 1951. Ph.D thesis.

Brock, Raymond Barrington, *Report No. 3 – Progress with Vines and Wines*, Oxted, Surrey: The Viticultural Research Station, 1961.

Brock, Raymond Barrington, *Report No. 4 – Starting a Vineyard*, Oxted, Surrey: The Viticultural Research Station, 1964.

Coombe, B. G., and Dry, P. R. (eds), *Viticulture Volume 1, Resources*, Adelaide: Winetitles, 1992 and 2nd edition, 2005.

Coombe, B. G., and Dry, P. R. (eds), *Viticulture, Volume 2, Practices*, Adelaide: Winetitles, 1995.

Domesday Books, 1086–1087.

D.S. *Vinteum Angliae: Or a New and Easy Way to make Wine of English Grapes*, London: G. Conyers at the Gold Ring in Little Britain, c. 1690.

Fielden, Christopher, *Is this the Wine you Ordered Sir?* London: Christopher Helm, 1989.

Gabler, James M., *Wine into Words – a History and Bibliography of Wine Books in the English Language*, Baltimore: Bacchus Press, 2004 (1985).

Heath, Tony, *Outdoor Grape Production*, London: Ministry of Agriculture, Fisheries and Food, 1978.

Heath, Tony, *Grapes for Wine*, London: Ministry of Agriculture, Fisheries and Food, 1980.

Hooke, Della, 'A Note on the Evidence of Vineyards and Orchards in Anglo-Saxon England', *The Journal of Wine Research*, 1(1), pp. 77–80, London, The Institute of Masters of Wine, 1990.

Hughes, W., *The Compleat Vineyard*, London: Will Crook, 1670.

Hyams, Edward, *The Grape Vine in England*, London: John Lane, The Bodley Head, 1949.

Hyams, Edward, *From the Waste Land*, London: Turnstile Press, 1950.

Hyams, Edward, *Grapes Under Cloches*, London: Faber and Faber, 1952.

Hyams, Edward (ed.), *Vineyards in England*, London: Faber and Faber, 1953.

Hyams, Edward, *An Englishman's Garden*, London: Thames and Hudson, 1967.

Lee, Roland, *Growing Grapes in the Open*, Birkenhead: Roland Lee Vineyards, 1939.

Lott, Heinz and Pfaff, Franz, *Taschenbuch der Rebsorten*, 13th edition, Mainz: Fachverlag Dr Fraund GmbH, 2003.

Louden J. C., *Encyclopaedia of Gardening*, London, 1834

Lytle, S. E., *Vines Under Glass and in the Open*, Liverpool: Horticultural Utilities Ltd, ca 1951.

Lytle, S. E., *Successful Growing of Grape Vines*, Liverpool: Horticultural Utilities Ltd, ca 1954.

Martin, Claude, *David Geneste – a Huguenot Vine Grower at Cobham*, Guildford, Surrey: The Surrey Archaeological Society, Collections Volume LXVIII, 1971.

Miller, P., *The Gardener's Dictionary*, London: P. Miller, 1771.

Ministry of Agriculture, Fisheries and Food, *Soils and Manures for Fruit*, London: Ministry of Agriculture, Fisheries and Food, 1975.

Ordish, George, *Wine Growing in England*, London: Rupert Hart-Davis, 1953.

Ordish, George, *The Great Wine Blight*, London: J. M. Dent and Sons Ltd, 1986 (1972).

Ordish, George, *Vineyards in England and Wales*, London: Faber and Faber, 1977.

Pearkes, Gillian, *Vinegrowing in Britain,* London: J. M. Dent and Sons Ltd, 1982, 1989.

Robinson, Jancis, *Vines, Grapes and Wine*, London: Mitchell Beazley, 1986.

Rose, John, *The English Vineyard Vindicated*, London: B. Teuke, 1672.

Salisbury-Jones, Sir Guy, 'Hampshire Vigneron' in *The Compleat Imbiber No. 2,* (ed. Cyril Ray), London: Putnam Ltd, 1958, pp. 89–95.

Salway, Peter, *Roman Britain*, The Oxford History of England, Oxford: Oxford University Press, 1991.

Selley, Richard C., *The Winelands of Britain: Past, Present and Prospective,* Dorking, Surrey: Petravin, 2004.

Seward, Desmond, *Monks and Wine*, London: Mitchell Beazley, 1979.

'S. J.' – A Gentleman in his Travels, *The Vineyard*, London: W. Mears, 1727.

Skelton, Stephen P., *The Vineyards of England*, Ashford, Kent: S. P. and L. Skelton, 1989.

Skelton, Stephen P., *The Wines of Britain and Ireland*, London: Faber and Faber, 2001.

Skelton, Stephen P., *Wine Growing in Great Britain,* London: S. P. Skelton Ltd, 2014.

Skelton, Stephen P., *UK Vineyards Guide*, London: S. P. Skelton Ltd, 2016.

Smart, Richard and Robinson, Mike, *Sunlight into Wine – A Handbook for Winegrape Canopy Management*, Adelaide: Winetitles, 1991.

Tod, H. M., *Vine-Growing in England*, London: Chatto & Windus, 1911.

Unwin, Tim, 'Saxon and Early Norman Viticulture in England', *The Journal of Wine Research*, 1(1), pp. 61–75, London: The Institute of Masters of Wine, 1990.

Unwin, Tim, *Wine and the Vine – An Historical Geography of Viticulture and the Wine Trade*, London: Routledge, 1991.

Vispré, F. X., *A Dissertation on the Growth of Wine in England*, Bath: F. X. Vispré, 1786.

Webster, D., Webster, H. and Petch, D.F. 'A possible Vineyard of the Romano-British period at North Thoresby, Lincolnshire', *Lincolnshire History and Archaeology*, 2, 1967.

Williams, G., 'A consideration of the sub-fossil remains of *Vitis vinifera L.* as evidence for viticulture in Roman Britain', *Britannia*, 8, pp. 327–34, 1977.

Wrotham Historical Society, 'The Wrotham grape', *Farming in Wrotham Through the Ages*, pp. 56–8, Wrotham Historical Society, 2004.

INDEX